Be Very
Afraid

Be Very Afraid

ONE MAN'S STAND AGAINST THE IRD

by Dave Henderson

Foreword by Rodney Hide, MP
Afterword by Graham Holland,
Commissioner of Inland Revenue

Published 2000 by FTG Press Inc.,
P.O. Box 1066, Christchurch, New Zealand 8015
Fax: (03) 351 5695, email: ftg@voyager.co.nz

ISBN 0–908578–72–5

"The power to tax carries with it the power to embarass and destroy."

Mr Chief Justice John Marshall,
Supreme Court of the United States,
Decision in McCulloch vs. Maryland.

Dedication

On 13 October 1996 Ian Lee Mutton drove to Otaki Gorge and ended his life. What led him to such drastic and tragic action was clearly set out in the suicide note he left attached to his body.

Ian was a self-employed air-conditioning mechanic. He was good at his job, but he fell behind in his tax. A simple series of misfortunes soon escalated to an unconfrontable debt. The IRD chased and hounded him. He had nowhere to turn, and no one would listen. Trips to the IRD for relief or help only ended in tears – his tears. He worked hard to pay off the debt. But he couldn't do it. The debt grew faster than his ability to pay it. His last act was to pen a suicide note addressed to the IRD. He graphically, and in no uncertain terms, laid the blame for his death on the tax department. He declared that he had now beaten them. They would get nothing more out of him. He was free.

This book is dedicated to the memory of Ian Lee Mutton, and to his thirteen-year old son Trevor who, inconsolable following his father's death, took his own young life. Ian and Trevor aren't the only people to have killed themselves because of an IRD beat up. Sadly, they are probably not the last.

Ian Lee Mutton.

Trevor Mutton (13 years old).

Acknowledgements

First and foremost, I want to record a debt of gratitude to my friends and family for their continued support over the last several years, and to my very loyal staff including Rick, Justin, Zach and especially Tracey who all stuck with me way beyond what I could have ever expected. Also thanks to Jackie for transcribing tapes, Suzanne Pollard for editing and communications advice, and my friends and business colleagues Bob Shaddick and Mike Wilson.

Special thanks must go to Simon Carr who, as a columnist in the *National Business Review*, fearlessly championed my case, and to Barry Coleman, his publisher, and all the other journalists and editors at the NBR who promoted and wrote about my story despite continual threats of legal action from the Commissioner of Inland Revenue.

Also thanks to my friend and lawyer Brian Palliser and his partners at Hill Lee & Scott in Christchurch and to Geoff Clews, barrister, for their support and assistance in dealing with difficult and complex IRD laws and processes and even more difficult and complex IRD personnel.

However, the real hero of this story is ACT MP Rodney Hide, to whom I and every taxpayer in this country are deeply indebted. Rodney's extraordinary political courage, perseverance and integrity have at long last put tax and cleaning up the Inland Revenue Department firmly on the political agenda. He is living proof that one person can make a difference. His personal commitment to my case is a real demonstration of the true role of a Member of Parliament.

Finally, I need to thank the creative people at Phillips for developing a simple device for recording my phone calls and meetings, without which I would not have been able to expose senior IRD staff.

Contents

Foreword

You should read this book. You could be next.

Our Inland Revenue Department is out of control. No one in authority cares or wants to do anything about it. Their only concern is that the money keeps rolling in and that the stories stay out of the papers.

The IRD took Dave Henderson aside and gave him a good, hard beating. They all but destroyed his life. Their only purpose was to teach him a lesson. No one cares. No one will take responsibility for what happened. New Zealand's top civil servants and top politicians have been made well aware of Dave Henderson's case – they have done nothing about it.

Dave Henderson is not about to stay out of the papers. The IRD this time picked on the wrong guy. Dave Henderson is tough. He is not going away. He is not giving up. He is going to be holding them all to account.

Dave Henderson's only crime was to be in business. His only mistake was to try to hold an IRD officer responsible for his actions. His only on-going error was not to back off in the face of state-sanctioned bullying and thuggery. These are strong words. I know of no other words to describe the IRD's actions.

Dave Henderson's story highlights how topsy-turvy our government's values have become. Our politicians and bureaucrats no longer value hard work, thrift or enterprise. Their attention instead is on the lazy and the unproductive. They get all the care, they get all the concern.

Our politicians and bureaucrats now view businessmen as villains, crooks as victims, and lazy losers as heroes. Our government's values are anti-capitalist and anti-enterprise. The values of our politicians and our civil service must be changed and be changed radically if New Zealand is to succeed as a productive and free nation.

Our tax laws need a radical overhaul to give taxpayers the rights that free citizens should enjoy. The IRD must be turned upside down and inside out to engender a culture of respect for those who pay its way. Our punitive penalties regime needs to be reformed and softened to ensure that tax law is no longer used as an instrument of oppression and fear.

More importantly, we must constantly remind our politicians and government officials that it is working people who pay their way. Government should not be stifling, threatening and strangling business. Our politicians and bureaucrats should be celebrating it, supporting it, and being inspired by it, because business is the very engine of our success and of our development.

Dave Henderson's story is a salutary lesson of just how far we have to go. What politicians and bureaucrats do now is just mouth fine words and high-sounding policy. That's no good. We need substance. We need action. We need results. That's why you must read this book. We need more people outraged. We need more taxpayers like Dave Henderson. We need more people standing up and telling our politicians and bureaucrats that they have had enough. That's exactly what must happen in order to engender a culture of enterprise and success into our government. And that's exactly what our country so desperately needs.

– Rodney Hide MP

ACT MP Rodney Hide.

Testimonial

I am a senior partner at the law firm Hill, Lee and Scott in Christchurch. I have known Dave Henderson for twenty years. I lived much of the story that Dave describes in this book. It's all true. It was for me an unbelievable experience. I have never been involved with anything like it in my thirty-year career and I certainly hope that I am never involved with anything like it again. I share Dave Henderson's and Rodney Hide's enthusiasm that this book may lead to a much-needed overhaul of the Inland Revenue Department and its operation.

– Brian Palliser (BA, LLB, AFNZIM, ACIT)
Barrister & Solicitor, Notary Public

Brian Palliser.

"Dave Henderson is the quintessential entrepreneur"

– IRD Report

I have wanted to be in business for as long as I can remember. I don't really know why. It's just the way I am. I started when I was ten years old. I began by chopping kindling wood and selling it around the neighbourhood. I bought and sold things – anything: pushbikes, record players, cars. With a friend I set up a little factory making belts and wristbands which we ran after school. It seemed to me that the world was full of opportunities. I still think that. I thought that by being in business I could realise these opportunities. I relish the opportunity to create and to build things. I also wanted to make money. I realised that with money I could have the things that otherwise would be beyond me.

By the time I was eighteen I was in business full time. I was happy. I had found my lifetime vocation. I was touring the country with a car full of clothing samples selling on commission to retailers. What a great life. I got paid by how well I did. If I didn't do well, I didn't get paid. If I did well, I got rewarded. It seemed a perfect arrangement to me. I loved it.

Since then I have had great successes and great failures. I have started over a hundred businesses in New Zealand, Australia, Canada and the United States. Some of them have done spectacularly well – others have done spectacularly badly.

My biggest success has always been property development. My first great property development was with a partner redeveloping a one-acre commercial block in the heart of Christchurch in 1981. We turned an old Motor Corporation car showroom into a block of retail shops, entertainment and car parking. That development is still there today, going strong.

I was then involved in converting the old Farmers' Co-op Department Store in Cashel Street to create Christchurch's first serviced office complex. It is still there today as I created it.

I set up several entertainment centres in Australia and New Zealand. I started an ice-cream chain called New Zealand Natural that is today one of the largest ice-cream chains in Australasia. I built a large tourist attraction called *Ripley's – Believe it or Not* on Australia's Gold Coast. I have started and operated numerous bars, restaurants and entertainment centres.

Not all of my businesses have been successful.

My biggest failure was probably the Sandwich Factory, a chain of lunch bars that I had created with my wife. This had been a great business. Sadly, it folded in the early 1980s after a long and bitter fight with the unions. Our staff didn't want to belong to the union. We weren't about to force them. Today we accept a worker's right to decide whether to join a union as a matter of course. But back in the 1980s, you had to force workers to join the union by law. We eventually collapsed what had been a very successful business rather than force workers to belong to a union that they didn't support.

Another failure was a company called Variety Leisure Corporation. This company had been active in the mid to late 1980s creating a number of entertainment facilities in Australia and New Zealand. It was bankrupted by the IRD in 1991 for a debt of $20,000 which was all penalties. That was after I had paid the outstanding tax and over $100,000 in penalites. The outstanding tax had arisen as a consequence of an honest GST mistake made by our accountants when GST was introduced and still new.

I have had failures. But the successes have far outweighed them.

In 1994 I was director and principal shareholder of a nationwide direct marketing company. With a partner I had built the company from scratch. It was turning over four million dollars a year and growing fast. I was involved in property development throughout New Zealand. I still had an ice-cream business supplying the New Zealand Natural chain throughout Australasia. I was 38 years old. I had worked hard all my life. I had done well. I had employed hundreds of people. I had paid millions of dollars in tax. The dream that I had of realising opportunities had come true. I wasn't a rich man by any means. But I had material comforts and I was freely pursuing my dreams and my aspirations. Most importantly, I was creating and running my own businesses. No one was telling me what to do. I was my own boss. I don't consider myself a clever person by any means. I know I lack a lot of the skills and personality traits needed to succeed in business in a big way. However, I do value and respect the concepts of hard work and enterprise. That's what got me to where I was.

I am now a bankrupt. All my businesses are gone. I have lost all the income I had. My life's work is gone. I am not allowed to run a business for three years. That's hard. The one thing that I am good at is the one thing that I am not allowed to do.

All this happened because an Inland Revenue Department audit went wildly off the rails. What should have taken four weeks took four long years. I was hounded and harassed by IRD. They made up claims. They said I owed a million dollars when I didn't. They destroyed me and my businesses. They put dozens of my staff out of work. They wrecked my life.

I had done nothing wrong. I hadn't broken any law. But that didn't matter. They did it to me anyway.

I am not the only one to have been affected in this way. I now know of many people in business who have been victimised and harassed just like I was. But this book is my story. It is about my fight with the IRD. It's about what the IRD did to me. And it's about what I did back.

"You have small wrists, we will only need small handcuffs"

Here's how it all started. At the end of 1993 my company Tannadyce Investments Ltd filed its two-monthly GST return. The only thing that was unusual about this GST return was that it was filed in Christchurch. All previous GST returns for this company had been filed in Wellington. Like many of our previous GST returns, this one claimed a refund.

The company had been involved in property development since its incorporation three years earlier. In a complex deal Tannadyce had contracted to buy the old Lower Hutt Railway Station from the Bank of New Zealand, established a bakery, a micro-brewery and a family restaurant, and turned the old disused station into a thriving retail complex called Station Village. Tannadyce had spent nearly three million dollars and was due significant GST refunds.

Over the preceding three years Tannadyce had been audited by the IRD Wellington Office on several occasions. My staff had worked closely with them and – together with our accountants – had always been able to provide them with all the documentation that they had needed to justify all of our refunds. The refunds were promptly paid. At the end of 1993 – with our involvement in the development in Lower Hutt at an end – we shifted the administrative tasks of Tannadyce to my home base in Christchurch.

On the 28 January 1994 we received a letter from an IRD auditor called Gordon Byatt who wanted someone from the company to contact him to "verify" the latest GST return. It all seemed pretty routine.

My office administrator Kath Cook collected up all the relevant invoices and – as she had done many times before – headed into the IRD to justify our refund. An hour later she returned to the office in tears, shaken and very disturbed. She told me what had happened. She had met with Mr Byatt. One of the first things he asked her was, "Is this one of Dave Henderson's companies?" She said it was. He then asked, "Are you sleeping with Henderson?" These comments set the tone for the rest of the interview. It was quite clear from what she described that Gordon Byatt's mind was made up that the refund should not be paid. He asked questions about the GST return that, despite her distress, Kath endeavoured to answer. He asserted that based on the computer print-out he was holding "this company should be dead". He was claiming that the company had incurred substantial losses. He then advised Kath that, "a short skirt and a big smile might work in Wellington but it won't work down here". He concluded the interview by asking Kath to hold out her hands. Naively she did. He looked at her hands and declared, "you have small wrists" he then looked her in the eye and said, "we will only need small handcuffs," A devastated Kath described Mr Byatt as a "middle-aged grease-ball with long silver hair, a false tan, and gold chains around his neck and wrists."

I was outraged. How dare he treat a female staff member doing her job with such contempt? I rang Byatt and called him, amongst other things, a "low-life scumbag". I demanded to know who his senior was and told him we would not be dealing with him any longer.

Kath wanted to lodge a formal complaint. I told her this was pointless. I said that they would all move to protect their own. I figured that if we protested all that would happen would be that she and I would end up suffering recriminations.

I realised that I couldn't send Kath back.

Kath Cook: IRD told her that a short skirt and big smile wouldn't work on them.

Gordon Byatt: Intimidated a female staff member with threats of handcuffs.

I had to deal with Byatt myself. I arranged to meet him a few days later. He was exactly as Kath had described. The interview was terrible. He was determined to maintain his dominant position. I went home and thought about the position. He had revealed to me the name of another auditor who was to be involved in the case, a Mr Chris Bond. I rang Mr Bond the next day. Bond asked for some further information that he indicated would tidy the whole matter up. I was keen to tidy it up and to receive the refund. I made immediate arrangements to obtain the receipts from Australia that he had asked for.

The transaction for which I was seeking the GST refund involved the company acquiring a vintage car as part of a property transaction. It had not been a happy transaction. The car we had received was a replica, not an original as I had believed. Mr Bond wanted the receipt for what we had paid for the car.

In March, Mr Bond told me that the Department was going to organise a valuer to value the car independently. I was happy with that. I explained that the car was now in Queenstown. He also asked for some additional information. I provided it immediately to him. He wanted details of payments and receipts for some subsequent transactions relating to some subsequent GST claims.

Bond asked me to meet again with Mr Byatt, which I did on 16 March 1994. Byatt told me that they were completely disallowing my claim. He explained that they had obtained a valuation and that this valuation was for thousands of dollars less than what we had paid for the car and that our claim would not proceed. I was later to learn that the valuation had not been obtained from an independent valuer, as required under the Goods and Services Tax Act, but had come from Philip Mills, a car dealer since discredited and delicensed for importing clocked cars. Philip Mills wasn't independent because it was he who had bought the replica from me. I had lost a bundle on the car because I had bought it believing it to be a genuine Stutz Bearcat. I had told Philip Mills the whole story and he took the Stutz replica as a trade-in for a BMW which turned out to have been clocked. I have never done very well out of cars.

Mr Byatt disallowed my claim because we had paid $150,000 for the Stutz which he said was now worth only $10,000. We had traded the car for $25,000 with Mills who had told me he was selling it to a clothing retailer in Queenstown. At this time all I knew about GST was that if you bought something for your business you got a GST refund on what you had paid and if you sold something you paid GST on it. I now know that I was right. I had been ripped off with the Stutz but I was entitled to the GST back on the full $150,000 because that is what I had foolishly paid and the transaction involved was at "arms-length", meaning that for GST purposes there were no improperly inflated values.

One of the ironies – and what was to become standard operating procedure – was that IRD were now telling me that I could claim GST back on only $10,000 for the car when in fact they were insisting I pay GST on $25,000 for the sale to Philip Mills. They weren't being consistent. Moreover, the true legal position was that no matter what I had sold the car for I was entitled to a refund on the full $150,000 that I had originally paid. Eventually Byatt suggested he might allow us to claim on $25,000 based on his "valuation".

It was clear to me from Mr Byatt's demeanour and tone throughout the entire interview that he was more focused on exercising power over me than exercising justice. I told him to "get stuffed" and stormed out of the interview. That was a mistake. I had crossed swords with him twice now.

I now know Mr Bond and Mr Byatt immediately started to make inquiries about the company's transactions over the last three years relating to the development of the Station Village.

I asked my staff in Christchurch to provide all documentation that the Department required. A few weeks later I wrote to Mr Bond complaining about Mr Byatt's behaviour and advising that we were not willing to deal with him. Mr Bond never responded to my letter. However, for a considerable period Gordon Byatt appeared to have nothing to do with the case. Mr Bond offered to increase the value of the Stutz against which we could claim GST up to $25,000. He told me that this was the correct interpretation of the law. In a desperate desire to clear matters up and conclude the audit I told him that I accepted. I was to later discover that Mr Bond was completely incorrect and that I was legally entitled to claim back the full $150,000 that we had paid for the car. I was out the door by $13,888.

The Tannadyce audit was off to a bad start. I had complained twice. The IRD were now giving Tannadyce special attention.

The "last remaining" issue

For the rest of 1994 we dealt with Kevin Jones – a technical officer with the Department. By comparison with Mr Byatt he was a pleasant and cheerful chap. But he was never especially professional. All he would repeat for almost a year was the mantra, "The audit is progressing. The audit is progressing". He never once gave any indication about where he was up to or when it might be complete. On several occasions he asked for more information and my staff provided it within days, if not hours, of his requests. He started an audit against every GST return we lodged that year. I had several phone conversations and meetings with Kevin throughout 1994 in which I offered assistance and pleaded with him to tell me where he was at and what the target completion time was. There were significant refunds now outstanding and, like any small businessman, I was anxious to haul in any cash that was owed to me.

I made the first Official Information request that I had ever made. I asked the IRD for all copies of any information they had received from the Bank of New Zealand – with whom I had made the deal to purchase the Lower Hutt Railway Station. I wanted to know what they were asking the BNZ in order to try and find out what was bothering them. Had the Department responded to that request – as the law requires them to – I would have identified what the Department was up to. This would have enabled me to assist them and to short-circuit what had become interminable delays.

On 28 November 1994 I wrote to the Department reminding them that the audit was approaching its first birthday, that we were being seriously inconvenienced as a consequence of delays, and offering to assist in any way we could to help to bring the matter to a close. On the 19 December Kevin Jones advised that he was, "making progress with the audit". He said

TANNADYCE • INVESTMENTS • LIMITED

P.O. Box 1066
Christchurch
New Zealand
Phone   64 3 351-8488
Facsimile 64 3 351-5695

15 December 1994

Kevin Jones
Business Audit
Inland Revenue Department
Private Bag
CHRISTCHURCH

COPY

FAX: 366 6654

Dear Kevin

I refer to my letter to you of 28 November 1994. It is now some eighteen days since that letter was sent to you, and despite your assurances on the phone we still have received no formal response to this letter. Obviously we are keen to obtain the information that we have requested as quickly as possible.

Can you please do the following:

1. Please provide the information requested in our letter 28th November 1994 as quickly as possible.

2. Explain to us why it takes so long to receive any response on what are relatively simple matters.

We also note for the record that the audit on Tannadyce Investments is coming up for its first birthday. Perhaps you would be so kind as to explain to us why it is taking so long for a very simple audit to be completed. I also want to record my advice to you on the phone the other day that we are ready and willing to help cooperate in any regard to provide you with any further information to bring this matter to completion. In particular if you advise us exactly what information you are waiting from the BNZ we would be willing to work with people we have an association with at the BNZ, and who have indicated their willingness to cooperate with us, to make this happen. Surely this would short circuit the whole thing.

I am very frustrated and disappointed that you are not interested in this offer for help.

I look forward to receiving all the above information and answers.

Yours sincerely

Dave Henderson

he could understand my frustration but that it was not uncommon for some audits to take longer than this. He implied it was nearing completion. He declined my offer of assistance.

Naively, I bought his warm assurances that the audit would be completed shortly and imagined it would be all over in the next few weeks. On the 23

Chris Bond: On one occasion admitted sending me a misleading letter through his personal incompetence.

January 1995 I wrote to him again and congratulated him on the fact that the audit had now reached its first birthday. I asked him if he was willing to tell me what information he needed to conclude the audit. He replied several weeks later by telling me that the secrecy provisions of the Inland Revenue Act 1974 prevented him disclosing what stage the audit was at.

The Department was keeping the lid jammed down on me tight. Unbeknown to me on 26 January 1995 they had sent a nine-page letter to the Christchurch CIB alleging eight charges of fraud against me concerning Tannadyce's GST returns. I knew nothing about these charges. The IRD never told me about them or of the concerns they had. What's worse, they had lodged this complaint with the police way before they had concluded their own investigation.

On 31 January 1995 I met with Chris Bond and another IRD staff member, Philippa Foulds, in a further desperate effort to determine where the audit was at and to find out what it would take to bring it to completion, what I could do to assist, and what the Department's timetable was. I wanted them off my back and I wanted the money that we were owed.

With the full knowledge of IRD's serious complaints to the police, Mr Bond estimated that 40 hours work remained and that this would be spread over the next four to six weeks. I was naturally unhappy with the audit still taking so long and asked why the 40 hours work couldn't be concluded in the next week. He wouldn't tell me.

TANNADYCE INVESTMENTS LTD.

Notes of interview, 31 January 1995, 10.05-10.45 am.

Attendees: Dave Henderson (s/h), Philippa Foulds & Chris Bond.

Mr Henderson had sought this interview to discuss progress on the audit of Tannadyce Investments Ltd, which has now been in progress for 12 months.

Despite the length of the interview, we were unable to give Mr Henderson an exact finish date for this job. We estimated that 40 hours work remains, possibly spread over 4-6 weeks.

Mr Henderson was not satisfied with our response. He wished us to assure him that the Investigator involved would work solely on this task until completion; Mrs Foulds said that she was unable to give that assurance. Mr Henderson then asked whether the assurance would, or could, not be given. Mrs Foulds said that she would not give that response.

P FOULDS.   31/1/95.   C BOND.

I heard nothing for a month. On 2 March 1995 I received a letter from Mr Bond telling me that a number of documents had been obtained and that these documents were "under legal consideration of their effect". He never told me what the documents were despite my requests in several phone calls, letters and Official Information requests. I wrote to him and said I didn't know what it all meant but "since it is three weeks since they went under legal consideration I am sure you would agree that they would have been fully considered by this time". I then asked again for an update of the status and time frame of the audit.

Mr Bond responded a few days later. He told me that the documents in question "are still under legal consideration of their effect".

In early April 1995 I rang Ross Gardiner at IRD, who I had identified as Chris Bond's senior. Ross Gardiner proved one of the more objective people at the IRD. Although his involvement was peripheral he was, over the next 12 months, to treat me respectfully and extend a degree of professionalism and empathy. I have since obtained under the Official Information Act his memo dated 12 April 1995 instructing Chris Bond to "contact the police to see where they are at and to see if they have any suggestions about how to put Henderson off for a while longer". The IRD wanted the police to tell them how they could stall me.

On 13 April 1995 Mr Bond wrote to me stating that the "remaining issue" being considered was the effect of section 60 of the Goods and Services Tax Act on the contract between the BNZ and Tannadyce. I was excited. The audit had been going for 15 months but at last I knew what was troubling them. I was frustrated that they had never told me what had been bothering them sooner, but I was pleased that we had now identified the "last remaining" issue. I shot down to Whitcoulls, excitedly purchased a copy of the Goods and Services Tax Act, and came home to study section 60.

The effects of section 60 were clear to me. It was all positive. Although our arrangements with the BNZ were a little complex they were quite unequivocal. Section 60 relates to the relationship of an agent to a principal in any transaction, that is, when someone acts for someone else such as an import agent or shipping agent acting on behalf of another businessman or an auctioneer selling goods for someone else. Section 60 provides for the agent to undertake and complete transactions, including the issuing of invoices and the payment of cheques on behalf of the principal, but it still holds the principal liable for the GST on those transactions.

My interpretation was that applying section 60 entitled Tannadyce to further refunds. The nature of the deal with the BNZ was that Tannadyce had been their agent in some aspects of the contract, e.g. for a period of time we had collected rentals on the property on behalf of the BNZ in return for a management fee. Tannadyce had paid the GST liable on those rentals. It was now clear that such liability for GST was strictly speaking the liability of the BNZ. I figured out we were now due an extra $10,000 in GST refunds.

I wrote to Mr Bond and asked him how he thought section 60 would apply, given the circumstances. Bond helpfully told me that it either applies or it doesn't and that the matter needed to be considered before the audit could be concluded.

At 8:30am on 20 April 1995 I rang Chris Bond. He told me that he couldn't progress matters and finalise the audit because he was waiting to receive the Tannadyce files from the Department's advisers. I assumed that these were the documents that were with their lawyers to be "considered as to their effect". I was to find out much later that the IRD wasn't seeking any legal opinion in respect of those documents or the effects of section 60 on them. Chris Bond was misleading me.

I then tracked down the head of the whole audit department in

Christchurch, Peter Sivertsen. He said he was familiar with my case, that they were waiting for an opinion from their advisers, and that he was annoyed that he hadn't received it. He assured me that he would speak to Chris Bond and get back to me straight away. He never got back to me at all.

However, the application of section 60 was about to become the least of my worries.

The Tannadyce audit is now fifteen months old. But there's progress. We had gone from "the audit is progressing," to there being "40 hours work left to do" and finally to "the last remaining issue". I was still confident it could be quickly resolved and our $60,000 GST refund paid to us.

The Fraud
Squad
bulldoze in

At 10:20am the same morning I had spoken to Sivertsen, I was stunned
to see three men in suits pull up in a car and park across my driveway blocking
my entrance. They marched down the driveway and hammered on my door.
I was scared. I didn't know who they were. I opened the door to be presented
with a search warrant.

The officers quickly explained that they were there to seize financial
records relating to my tax affairs. I was stunned. For over 15 months I had
been offering the Department any and all records they wanted. They had
repeatedly assured me that they had all that they needed and that if they
wanted anything more they would let me know. Now I had the police in my
home to search and to seize those same records.

I asked them to wait in my hallway while I went and collected up the
information they wanted. I had no reason or desire to hide anything. I soon
found the police wandering through my dining room and living room. I
asked them to go back to the hallway. They gave me a quick lesson about
search warrants, tersely explaining that they had the right to go anywhere in
my house and go through anything that they chose to. All they would say
was that they were acting on complaints lodged by the IRD. They would
not explain further.

I provided them with all the documents they required. They took them
away after issuing me with a receipt.

I was shattered. Later that afternoon – after I had settled down – I phoned
Bond.

I wanted to meet him to find out what was going on and why the IRD
had involved the police. I was confused as to why he had told me that
morning that "the last remaining issue" was still the section 60 matter.

He told me dismissively that he wasn't working to my timetable but to his own. He was very arrogant, but the happiest and most confident I had ever heard him.

Two days later I called Peter Sivertsen again. He agreed that he would speak to Chris Bond and arrange to pay a partial refund of the $60,000 that we were claiming as some of the matters in question had been resolved. I was totally confused. I had just had the police storm through my house and now the Department at long last was offering to settle a part of our long-claimed refund.

The next day it got weirder. I got a letter from Mr Bond telling me that the company had approximately $11,000 in credits that were not disputed, but he did say that the effects of section 60 might negate these sums, and he sought further information about the details of the BNZ deal. I replied the same day, giving him the details he wanted. I asked him again about the documents that he was appraising, and explained that the application of section 60 meant that we were owed more money, not less.

The following day I set up a meeting with Chris Bond and his boss Ross Gardiner. It took place on 26 April 1995 in a meeting room on the fourth floor of the IRD office in Cashel Street – a room where I had been many times before and which I was to become very familiar with over the coming years. I opened the meeting by asking Mr Bond and Mr Gardiner to explain why they had lodged a complaint with the police. Both denied having anything to do with it. They told me that I would have to discuss it with Mr Sivertsen as he had lodged the complaint. I later discovered Mr Bond had been actively involved with all the matters relating to the police complaint. At the time I didn't know this and I accepted his explanation.

We discussed the significance of section 60. We appeared to agree on how section 60 should rightfully be applied to the relationship between Tannadyce and the BNZ. I then pointed out that as a consequence of that application Tannadyce would now be due additional GST refunds. Mr Bond appeared troubled by this, frowning and going over his file and notes. I then discussed how we might proceed. Mr Bond told me that we would need to go back virtually to the start of business for the company and to redo all our figures. This would be a costly and expensive exercise. It also seemed to me to be possibly a complete waste of time. Any extra GST paid to us by the Department could be claimed back from the BNZ. The BNZ might then make a claim against Tannadyce for that money. There was possibly nothing to gain. Technically there was no tax outstanding. Overall it was a wash.

I suggested to the Department that we call it quits, forget the application of section 60 and let all matters lie where they were.

Mr Bond was not happy with this and kept on insisting that if Tannadyce was due extra money then we should get it. I explained to him in quite graphic detail the amount of work that would be involved. He seemed to have no concept of the cost or work involved for us. However, he did assure me that as soon as we had reworked these figures and filed them with him, the audit would be at an end. That assurance was enough to motivate me to do it. We concluded the meeting by the Department agreeing to release immediately to us $11,000 of the GST credits that we were waiting for. Mr Bond gave me his personal assurance that as soon as we faxed through our bank account details, he would arrange for an immediate direct credit of that sum. I have his note of the meeting in his handwriting confirming all these arrangements.

I returned to my office very enthused. Despite the ongoing police inquiries, I had reached agreement as to the conclusion of the audit and we were to receive some much needed funds.

I met with my staff and made everyone understand the importance of reworking the figures in accordance with the agreement I had made with Mr Bond. We estimated that it would take one person approximately twenty days. It was a massive task, involving hundreds and hundreds of transactions. Although we were under a lot of pressure from other business commitments, we started immediately to rework all these records.

Peter Siverston: In charge of the audit for over 3 years.

The next day I phoned Mr Bond at ten past three in the afternoon to confirm that he had deposited the GST refunds in our account. He told

INLAND REVENUE
TE TARI TAAKE

IR234

26 -04- 95

TANINADYCE INVESTMENT LTD

Meeting with Steve Henderson, Ros Gardiner, & me.

We traversed the issues in my letter of 21 April, re agency & BNZ. I made pages from O. wife. copy of Tech Rulings available to H.

H advised that expenditure was not incurred as an agent although rents were collected on behalf of BNZ, & further advised that management fees were never drawn by Tannadyce. As a consequence, re-assmts of T.S. returns to exclude the outputs from rent may well result in further refunds. The documentation referred to in my letter will be supplied as soon as possible, possibly by early in the week commencing 1 May.

We agreed that the identified credits totalling approx $5000 would be released asap. T.S. is to fax its bank A/c number, to facilitate direct crediting.

A number of other general issues were traversed.

me that he had not, despite his very firm minuted agreement the day before. He explained that he had discovered that we had not filed income tax returns for 1994 and 1995 and that any income tax owing might wipe out the refunds. I pointed out to him that the company had made significant losses and therefore no income tax could be due. I was later to find out that in their letter to the police some months earlier, the Department had advised the

28

police that in their assessment the company had up until that time incurred losses in excess of $2 million. The IRD knew that Tannadyce had made substantial losses. Byatt had even asserted this to Kath Cook. But now they were claiming that they wouldn't pay out on part of the GST refund because there could be income tax to pay. It didn't make sense.

Bond asked that I confirm in writing the loss position and said he would see if the Department's position could be reversed. I wrote that letter the next day, but it made no difference. We never received the promised, and much-needed, refunds.

All through this period, and right into early May, my staff worked hard to complete the information Mr Bond had requested. In mid-May the reworked financials, together with all the supporting invoices and documents, were delivered to the Department. The new schedules showed that over $20,000 additional GST was due to the company. But I was nervous. Knowing the mentality of these people, I feared that the prospect of having to explain to their seniors that the audit had resulted in a greater – rather than lesser – refund would prompt them to drag matters out further. After all, they had by now spent many tens of thousands of dollars for no result.

As time would tell, my fear was well-placed.

The police are now involved. I am under investigation for fraud. No one will tell me why. The IRD promise a part refund. They fail to keep their word.

IRD use phantom credit note

By mid-June 1995 – a month after we had delivered the required information to Mr Bond – I phoned him to see what progress he had made. It appeared nothing had happened. My hope of the audit being brought to a close in a few weeks – as Mr Bond had said it would – was fast melting. Mr Bond advised that he was putting my old friend Mr Byatt back on the case. I protested. I didn't think that Mr Byatt should still even be working for the IRD, let alone be put back onto our audit. But given Mr Bond's assurances that this was the last remaining issue, and given the fact that it was quite plain we would be due an additional refund, I reluctantly accepted Mr Byatt back. I didn't really have any choice.

About this time the IRD started yet another audit on another company of mine. Kath Cook was handling that matter. She met with an IRD employee called Michelle Lonsdale to resolve the issues involved. Kath found this woman quite professional, and described in detail the sexist and intimidating comments Gordon Byatt had made to her eighteen months earlier. As Kath relayed it to me, Michelle Lonsdale appeared shocked by Byatt's behaviour. She encouraged Kath to lodge a complaint, assuring her that the matter would be fully and properly investigated. When Kath returned to the office she prepared a letter of complaint and faxed it to the Department. She has never received a reply.

The only response to Kath's complaint was a letter written to me telling me, once again that, Byatt would be taken off the case. I was to find out a year later that he was still working on it.

The Tannadyce audit kept dragging on through August and September that year with Mr Byatt raising nit-picking matters like what was the taxable activity of the company. These nit-picking questions didn't square with IRD's assurance that there was only "one remaining issue". Nonetheless, we continued to co-operate and to provide further information. What Mr Byatt did produce was a set of schedules that he had prepared from the information we had given to him in May. These schedules confirmed our own figures and, in particular, confirmed my conclusion that applying section 60 would generate additional refunds. My original estimation of an additional $10,000 had been wrong – the department's own schedules showed that an extra $20,000 was now due to us. The Department refused to discuss this extra refund until December that year.

By November that year it seemed that the Department was desperately looking for ways to avoid paying our refund. I began to wonder if this audit would ever end. It was now 22 months old.

By this time we had spent way more than the refund we were due in time and expenditure. I had been further involved with police interviews but still had no clear idea of the nature of the complaints that the IRD had laid with them. The police would ring me up and ask me in for questioning. I went regularly to the police station with a lawyer in tow. They would question me about the nature of some of our transactions, but it was never clear to me what they were trying to find out and what I was suspected of having done wrong.

I employed a barrister named James O'Neill and briefed him on what had happened. He would come with me to the police station and argue with the police, for example, about whether they could video me as they questioned me. James O'Neill was as mystified as I was as to what the police wanted.

The questioning seemed to focus on the Stutz motor car. Interpol had interviewed Michael Wilson, a business associate of mine, in Sydney. He had been very intimidated by their arrival and even more concerned when they told him that I was under investigation for 22 counts of fraud. They asked him if he owed me any money and took a statement from him. He said he didn't, which was quite true as he owed the money to Tannadyce Investments Ltd. The Department sometime later was to try and make a big deal out of this without making the proper distinction between myself and Tannadyce, a limited liability company. At the same time the police were executing search warrants on several law firms around Christchurch with whom I had done business.

From Michael Wilson I now at least knew that I was supposedly facing 22 counts of fraud.

All of this was taking a huge emotional and financial toll on me. I was under investigation by the police. I was owed a very significant amount of money by the IRD. I had an audit on my hands that did not appear to have an end-point. I was spending money on lawyers and accountants. I was having to neglect my other business responsibilities.

At the end of November 1995, I resolved to work full time on all these tax matters until they were finished. I couldn't fulfil my other obligations as long as these matters were outstanding.

I deluded myself that somehow my businesses would hang together without my constant involvement. On reflection, the only justification for this was my belief that somehow all the IRD matters could be resolved promptly. As the audit stretched out, my businesses, desperate for cash and my time, could no longer be sustained. Eventually they were all to close down.

One of my most significant ventures was Radio Liberty. This was a niche radio station broadcasting in Auckland, Hamilton, Wellington and Christchurch. As a new venture operating in a highly competitive marketplace, it was always going to need my intense focus and maximum energy to have a chance of succeeding. The drain of the audit meant that I was putting little or no time into this venture. It was eventually to succumb. Radio Liberty was a significant financial and emotional loss for me.

On 1 December 1995 I rang Bond and insisted that he meet me to establish exactly what was going on and to establish exactly what it would take to conclude all issues. He agreed to the meeting but said that he would have a number of questions to prepare, the answers to which would help bring the audit to an end. In a later phone conversation he told me he had fifty more questions to put to me. It made me extremely suspicious to learn that the Department still had fifty questions despite having worked on the audit for two years and despite having lodged significant complaints of fraud to the police. I asked Mr Bond to fax me the questions. He refused to. I wanted the questions so that I could get the answers for him by the time of our meeting.

After some discussion we finally agreed to meet on 12 December. I was back at the fourth floor meeting room. At the meeting were Mr Bond, Mr Gibb Lee who was, I was told, taking over from Mr Byatt, and a stenographer. The meeting took three hours and we had to agree to continue for another three hours the following day. I have the stenographer's record of both meetings. The meeting was opened by Mr Bond accusing me of not having filed a credit note of approximately $30,000. I was stunned, especially in light of the ongoing investigation for fraud. I asked Mr Bond whether he had a copy of the credit note. He assured me that he did have it but he refused to show it to me. Mr Bond made great capital alluding to the fraud involved in not declaring the credit note.

The remaining questioning through that meeting, and over the continuation the next day, related to a whole raft of new issues mostly unrelated to section 60. Mr Bond could not reconcile for me his previous assurance that there was only one remaining issue with the Department now having in excess of fifty further questions.

That night I went back to my office and worked through until after 2.00am searching for the details of the alleged missing credit note. I knew nothing about any credit note, nor did any of my former staff. The meeting the next day was as acrimonious as the first. Mr Bond and Mr Lee endlessly focused on very minor points and continually refused to justify their purpose in doing so.

These two IRD officers went on for some time asking me what was Tannadyce's taxable activity, and who had made payments on a small number of invoices of minor value. They wanted details of advances from Tannadyce to an associate company. They were insisting they weren't advances but fees. All these matters had long since been dealt with satisfactorily. But I co-operated as best I could, provided the information they needed, and agreed to provide the further information that they specified. They in turn agreed to provide me with some information including a copy of the $30,000 credit note that they assured me they had.

Mr Bond made it clear that I was to deal with Gibb Lee. Mr Lee appeared very uptight. He was overtly agreeing with everything Mr Bond said, or suggested, and clearly had a bad attitude towards me. He displayed what I considered to be a completely unprofessional demeanour. In my view, Mr Lee was not approaching me or the audit with an unbiased mind.

On 13 December 1995 Mr Bond admitted that a previous letter he sent to me had defined a single unresolved issue, when in fact there were more. Mr Bond said "This problem was my own personal incompetence." This is recorded in the Department's own record of the meeting.

At the end of the meeting I asked for an off-the-record conversation with Chris Bond. Having got his complete assurance that it was off-the-record I proceeded to make a proposal to him. I explained that I would be willing to negotiate a settlement with IRD to bring the matter to a close if they would be willing to withdraw the complaint to the police. I explained to him that to date I had already spent more than any refund I would receive and that the affair was taking a heavy toll on me emotionally, physically and financially. Mr Bond told me that he would consider my proposal and discuss it with Peter Sivertsen. I later obtained his notes on file recording our off-the-record conversation.

The following day I chased up Gibb Lee to get a copy of the credit note for $30,000 that he and Mr Bond had accused me of not providing. After several calls he had to admit that no credit note existed. Mr Bond and Mr Lee had both been deceiving me. They had entirely made up their claim about the credit note. But rather than apologise, and humbly retract, Mr Lee continued to assert, without justification, that Tannadyce could not claim the original $30,000 expense and that they were going to deduct it anyway.

This to me typified the unprofessional conduct that I had had to endure for the previous two years. There was no willingness even to consider that they might be wrong. I believed that there had to be someone in the IRD who was professional enough to understand my position and demand that my audit be completed.

That day I rang Peter Boerlage. He confirmed that as Acting Manager (Taxpayer Audit), Mr Bond and Mr Lee were answerable to him. He agreed to meet me at 4pm that day. I trudged once again to the fourth floor meeting room. Also present was Philippa Foulds, a senior manager at the IRD. In great detail I explained to them the history of the audit, how it had started two years ago, how I received assurances nine months earlier that section 60 was the last remaining issue, and how we had had meetings this week where another 50 minor issues had been raised. I explained to them about the phantom credit note that I had been accused of withholding, and I spoke about the massive personal cost that it was all having on me. I pleaded with them to find a way to bring the matter to a close.

They seemed unwilling to accept that my views had any credibility. But they assured me that they would go back to Mr Bond and seek further clarification as to what was going on.

Over the next few days I provided more information that the Department was seeking and I made further written appeals to Mr Boerlage to find a way to expedite matters. None of these appeals bore fruit. The Department, as always, closed down for the Christmas period.

On the 10 January 1996 I received a letter from Peter Consedine, the acting District Commissioner. He asked me to stop ringing staff members at home. During the Christmas period, while I was still working on the audit, and in need of clarification of questions, I had taken the liberty of phoning two staff members at home. Generally, they had been very unhelpful. Mr Consedine went on to assure me that the staff involved on my file were working on identifying the remaining issues and would have those identified and detailed to me by 31 January 1996.

So here we were approaching the second birthday of the audit. The Department was advising that they had two staff members working full time for a month to identify the remaining issues in the audit. All this despite the fact that they had assured me, in April 1995, that the application of section 60 was the last remaining issue, and then, in December 1995, that the fifty questions were the last remaining matters.

I pleaded with them to explain immediately to me exactly where they were at, what information they were looking for, what actions were needed to bring the audit to completion, who was working on the audit and what priority it had within the Department.

Mr Consedine appeared intransigent. The IRD would not provide me with any more information until 31 January when they would provide me with a schedule of all outstanding issues.

On 29 January I received an eight-page letter from Mr Bond setting out the third set of "remaining issues". Much of this was just petty nonsense, with the Department wanting invoices for amounts like $60 and $70. Besides, we had already provided the Department with copies of all our invoices for the periods in question. Nonetheless, I set to work. The very next day I responded in full providing the information to all the significant issues raised.

I also phoned Mr Bond at home, as I couldn't get him at the office, to try and set up a meeting. I made this call at the suggestion of Mr Lee, but despite that Mr Bond lodged a formal complaint with the Telecom Malicious Calls Centre complaining about "nuisance phone calls" from me. On 2 February 1996 Mr Bond issued a section 17 notice demanding even more information. This is a notice issued pursuant to the provisions of section 17 of the Tax Administration Act. Section 17 provides departmental officers like Mr Bond with the power to demand information, in the course of an investigation, and threatens taxpayers with massive penalties if they don't comply.

As I had now been working full time on the audit for a couple of months, and as I appeared to be making no progress, it was time to rethink my whole approach and strategy. The audit was now two years old. I had received many worthless undertakings and assurances from senior staff. My health was continuing to decline. I was still under investigation for fraud. My businesses were crumbling around me. I desperately needed the refund but was being forced to spend significant amounts of money trying to bring the matter to an end.

I carefully weighed my options. I could pull out now, put Tannadyce into liquidation, and get on with rebuilding my life. Or I could persevere through this affair, work to bring the police investigation to a close, bring the audit to an end, receive my refund, and get on with my life at that point. Somehow it just didn't seem right to give up and walk away from $60,000 or $70,000 worth of GST refunds. Most importantly I believed that if I did give up and walk away from it, then that might make me appear guilty in respect of the IRD's complaints to the Fraud Squad. But there appeared to be no one in the IRD who I could reason or even negotiate with.

I realised that I was up against a number of senior IRD staff who had so much personally at stake in this audit. It would be a massive leap for them to explain how it was that they had spent two years, and hundreds of thousands of taxpayers' dollars, on an audit which generated nothing.

A firm of accountants advised me to concede something significant to the Department. They had seen audits of this nature before, with the auditors becoming so entrenched and so driven by their own personal feelings that you have to allow them to save face. They encouraged me to give way on a couple of significant points no matter how right I was, because such concessions might allow the auditors to justify their actions to their seniors. I found all of this repugnant.

I couldn't help but think of the thousands of small business people each year who face audits of this nature and who are forced to give up hard-earned money, unjustifiably, because of the Department's unprofessionalism and bias. I resolved to go the distance. I believed up until that date that I had co-operated fully with the Department, providing them with all the information they had ever requested and offering every assistance. My new strategy was to continue to follow the rule book exactly, but also to demand specific timetables, and to hold IRD staff to account for every undertaking and agreement they made. I also resolved to appeal at the highest level of IRD management with a hope that someone somewhere would understand what was going on, see how outrageous it was, and move to fix it by bringing this audit to a close.

I couldn't help but reflect on Mr Bond's personal assurance to me of over a year ago that the audit had only another forty hours work left to complete. I thought about how the Department repeatedly told me that I was a "customer", yet continued to treat me so contemptuously and unfairly.

The decision to see it right through was not one I took lightly. I realised that I was probably buying the fight of my life. Little did I know what was to come.

The audit is two years old. I am now working full time to resolve it. The IRD have introduced a large number of new issues and have falsely asserted the existence of an unreported credit note.

"We are sorry for the delays..."

The next day I rang the South Island District Commissioner, Marie Fahey. She seemed aware of my case. In a lengthy discussion she expressed concern about the allegations I was making to her. She assured me that if I took the time to set out my allegations in writing she would investigate them and respond to me. I was frustrated by this, but took the trouble to prepare a lengthy letter which I sent on 5 February 1996.

In mid-February I was advised that she had assigned a senior staff member who had had no previous dealings with the case to review it. I found out later the reviewer was Martin Herriot.

On 6 March 1996 I met with Chris Bond and Gibb Lee. They were more co-operative and it was clear there had been an attitudinal shift. I assumed that the District Commissioner had issued instructions that there needed to be a sharp lift in performance.

On 8 March I received a four-page letter from Philippa Foulds. The letter was a response to my letter of complaint to Marie Fahey, the District Commissioner, and followed the Department's internal review. Most of my complaints appeared to have been treated lightly. But the Department did apologise for Mr Bond's credit note mis-representation and for all the delays in the audit. Furthermore, and of greatest importance, the Department undertook to ensure that there would be no further delays in completing the audit. This was the most significant development in the audit to date, given that it had come from a very senior officer and followed a review ordered by the District Commissioner. I felt tremendous confidence that the outstanding matters could be concluded swiftly.

The Department now started hounding me over some remaining personal income tax. I had paid off a considerable amount of this but was left with a residual amount which was difficult to pay as I didn't have the money. In an effort to deal with this I once again met with Ross Gardiner, IRD's Acting Manager Taxpayer Audit. I proposed to him that – given the status of the Tannadyce audit, the interminable delays in dealing with it, and his acceptance that there may well be tax owing to us – that any action with regard to personal bankruptcy be held off until the Tannadyce audit had reached conclusion. Eventually he agreed to this and sent me a letter confirming the Department's acceptance. I thought that this was fair and practical. I immediately signed it and sent it back to him.

I continued to deal with Gibb Lee and Chris Bond, pursuing the few outstanding Tannadyce audit issues. Despite the Department's written undertaking ten days earlier that there would be no further delays, Mr Bond and Mr Lee refused to return my calls and, when I did get to speak to them, they freely acknowledged that they hadn't read or dealt with important correspondence that I had sent them. I was particularly frustrated because the audit was at a point where, if the officers concerned focused on it, everything could have been brought to a conclusion within a week.

Through February I had read and studied the Official Information Act. I wanted a clear understanding of what the Department's obligations were. On 7 March I lodged Official Information requests for all documentation relating to the police complaint.

Ross Gardiner provided a prompt response but the information he supplied was heavily edited. Despite that, I was able for the first time to get some understanding of the Department's claims of fraud against me. I was outraged. Their allegations were spurious and could have been easily cleared up and dealt with. Virtually none of the matters that they had accused me of had ever been discussed with me in any of the meetings we had had. This was in spite of me having offered, from the very beginning, to help in any way, to provide any information and to answer any questions.

There were also significant factual errors in their letter of complaint to the police. Dates were wrong. Amounts were wrong. Other significant points of fact were wrong. I sought immediately to discuss these issues with the Department. They refused to deal with it, hiding behind the excuse that the matter was now in the hands of the police. It was to be many more months before the police finally gave up the investigation and closed the file.

I also discovered for the first time that the letter of complaint to the police had been signed by Peter Sivertsen. This surprised me because it

INLAND REVENUE	165 Cashel Street,	Christchurch

INLAND REVENUE
TE TARI TAAKE

FAX

Date: **18/03/96**
Number of pages including cover sheet: **1**

TAXPAYER AUDIT

To: **Dave Henderson**

From: **Ross Gardiner**

Phone _____

Fax phone: **351 5695**

CC:

OfficePhone. **(03) 379 6060**

Fax phone **(03) 366 6654**

REMARKS: ☒ Urgent   ☐ For your review   ☐ Reply ASAP   ☐ Please comment

Further to our discussion last week and your request that we withhold any further bankruptcy action until the current audit is completed. I have discussed your request with Ray Healy in whose hands the tax recovery matter sits. We have agreed that it would be proper in the circumstances to agree to your request but subject to several "conditions" designed to protect the revenue.

Firstly, on the assumption that on completion of the audit there MAY be credits available to Tannadyce, we would ask you to authorise us to transfer sufficient of those credits to clear the balance of your personal account. Secondly, you authorise the transfer of any remaining credits to the Omnivox arrears account.

As I mentioned to you there have been a number of assessments raised on Tannadyce in the absence of GST returns. These returns need to be furnished to establish the exact liability for the periods in question for until that is done any credits becoming available will be absorbed, at least partly, by the default assessments for the missing return periods. Details of these assessments can be obtained from Ray Healy and your authorisation should also be faxed to him.

Apart from dealing with your information request my role in your affairs is an advisory capacity only and any requests/complaints etc concerning the audit, for example, should be made to Mrs Foulds. I can tell you though, that it has now "made it clear" that your responses are to be given priority by Messrs Bond and Lee.

PS. *This fax was drafted prior to your call this morning.*

---

appeared to me from our few discussions that he knew virtually nothing about the facts of the matter and, as time would show, had great difficulty in grasping any of the legal and commercial concepts involved. Recently, another senior IRD staff member advised me, in writing, that in respect of Mr Sivertsen's letter of complaint to the police that Mr Sivertsen's comments did not represent a considered appraisal.

On 21 March 1996, with matters grinding to a virtual halt, I met again with Ross Gardiner, Philippa Foulds and Chris Bond. I suggested to them that I had a logical and constructive way forward. I identified five major issues that needed to be dealt with. I spelt these out and got their agreement that they were the last five remaining issues. I then proposed that we work through each remaining issue in order, bringing each to its conclusion before we started on the next. Ross Gardiner and Philippa Foulds seemed particularly enthused about this process. Chris Bond appeared to have reservations and looked uncertain. Ross Gardiner and I agreed that we would work together to resolve the first issue, which was the Stutz motor car.

One of the key points here was whether or not the holding of a Power of Attorney fell within the legal definition of an associated person. I held Power of Attorney for Michael Wilson from whom I had technically bought the car as a settlement of a debt. The original owner had sold it to Mike as part of a property deal. I had also been involved in that original transaction as Mike's attorney. I had taken the Stutz off him in good faith believing it to be authentic. Mike had relied on my judgement. Bond maintained that as the term "trustee" was included in the definition of "associated persons" that the holding of a Power of Attorney and trustee were one and the same thing. I asked Mr Bond to support this irrational assertion. He said he had several dictionary definitions where Power of Attorney was included in the definition of trustee. He subsequently faxed through a couple of dictionary definitions, none of which came close to supporting his argument. Ross Gardiner appeared embarrassed by Bond and continued to work with me to conclude the Stutz issue. I advised him that I had information at my office that supported our position on the matter. He visited my office to go through this information. This was the first time in two-and-a-half years of being audited – despite my repeated invitations – that anyone from the IRD had bothered to visit me and inspect the records we held at our premises. So desperate was I to bring the matter to a conclusion that I even offered in writing for the Department to treat Wilson and me as associated persons. I was willing to suffer the financial disadvantage (if any) that might flow from this in an effort to bring the matter to a close. They never took up this offer.

Another offer I made was for the IRD to phone Mike Wilson and speak to him directly. They agreed to do this, obtained his number from me, and then never did a thing. Later they told me that they had made arrangements with the Australian Tax Office to interview Mike in Sydney. Mike was willing to co-operate in every way. He offered to swear affidavits to confirm the facts. They also declined this offer. It was to take almost nine months before the Australian Tax Office interview took place. Two Australian Tax Office officials drove down from Newcastle and met with Mike at his office in Sydney. They interviewed him for just over an hour and at the end of the interview apologised to Mike and told him that they were embarrassed by the questions which were repetitive and seemingly pointless. The questions had been prepared and sent to them by Chris Bond.

Despite Mr Bond's best efforts, Ross Gardiner reached a conclusion on the Stutz issue. He recommended that my position on this first point of the new agenda was correct. I was to find out later that Sivertsen never accepted this.

The next issue on our list was section 60. I was back dealing on this with Bond and Lee. There continued to be delays. Once more I had to complain to Philippa Foulds. She argued that the Department was under pressure and lacking resources. She accepted that her undertaking of 8 March was regularly being broken. She was not comfortable about this and an internal memo from her to Mr Bond and Mr Lee at this time confirms her displeasure with them for not performing. She said that, "under no circumstances was the Department to be seen to be responsible for any delays in the audit". Shortly after this she was removed from the case and was never involved again.

Around this time another curious incident occurred. A particularly irate staff member of mine from Auckland phoned me claiming falsely that he was owed thousands of dollars in wage arrears. He threatened that if I didn't pay him this money, none of which was actually owing, that he would visit the IRD in Christchurch and "tell them all about me". He went on to tell me that he already had had discussions with the Department and that they were very keen to meet with him. He was Arch Tambakis, talkback host, well known for making outrageous allegations. I told him to go for it and that I wouldn't be bullied or intimidated by baseless threats and allegations. I never thought any more about it until a few days later when I was walking down Cashel Street on my way to a meeting. I was stunned and amused to see Arch Tambakis sitting in a coffee shop directly under the IRD offices enjoying a cappuccino with senior IRD officer Don Gray. Tambakis was virtually blind and Gray didn't know me so I had a good opportunity to observe them both and get a clear record of what they were discussing.

The IRD didn't have the resources to clean up my audit but they had all the time in the world to hear nonsense smear stories from some whacko from Auckland. Tambakis was later to feature on the Holmes Show for

Senior Technical Officer

Copy to : Gibb Lee
          Investigator, Business Audit

From: Philippa Foulds
           Acting Manager, Taxpayer Audit

Subject: Tannadyce Investments Ltd
          Dave Henderson

Friday 15 march I received a call from Mr Henderson.

He was extremely angry and vented this anger upon me, in no
uncertain terms.

A letter was sent by me , 8 March 1996, copy attached. I had
discussed the contents of this letter with you before I issued it.

Para 6... " The department undertakes to ensure that there are no
          further delays in this audit."

Mr Henderson's anger culminated in a charge that I was a downright
liar.

A letter was faxed to the department on the 11th. He had yet to
receive an acknowledgment or reply, as at 15 March. In speaking to
Gibb he became aware that no action would take place until after
the 15th upon your (Chris) return.

He quite rightly charges that I made a false statement in my
letter of 8 March.

I am not satisfied with the manner in which Mr Henderson's letter
of 11 March was handled. At a minimum Mr Henderson should have
received an acknowledgement. If the material his letter contained
was insufficient to make a decision, this should have been
conveyed to him also.

Under no circumstances can we afford to be responsible for delays
in progressing this audit.

Please address the issues of the letter of the 11th with urgency
and ensure Mr Henderson is kept informed of progress.
I would expect a reply to be issued to Mr Henderson by midday
Tuesday 19th March.

I would also ask that in the future, I be kept informed of any
correspondence which is received from the taxpayer and the
timeframe required to respond to issues involved.

P Foulds
Acting Manager, Taxpayer Audit
Christchurch
18/3/96

running a scam on old-lady callers to his Hamilton talkback show.

On 3 April, less than a month after their undertaking that there would be no further delays, Peter Sivertsen, by this time manager of the Technical and Legal Support Group, wrote to me demanding that I deal exclusively with Gibb Lee. This was totally contrary to our agreement to resolve issues sequentially with the relevant officers. Gibb Lee by this time had become the local shop steward for an IRD union that had broken away from the PSA. This meant that he was often away in Wellington for several days at a time negotiating pay and conditions for IRD workers.

It was inevitable that having only Gibb Lee working on Tannadyce would slow everything down even more. I wrote back to Peter Sivertsen the next day pleading with him not to do this to me, but to no avail.

Through April I made several further pleas to Peter Sivertsen to have outstanding issues addressed. The Department remained adamant that everything was to go through Mr Lee.

Finally the Department agreed to hold a meeting on 23 April 1996 at 2pm. The meeting was chaired by Peter Sivertsen. Also present were Messers Bond, Gardiner and Lee. It was the first time that I had met Sivertsen. He was at the meeting in his capacity as Manager, Technical and Legal Support Group. What particularly amazed me was that he appeared unable to grasp the simplest of technical or legal points. He appeared to be well past his use-by date and certainly not management material. After a very short period his attention waned and it was obvious he did not want to be there.

Nonetheless, the meeting went smoothly for a couple of hours, slowly making progress through the issues until Bond stormed out. It was clear that there was a dispute between Bond and Gardiner and that Bond was uncomfortable with some of the positions that Gardiner was agreeing to. At Peter Sivertsen's suggestion we brought the meeting to a close and reconvened the following Monday.

Still clearly miffed, Bond did not show up. The other three did. I repeated the four key issues that we still needed to resolve. I believed the issue relating to the Stutz had been resolved. In respect of section 60 I revisited the schedules prepared by us in May 1995, and confirmed by Mr Byatt in August 1995, that showed that we were due significant further refunds. Everyone present at the meeting accepted that the schedules appeared to be in order and there appeared to be little difficulty in resolving the other issues. I then wanted to produce a nine-page schedule that I had prepared documenting all the delays that had occurred in the 27 months that the audit had been

Mike Wilson: Australian property investor, for whom I held Power of Attorney.

running.

Sivertsen became very restless, had no interest in my complaints and was desperate to wrap the meeting up. Gibb Lee kept on whining that he had only been involved since December 1995 and he therefore could not have been responsible for the delays in the first two years of the audit. In short, my complaints of delays and Departmental shortcomings were of no interest to these senior personnel.

Despite everyone's agreement that we had effectively finished the section 60 matter there was still no finalisation. On 15 May I met yet again with Ross Gardiner and Gibb Lee. Gibb Lee presented a bizarre notion that there was a letter written by the BNZ on file that he had discovered which stated that all GST refunds for the development of the complex were to the advantage of the BNZ. He undertook to get this letter to me as soon as possible. I was stunned by this and particularly amazed that the Department would ignore the law and rely on a letter from one party to another in a commercial transaction as determining legal tax liability. Once more, Chris Bond had not attended this meeting. Ross Gardiner expressed frustration about this.

I repeatedly asked Gibb Lee for details of the Department's own legal opinion on section 60. Highly embarrassed, he had to acknowledge that the Department in the whole 27 months had not bothered to obtain any legal opinion. Ross Gardiner was stunned and freely expressed his amazement. He then undertook to have a staff solicitor summarise all the points supporting the Department's position and to make sure that this was forwarded to me. To this day I have never received that summary.

In another desperate attempt to bring the whole affair to a close I freely offered to settle or compromise on several issues, even though the Department was wrong, if that would help. I was being driven down by the ongoing costs and the ongoing personal toll.

Several days after that meeting I chased Gibb Lee for a copy of the letter from the BNZ that he claimed to have relied on to support his view on the section 60 issues. He could not produce the letter and eventually had to acknowledge it didn't exist. He had made it up.

Once again I phoned Philippa Foulds to express my disappointment that her undertaking that there be no further delays was being continually breached. She explained to me that she was no longer able to comment on the audit and that I was not to phone her again. She terminated the call by telling me that the new manager for Taxpayer Audit was Adriaan Geerlofs.

Adriaan Geerlofs: Told the court assessments had been issued, when they had not been.

On 22 May I received a letter from Peter Sivertsen telling me that their legal section had now done an opinion on the ramifications of section 60 and that the Department's position remained unchanged. I immediately rang Lee, eagerly trying to obtain a copy of the opinion so that I could understand their position and hopefully resolve the matter. Lee refused to provide me with a copy of the opinion or a summary of it. He never explained why I could not see it. I was later to be advised that no legal opinion was ever obtained.

On the strength of Philippa Fould's advice I made my first contact with Adriaan Geerlofs. He was a dry character, recently transferred to Christchurch from Wellington.

He seemed genuinely interested in my case but certainly didn't appear to accept the gravity of my allegations. He assured me that he would address matters and would try and move it forward.

One step forward, two back. The IRD had apologised for the delays but there were still continuing delays. They still had no legal opinion on my tax position – despite saying that they had – and were still asserting reliance on documents that didn't exist.

...Even more delays

Finally I received some schedules from Gibb Lee on 13 June that for the first time identified specific positions the Department was taking. These schedules were bizarre. When we were doing our development work on the Station Village project we had established a number of businesses such as a restaurant, a large bakery, a micro brewery and bar. We wanted to create anchor tenants that would generate foot traffic and hopefully attract further tenants to the complex. To operate and manage these businesses we set up separate limited liability companies. But it was Tannadyce that had incurred the expenditure in the development of the premises and the setting up of the businesses. It appeared that Mr Lee had spent a great deal of time itemising all Tannadyce's expenditure on the development and reallocating the expenditure attributable to the establishment of each business away from Tannadyce, who had spent the money and owned the asset, to the separate operating companies. For reasons never divulged to me, Mr Lee had also allocated almost half-a-million dollars of expenditure away from Tannadyce to a company that had never even traded. Repeated requests by me to Mr Lee for an explanation came to naught. I wrote to Mr Sivertsen seeking urgent clarification of several of the points in Mr Lee's schedules.

A great deal of work had been done reallocating the expenditure in these schedules. What stunned me was the arbitrariness of the reallocation. Logic, and my own way of approaching these things, suggested that before any reallocation occurred, the principles, technical positions and legal propositions involved should have been thoroughly canvassed. There should have been an attempt by the Department to agree with me and my advisers on this before proceeding to spend hours completing schedules that were completely unfounded.

It was clear, even from casual observation, that this rescheduling would have a dramatic impact on Tannadyce's GST position. Instead of an increase in our refund – which was to be expected from the schedules the Department had provided in 1995, these new schedules and reallocation had the effect of negating completely all of Tannadyce's refunds that were due.

I couldn't help but rekindle my earlier fears that, given that the Department by this time must have spent in excess of quarter-a-million dollars on this audit, that there would be increasing pressure on the officers involved to find something to negate my refund and justify their time and expenditure.

My fears were further fuelled because the only consistent principle that appeared to be driving the reallocation was that it was always and everywhere to be to Tannadyce's detriment. There would be no extra tax to be gained by the IRD in all this even if the Department were right – these other companies could have claimed back the GST. What would make a significant difference would be the interest and penalties that would be added with the reversal of the refunds made to Tannadyce.

Also at this time, I had completed and filed an income tax return for Tannadyce. The Department immediately began an audit of that return. It showed the first of our losses at approximately a quarter-of-a-million dollars. The audit of that return was concluded in November 1998 (two-and-a-half years later) with the Department confirming the losses that we had claimed to the cent. When the Department started that audit they had assigned it to a keen young auditor called Philip Lynn. Poor Lynn didn't have any concept of what he was getting into. The senior management of the IRD had sent the new boy to audit Dave Henderson. To give him credit, at least he had the good manners and professionalism to come to my office to discuss the matter with me. I explained to him, deliberately understating the fact, that I had had some difficulty with IRD personnel involved in a current GST audit of the company. I asked him to sign a pledge with me confirming unequivocally to adhere completely with the Department's own protocols for conducting audits as outlined in the Department's pamphlet IR 297 published in May 1995. Those protocols included such tough constraints as requiring IRD staff to be professional and courteous, fair and impartial, and prompt and efficient. Lynn seemed to think that signing this pledge was a reasonable thing to do. But he asked if he could take it away and study it some more.

He came back a couple of days later with his own reworked version of my pledge hand-written on Departmental stationery and ready to sign. I requested a couple of changes, which he agreed to, and he promptly returned with a second draft. I told him I would be happy with this and that as soon as he signed it we could get underway. I heard nothing for several weeks.

Finally I got a phone call from Lynn very nervously explaining that Adriaan Geerlofs had advised him not to sign this pledge. Subsequently, Geerlofs wrote advising me that Lynn would not be signing the pledge, that it was Departmental policy not to make such written commitments and he chastised me for having proposed the pledge as a condition of Lynn commencing his audit. Tannadyce's income tax audit was soon passed to another more seasoned auditor.

Having spent a few days in late June 1996 studying the schedules prepared by Gibb Lee, I decided to go back to District Commissioner Marie Fahey. I wanted to explain to her that in the five months since we had last talked that there had been considerably more delays and, more importantly, there had been considerable regression in terms of the audit. I found that she had retired. The Department had since been reorganised again and the office of District Commissioner had been superseded by the office of Service Centre Manager. The new Service Centre Manager for the South Island was Carson McNeill. I contacted him, explained who I was, and said that his predecessor, Marie Fahey, had left an invitation open to me to contact her again if I was encountering difficulties with the Department. I asked him to meet with me. He was extremely reluctant to have anything to do with me or the case and kept assuring me that everything was fine. I kept on assuring him that it wasn't. Reluctantly he agreed to meet me a few days later.

On Friday 21 June 1996 at 9:30am I met with Carson McNeill in his office. He once again advised me strongly that he was not willing to become involved in this matter. He confirmed that Peter Sivertsen was in charge of the audit. I expressed my reservations about Siversten's ability to grasp the issues involved but he was completely unwilling to accept that proposition. We wrapped up the meeting with him assuring me that Sivertsen would contact me the following Tuesday to advise me the terms of reference for the way the audit would be completed, the timetable for completion, a time-table for dealing with outstanding correspondence, and an update on a number of Official Information requests that I had lodged that the Department had not bothered to respond to. I left the meeting feeling pleased. This seemed like a positive development, particularly the concept of having a timetable that we could now work to.

By close of business on Tuesday 25 June I still had not heard from Sivertsen, as Carson McNeill had assured me that I would. So I rang his office and all they would tell me was that he was out of town. I knew he had responsibilities in other regions, and I guessed he might be in Nelson. Opening the Nelson phone book I picked the most expensive hotel that I could recall and rang there. Bingo! He was registered in the hotel and they put me through to his room. I spoke to him and reminded him of Carson McNeill's commitment for him to phone me. He stuttered and stammered, as he was prone to do, and confirmed that McNeill had briefed him. I could hear him rustling for papers. He then started to quote me the timetable that had been agreed upon. The GST audit was to be completed by 5 July. That was still ten days away. It seemed to me too long and I protested. He said there was nothing he could do to change it. He said the Income Tax audit would be completed by 2 August. I protested that too. I wanted to discuss the other issues. He told me that he was too tired (this was at 6 pm!) and could I phone him in the morning at the Nelson IRD office.

I rang him at 9:15am the next morning. He was willing to talk and I opened the discussion by affirming my belief that every issue could be cleaned up swiftly with a little bit of goodwill on both sides. He asked me to identify the major issues. I had done this at least ten times before with senior IRD staff including himself. To demonstrate goodwill I stated them again. His own notes of that telephone conversation record the clear and specific detail with which I set out the remaining four issues.

His notes also record that I pleaded with him to send staff to visit my offices to inspect documents, agreements, contracts, and similar, that would help establish the principles and the nature of the relationship between all the parties in the Station Village Development. These would show why Gibb Lee's reallocations were completely wrong. He gave me his personal assurance that he would arrange for staff to come to my office and look through these documents. No one ever did.

Carson McNeill: Broke many of the undertakings and agreements he entered into with me.

50

707

Discussion with David Henderson 26 June 1996 9.15 am

David rang me following our conversation last evening and stated his belief that every issue could be cleaned up with a little bit of goodwill on both sides.

I asked David to list for me the five most critical issues that he believed needed to be attend to. These are as follows :

1   Section 60 GST Act

   ○   Ramifications on the Agency. This is already done.

   ○   Chris said he had accepted the figures from Kath Cook which were audited by Gordon Byatt.

2   The lease arrangement between Tannadyce Investment Limited and BNZ

   ○   Rolls credit notes

   ○   No one has ever dealt with the BNZ on this one

   ○   He can get an invoice from the BNZ which would make his input claim legitimate. He had spoken about this to Gibb but Gibb made no comment.

(Both of these issues could have been dealt with 18 months ago, he said, or at least at the beginning of this year)

3   The Issue of Fees

   ○   This is a genuiue dispute

   ○   Is willing to accept some adjustments

   ○   But no one is willing to get back to him on this.

4   The Stutz Issue

   ○   Two or three sub issues arise out of this.

   ○   He has no faith that the ATO will attend to this within a year or even two.

   ○   He is not afraid of the issue and wants to discuss it and have it out.

5   Immediate Discussion

Henderson wants IRD to acknowledge that it has spent 31 months on this audit.

- show him in what way he has not helped, or provided information that was requested.

- there had been gross incompetence in this Department, Chris has acknowledged this.

- He assures us that there is goodwill on his part, he wants to get on with his life.

- Ross is the only person who has ever bothered to come across to his office.

- If any one had come to inspect the records in his office (and there are boxes of records available) they could have sorted out the issues.

- The records are available now. These would sort out the issues in the schedule sent out by Gibb.

6   Nonsense, nit picking. He wants this to stop.

David concluded by saying that there are only two possible options to this audit.

a   we work it out with goodwill and sit down to draw up a determined programme for the conclusion and wrap up of the audit.

b   we slug it out in Court and he brings an action against several people in the Department. This will take months possibly years.

His concluding comment was why can't we sort out the 1992 income tax return in a very short time and why does it takes 6 weeks. (I pointed out that we don't want to look at one return in isolation.)

I did however assure David that if there were records available that would help sort out the issues and these were accessible now then I would arrange for people to call and talk to him at his office and look through those invoices. His phone number is 03 3654125.

Peter Sivertsen

CHRONOLOGY
THURS 8.30.

Later that week I had further discussions with Adriaan Geerlofs, trying to get my mind around the bizarre figures and schedules prepared by Gibb Lee. On 2 July 1996 Mr Lee wrote to me apologising for his errors and trying to explain the correct position. I was even more confused. I rang McNeill again. He made no secret that he was completely frustrated with me. He appeared to be implying that I was either slow or was deliberately misunderstanding Mr Lee's schedules. He finally agreed to set up a meeting with Peter Sivertsen, Adriaan Geerlofs, Chris Bond and Gibb Lee, who would all explain to me in clear detail the rationale for the position the Department was taking in relation to the audit. Once again I was enthused. I still believed that given a couple of hours and goodwill on the side of the Department all the issues could be resolved and the principles for finalising the audit properly established. Given the seniority of all the people involved, I still thought that reason would prevail and that a swift and positive outcome was possible.

The schedules allocating expenditure issued by IRD were bizarre – the only principle guiding them was that they were to be to Tannadyce's detriment. Tannadyce also had an income tax audit to deal with. Sivertsen had undertaken once more to take a fresh look at matters.

Gibb Lee dumps on Henderson. Then takes a holiday

We set up the meeting for 1.00pm on Thursday 4 July 1996. Bond and Lee were not there, despite the Department stating that this was an all-important meeting.

I was committed to making the most of the meeting. I honestly believed that at the end of this day I would walk out with the Department freely acknowledging that their positions and schedules were wrong and with them holding a clear view of the reality of Tannadyce's relationships and transactions.

I had asked for a whiteboard to be available in the meeting room. I had framed up in my mind how the meeting should flow and how I would logically and dispassionately set out all the relationships, the specific nature of the transactions, the flow of events and how everything linked together. It was vital for me to conduct this meeting properly and thoroughly to try and bring this nightmare to an end.

I commenced the meeting by advising that I had records available at my office to support everything that I was going to detail. I offered to have staff deliver any of these records that they might need to substantiate my position.

I spent the first two hours on the whiteboard. I would ask myself the questions that I believed the Department's auditors should have been asking

31 months ago. I answered them clearly and honestly drawing diagrams and flow charts to support everything that I was presenting. I dispassionately set out my view of the principles and the exact nature of all the relationships. I became concerned that Peter Sivertsen was not even grasping the simplest of my explanations. He was becoming very restless and regularly yawning. However, Geerlofs was taking copious notes and asking questions. When I had explained what I thought were all the principles and legal propositions involved, and the exact nature of all the relationships of all the parties, I wrote on the whiteboard the remaining issues that needed to be concluded to bring the audit to an end. I went through each issue setting out clearly my viewpoint. I gave detailed explanations, and given that some of the concepts were a little bit difficult to grasp, I took the time to allow each of them to understand them. Furthermore, I continued to set out my conclusions and positions on the whiteboard. At Sivertsen's request the meeting concluded at 4:30. Both Geerlofs and Sivertsen agreed to meet with Gibb Lee and Chris Bond the next day, Friday 5 July, and to meet with me again on Monday 8 July to try and wrap the matter up. Once again, albeit reluctantly, I expressed my willingness to compromise, if necessary, to conclude matters.

Over that weekend I took time to go back over all my files. I was highly optimistic about the meeting on Monday and I wanted to be sure that I hadn't missed or misrepresented anything.

On Monday 8 July we met again at 2pm and again Gibb Lee and Chris Bond weren't there. Mr Sivertsen opened the meeting by saying that he was only willing to be there for less than an hour. He didn't explain why he couldn't be there longer. Both he and Adriaan Geerlofs appeared uninterested. This was also not a good sign. They very abruptly explained to me that they had met with Mr Bond and Mr Lee, that they had gone over all my propositions and explanations and that as a consequence the Department's view was unchanged. I was shattered.

They concluded by advising me that assessments would be issued in the next few days and I would have to go through the Department's formal objection process if I didn't accept those assessments. The meeting was over in 45 minutes. They had no questions for me. They refused to provide me with any justifications or explanations for the irrational positions that they were taking.

Some weeks later I was to obtain copies of Adriaan Geerlofs' notes of these meetings. It was clear to me by studying those notes that he had not understood or grasped the simple explanations that I had put forward.

It was disappointing that neither he nor Peter Sivertsen had asked for any of the records I had offered to substantiate my position.

Also around this time, I had been chasing responses to Official Information requests I had made to Mr Bond over three months earlier. The Official Information Act exists to provide more openness in government and to make government and government departments more accountable. It provides for the public to request information from Ministers and government departments and the recipient of such a request is obliged by the Act to respond with the relevant information in twenty working days. The spirit of the Act is that the recipients of a request are to assist and to help the person making the request and to co-operate in all reasonable ways to make information available. With one exception, my experience throughout all my dealings with the IRD was 180 degrees away from what is embodied in the Act.

The Department says in its brochures that taxpayers can expect to receive copies of notes of meetings and phone conversations with IRD staff. I had to resort to making Official Information requests to obtain such copies. On most occasions the Department would not even respond to these requests. It would take several appeals to senior staff before I would get a response. Most of those responses were outright refusals.

In this particular instance, Mr Bond tried charging me for his time in accessing and copying the copies of meeting notes that I sought. I kicked up a fuss about this and eventually the proposal to charge me was dropped.

By this time my life was a nightmare. I had devoted almost eight months of my life full-time and two years part-time to dealing with this extraordinary affair. I had also committed a huge amount of resources. I was battling with a number of corporate creditors, some of whom I had provided with personal guarantees. The IRD were also moving to wind up the operating company for Radio Liberty, Omnivox International Ltd, based once more on false claims. I was too embattled to deal with this. The $60,000-70,000 that Tannadyce was due would be a huge help. I sensed that maybe I was being imprudent by not focusing on producing money to deal with these debts and to deal with my own day-to-day living requirements. But I was committed to finalising the audit.

On 9 July, the day after our disappointing meeting, I wrote yet another long letter to Peter Sivertsen pointing out how and why the Department was making a grave mistake with their proposed expenditure reallocation. I highlighted for him the history of the Department's position on section 60 over the preceding 31 months, in particular showing how the Department had held a number of differing viewpoints and had never once obtained any legal opinions even from its own staff lawyers. I still believed that I was only one intelligent and fair IRD staff member away from having everything resolved. All I needed to do was to find that person.

Peter Sivertsen was the manager of the Technical and Legal Support Group. As its name implies, this group exists within the Department to assist auditors and investigators to arrive at the correct legal and technical position with the audits they are working on. Yet Sivertsen never made a robust effort to ensure that in this case the correct technical and legal positions were identified. As time went by it was clear to me that he himself did not understand any of the concepts involved and yet he had signed the letter of complaint to the police.

On 10 July 1996 I received one of the most significant pieces of correspondence to that point, a letter from Gibb Lee. He referred to his earlier work sheets and schedules and to my letter the previous day addressed to Peter Sivertsen. He told me that amended assessments for the various GST periods were being prepared and that they would be issued shortly. He asserted that the "underlying bases for our amended assessments have been discussed with you on a number of occasions and set out in our letters of 29 January and 2 February 1996. To ensure clarity I will list them again". The letters he referred to contained no explanations as he asserted. They were simply requests for further information. That on its own was contemptuous enough. But the further explanations in Mr Lee's letter to "ensure clarity" showed absolute disdain.

It was clear that the most central and significant issue was that relating to section 60 and the Department's reallocation of expenditure. To explain this Mr Lee advised, referring to BNZ, Tannadyce and associated entities that, "income and expenses have been allocated amongst these various entities in relation to their identified involvement in the complex". The complex, of course, was the Station Village Development. He went on to explain: "The allocation is based on documentation from various sources, in accordance with section 60 of the Goods and Services Tax Act 1985 and the relationship between Tannadyce and the other entities". The most significant parts of this were "identified involvement" and "relationship". I had explained clearly with supporting documentation the identified involvement of each party and their specific relationships. Despite several appeals, the Department had never provided me with any detail of their perception of the involvement or relationship of the parties. Nor had they rebutted or provided me with opposing arguments. They had never scheduled or specifically referred to "the documentation from various sources". Their position was completely wrong. As I have explained earlier, as one specific example, they were reallocating expenditure from Tannadyce, that it had legitimately incurred, to a company that had never traded. They were not open to any evidence or opposing arguments from me – they were simply bulldozing a position on to me.

On reflection this letter is one of the most oppressive pieces of communication I have ever received. What made it worse was that on the day after I received it the author, Mr Lee, left on an eight-week overseas holiday. He said in his letter that he had explained the Department's position to me knowing full well that he never had. With the full knowledge that his reallocations had no foundation in reality, and completely contradicted all that I had put before him, Mr Lee, with the express approval of his seniors, was going ahead to issue nonsense assessments.

He also recorded in that letter that if I chose to object to these assessments then "the objection must be lodged by 30 September 1996".

I was shattered. Up until this time, I had not actively involved lawyers or accountants. I had used them on the periphery to seek opinion on technical and legal points. I had done this for two reasons: firstly, to avoid running up massive expenditure; and secondly, because I had naively believed that I was going to have the matter solved on my own long before this. I now needed professional help.

The IRD had made up nonsense schedules. The officer I had to deal with was overseas for two months. The only process available to me was to object formally to the assessments. I had a date I had to object by. The trouble was the assessments hadn't been issued.

IRD issue multiple false and contradictory assessments

The next day my friend and lawyer Brian Palliser came to see me. Brian is a senior partner in a well-established Christchurch law firm, Hill, Lee and Scott. He is one of the most big-hearted people I know. If he builds respect for you he will do anything and everything to help you in any way he can at any time. I had met him many years earlier when he was acting for a creditor of my ill-fated business, the Sandwich Factory. He had turned up at my doorstep serving summonses and I had on more than one occasion invited him in for a cup of tea. We had enjoyed each other's company. He seemed stunned some months later after the Sandwich Factory had gone into liquidation that I turned up in his office with a bundle of cash to pay his client in full. While I had done this as a matter of personal responsibility, as I had done for all that company's creditors, he seemed taken aback that someone would bother paying a debt for which they had no legal liability. This action clearly endeared me to him and from that day on Brian has always been ready and willing to assist, sometimes in extraordinary ways and without payment, with any difficulty that I may have.

Although he was familiar with some of the elements of the tax dispute, I had never told him all the fine detail. He knew I was distressed and he wanted to help. On this day we set aside a couple of hours. Without the benefit of a whiteboard I repeated almost verbatim the exact analysis I had given to Geerlofs and Sivertsen a week earlier. Brian asked probing and important questions about the transactions and the deals Tannadyce had done and gained a full and complete understanding of all the issues involved. I quickly brought him up to speed with all the correspondence. He too was stunned by the Department's position, how it was dogmatically adhering to a view that not only appeared to be inexplicable but also defied logic and commonsense.

He was enthusiastic about being quickly able to deal with the Department and sort matters out. He identified the possibility that there may be a personality clash between myself and the senior IRD officers and suggested that he communicate directly with Carson McNeill to identify the issues, and insist on an immediate resolution. As time would evidence, the Department were to treat him with just as much contempt as they were treating me.

I continued to receive correspondence from the Department on some other peripheral issues. With Mr Lee away for eight weeks, I contacted Peter Sivertsen to enquire as to whom I could deal with in Lee's absence and how we might advance issues. Sivertsen refused to deal with any further matters and insisted that nothing happen until Lee returned from his overseas holiday.

I was becoming desperate. I urgently needed the refund and audit issues resolved. I was involved in fighting rear-guard actions to stop creditors pursuing me for personal and corporate debts.

A week after receiving Gibb Lee's oppressive letter I still had not received the assessments that he had promised me. I didn't know how to access them because he was away on holiday. I rang Sivertsen and Geerlofs on a number of occasions. As usual, they undertook to deal with the matter and get back to me and, as usual, they never did. I followed these calls up with letters which didn't get a response.

On 19 July 1996 I received the letter shown overleaf from Peter Sivertsen:

This letter typifies my dealings with the IRD. I was being asked to deal only with a staff member who was overseas for a two-month holiday. I was being asked to object to assessments and adjustments of which I had not received any details. And I was being asked to provide written factual evidence to support my opposition to circumstances that the Department refused to detail for me.

It was clear to me that this contemptuous mode of operation was not only in clear contradiction of all IRD's stated policies and procedures but it

Inland Revenue
Te Tari Taake

Christchurch Service Centre

Charter House
165 Cashel Street
Private Bag
Christchurch
New Zealand

Telephone 03-379 8500
Facsimile 03-366 6654

19 July 1996

Mr David Henderson
Tannadyce Investments Ltd
Box 1066
CHRISTCHURCH

Dear Sir

I observe that despite the request in my letter of 11 July 1996 that you confine your contacts to the case officer involved, you have continued to call both Mr Geerlofs and me after hours at our private residences. You have also rung me on a number of occasions after we had had discussions on an issue despite receiving an assurance that I would respond when I had consulted other officers.

Not content with this you have also rung various officers around the Department seeking my whereabouts.

I remind you that you have also pursued me at various venues when I have been away from my office, including phone calls to Nelson when I was working there.

In addition you have continued to address correspondence to both Mr Geerlofs and myself. I must ask you again to put your energy into providing a substantive objection to any adjustments that you disagree with and to provide written factual evidence to support your objection. I am not prepared to enter into any further discussions with you on the conduct of the audit nor in respect of the numerous other assertions you have made. You have had the benefit of an independent review and full consideration of your views by Mr Geerlofs and myself, which confirmed the findings of the investigators.

Yours faithfully

P Sivertsen
Manager
Technical and Legal Support Group

spat in the face of the concepts of natural justice. But as I discovered there was nothing that I could do to change it. The Department held all the cards. A few days later I received yet another letter from Peter Sivertsen reasserting the Department's position. He made the bizarre observation that "I cannot accept that you have never been acquainted with the Department's position with respect to section 60 matters and the relationship between the BNZ and Tannadyce Investments Ltd. In essence, the Department's position is quite simple on this matter viz, that the various agreements in their entirety lead us to the conclusion that an agency relationship existed between BNZ and Tannadyce".

So Sivertsen is now saying that the Department's position is exactly that which was accepted by Chris Bond and myself in April 1995 some 16 months earlier – a position that the Department confirmed a few months later with their own schedules that showed that Tannadyce would be due additional GST refunds. This letter totally contradicts what Gibb Lee had been putting to me with his reallocations. Before signing off his bizarre letter, Mr Sivertsen issued the following instruction to me, "What is now required is that you prepare a formal objection to the assessments that had been issued". The trouble with this advice was

Brian Palliser: Only took a couple of hours to understand clearly all the issues.

that no assessments had been issued. I hoped that the receipt of the assessments might provide further clarification.

Of course, I would phone Peter Sivertsen several times over the next few days trying to get hold of the assessments. Mostly, he would hang up. I would then phone his boss, Carson McNeill, who would give me soft assurances that would come to nought.

The time I had been allocated within which to lodge objections was fast ticking away.

But I did around this time ascertain from Adriaan Geerlofs that, contrary to all I had presented to them, the Department had arrived at the belief that the businesses that Tannadyce had developed at Station Village were for and on behalf of the BNZ and therefore the expense incurred by Tannadyce was to be accrued to the benefit of the BNZ. As always when matters like this arose, I dealt with this instantly. I rang the law firm Buddle Findlay in Wellington and spoke to Justin Toebes, the partner in the firm who acted for the BNZ, and with whom I had dealt. He was astounded by this proposition. He immediately wrote a letter rejecting it and faxed it to me. I had the letter delivered to Adriaan Geerlofs and once more naively sat back believing I had finally solved the audit. Of course, it didn't change a thing.

A few days later I managed to secure a meeting with Carson McNeill. I pressed upon him with every ounce of persuasion I possessed that the

Department was making a grave error in proceeding as they were. I explained that I had never received a proper explanation of the Department's application of section 60, nor had I received the assessments setting out the new position. He didn't accept either of my claims. He made it very clear to me that the Department would not entertain any further discussion in respect of the audit. Despite all the errors they had made to date, and all the delays, the Department was not prepared to grant me even the smallest benefit of the doubt.

Carson McNeill kept on assuring me that he had complete confidence in all his staff who had worked on the file and that they had acted completely in accordance with Departmental procedure and policy. I faced the fact that all my avenues of communication had been completely shut down. Brian Palliser's letter had not been responded to. The objection period was fast being whittled away and no assessments had been issued or further detail provided.

Over the next three or four weeks I wrote many letters pleading with the senior IRD staff in Christchurch to provide me with explanations and the assessments. Once more, I received a variety of baseless assurances and undertakings. For example, on 30 July 1996 at 8:15am I had a telephone conversation with Carson McNeill. He gave me his personal assurance that he would ensure that I would receive full detail on the Department's position on section 60 and the reallocation of expenditure shortly. I never received this.

It was my observation that Carson McNeill, the IRD's most senior South Island officer, had little or no control over his staff. Over the course of two years of dealing with McNeill he would break with impunity the greater number of agreements and undertakings that he gave me.

In the last week of July, I did start receiving GST statements of account and some GST assessment notices. That week I received nine different assessments for Tannadyce, all covering the same period, all with different figures. There were no discrepancy notices accompanying any of these assessment notices. I had got into the habit of ringing other IRD offices around the country. I would indicate to them that I was a taxpayer in their local area seeking some direction and advice. I would regularly find that the advice I would get from, say, the Tauranga office, would conflict with what the senior officers in Christchurch were telling me. For example, an IRD staff member in the North Shore office explained to me that they would never

CHRISTCHURCH SERVICE CENTRE

DATE	:	1 AUGUST 1996
TO	:	ADRIAAN GEERLOFS AREA MANAGER BUSINESS LINK
FROM	:	CARSON MCNEILL SERVICE CENTRE MANAGER
SUBJECT	:	**HENDERSON**

This is a record of conversation I had with Mr Henderson on Tuesday 30 July 1996 at 8.15 am approximately.

Mr Henderson rang in relation to assessments received and the fact that no detailed discrepancy notices had been attached. I referred Mr Henderson to a letter he had received on 10 July in which those discrepancies had been explained and that he now had every right, if he needed to, to raise objections, in which at least two months would be given.

Mr Henderson went on further in relation to section 60 adjustments on one hand and secondly the undertaking that he had understood from Ross Gardiner and Ray Healey that the department would not take any action of bankruptcy against him.

In respect of the section 60 adjustment I said that I would ensure that he would receive adequate detail for him to decide on whether he wished to agree or disagree and thus take objection (Peter Sivertsen already has this underway).

In respect of the question of bankruptcy action being taken I explained to Mr Henderson that no one could premeditate the future action of the department in respect of outstanding liability. What was important was that the liability is first established hence the reason for the assessments which was the department's belief as to the correct liability.

Carson McNeill

---

issue assessments involving significant changes without providing the taxpayer with a detailed discrepancy notice.

But that was not the worst of it. Of greatest concern with these assessments is that they covered only fifty percent of the periods involved and they showed a debt owing by Tannadyce of up to $450,000. Of course, the amount varied depending on the statement received that day. This was a massive shock to me. My $60,000 refund had now been turned into a nearly half-million dollar debt.

It is also important to remember that the bulk of these periods now being reassessed had already been the subject of audit by the IRD in Wellington. During those audits – as the Department has subsequently confirmed – we co-operated fully with the Department giving them access to all our records. The GST returns that were now being reworked had been completed by a national firm of chartered accountants called Kendons from Lower Hutt. Staff at Kendons had worked with the IRD through virtually all these audits.

It was the end of July 1996. I had received a variety of varying assessments and statements. Gibb Lee was sitting in the South of France. Brian Palliser was being treated with contempt. I was now advised that Tannadyce owed the Department half-a-million dollars and I was battling to get any meaningful response from anyone in the Department. To my amazement I was served with a notice from the Department formally advising that they were petitioning the court for my personal bankruptcy with respect to my personal debt to them.

It's now serious. No one will provide explanations. IRD have delivered nonsense assessments. Tannadyce owes half-a-million dollars. They are now pressing me for personal bankruptcy.

"Henderson owes a million" — Not

In March 1996 I had entered into an agreement with the Department that they would not pursue me for this personal debt until such time as the Tannadyce audit was complete. The Department had confirmed this arrangement in writing (see page 40). But despite this very firm and clear agreement, they were now proceeding with this bankruptcy action. It involved approximately $10,000.

Naturally, I complained and endeavoured to appeal to some sense of reason and fairness. In particular, I spoke at length to Ross Gardiner. Ross was the person with whom I had made the agreement and he had confirmed it with me in writing. He was still a senior officer with the IRD. He suggested that the audit had now been completed and that it appeared that no refunds would be available. I explained to him that the audit had definitely not been completed and I pointed out that there were several periods for which I had not yet received assessments. I asked if we could have an off-the-record discussion. Like all my other off-the-record discussions I was subsequently to find a record of it in the Department's files.

In that off-the-record discussion I pleaded with Ross to help me with the Tannadyce audit. He said he could be of little help. But he did make it very clear that I was entitled to know the full reason for any positions that the Department held particularly in respect of the section 60 issue and that the Department had an obligation to set out fully the basis for its assessments. He went on to tell me that there was nothing further that he would or could do and he confirmed that the only avenue of complaint for me was with the senior IRD officers with whom I was already talking. He did appear to be embarrassed that the Department were going back on an agreement that he had made with me but he kept on asserting that "it is out of my hands". I was left with no choice but to issue instructions to my lawyers to try and defend the IRD's bankruptcy proceedings.

Ross Gardiner was later to advise that he was "off the case" and he had been told to "pull his head in" in relation to my matters.

Also at this time I had taken to accumulating all the literature published by the Department that set out what standards a taxpayer should expect from the Department and its staff when being audited. I made a number of approaches to IRD National Office in Wellington to discuss these publications with the people responsible for putting them together. These brochures would, for example, offer taxpayers the warm assurance that all audits are to be conducted in a "prompt" manner. Given that mine wasn't, and given that none of the senior South Island staff cared that it wasn't, I thought that I may somehow have misinterpreted what the word prompt means. The people who produced the brochure couldn't help me. They refused to provide me with any Departmental definitions of the word "prompt". They insisted that I direct all my inquires to IRD in Christchurch with whom I was already dealing. I did discover, though, that a Dave McDonald, from IRD's Christchurch office, had actually written the brochure that was promising prompt service. I naturally contacted Mr McDonald. He too refused to elucidate what "prompt" meant when a taxpayer was being audited. On 5 August 1996 I wrote to Adriaan Geerlofs asking him to provide me with a formal definition. In that letter I told him that all the dictionaries I had defined it as "immediate, without delay". My letter was never responded to.

However, a week later, in a phone conversation, Mr Geerlofs told me that he was not going to give me a formal definition as he did not trust my motives. I pushed him and eventually he acknowledged that as far as the Department was concerned the word "prompt" is defined as "as quickly as our resources allow". He went on to explain that IRD staff worked with many taxpayers simultaneously and therefore it was not possible to focus on just wrapping up one audit. I asked him for further definitions in respect of IRD undertakings. He refused to discuss these with me, told me I was wasting his time, and hung up.

The bottom line is that these sweet sounding brochures are nothing but words on a page. They mean nothing to the IRD, to the staff or to the management. My point was not to get a definition of a simple word but to highlight to senior staff that there was a serious gap between their public relations and what happens in reality. It was clear that this gap was of no concern.

I continued throughout August 1996 to plead with the Department for clarification and explanation of their application of section 60. I was continually met with fob-offs, outright refusals and occasionally confused ramblings. Sivertsen's position on it was moving rapidly. Previously he had said it only related to our relationship with the BNZ. On 5 August he said in reference to Tannadyce and its associated companies that "while Tannadyce drew on these monies, it is clear that it has incurred a significant proportion of this expenditure on behalf of those companies".

I also continued to request the assessments that I had been promised a month earlier. Although I had received half of the assessments, and they did indeed show a liability for Tannadyce of half-a-million dollars, I still naively believed that the other half of the assessments might wipe out that liability and still show a credit. I wrote many, many letters to all the officers involved variously pleading, asking politely, and demanding an explanation, all to no avail.

The Department repeatedly told me that they could not provide me with the figures but that the assessments would be issued shortly. Brian Palliser continued to write to the Department and had also by this time resorted to phoning Peter Sivertsen. In those phone conversations he tried to point out respectfully that they were wrong in their application of section 60 and he respectfully requested that they defer their bankruptcy action against me. This too was to no avail. His requests were always met with the Department's now standard line that it was our job to prove the Department wrong through the formal objection process. There was a problem with this: I still didn't have the assessments and the time given to me to lodge that objection was fast closing.

In mid-August, desperate for a way to awaken the Department, I prepared a six-page analysis of the Department's shifting positions on section 60 over the last 32 months. I was careful to set out exact dates and exact quotes from departmental correspondence. Once more I was hopeful that these incontrovertible and embarrassing facts might spark someone within the Department to do something. They didn't.

The Commissioner has subsequently attacked me publicly for writing too many letters and making too many phone calls. He has never once chastised his staff for not providing the explanations that those phone calls and letters sought.

Over a three-month period, commencing 1 July 1996, I wrote 61 letters to the Department. Those letters were addressed to eight separate IRD staff members. I don't know whether that is excessive or not. What I do know is that I would rather not have had to write a single one of them. They were gut-wrenching times. I had had to drag myself into the office each day, confront this unbelievable situation that I found myself in, accept the extremely limited options that I had and try and make something positive of it. I wrote the letters for two reasons. Firstly, to contribute towards a complete record of what transpired in the way I was treated. Secondly, because it was the only avenue available to me to try and find one person in the Department who might deal with these issues properly and professionally. The Commissioner never makes the point that I would have needed to write only one letter if my reasonable questions had been answered. The Commissioner claims that my constant pleas for help, clarification and for the assessments themselves were a good part of the cause for the delays.

Brian Palliser made his own appeals to the IRD solicitors for them to defer their personal bankruptcy action until the end of the Tannadyce audit as was set out in IRD's written agreement. The IRD kept asserting that the audit was at an end and that there was no refund available for Tannadyce to offset my personal debt. Furthermore, the Department started arguing that Ross Gardiner, with whom I had made the formal agreement to defer bankruptcy proceedings, lacked the authority to make such an agreement and, therefore, it was of no legal effect. At the time we made the agreement, Ross Gardiner was Acting Manager, Taxpayer Audit. On the morning of 16 August I phoned Ross Gardiner and put this proposition to him. He told me it was "crap". He went on to say that unfortunately he had no authority to act in any way in respect of the case now.

The bankruptcy hearing was set down for 19 August in the Christchurch High Court. My solicitors prepared an affidavit for me to sign setting out my position and, in particular, drawing the court's attention to the written agreement with the Department. With some considerable difficulty I scraped together the $9,000 needed to pay the Department and settle the debt if things didn't go well for me at court. I made sure that this was in cleared funds so that my solicitor could go to court and if necessary confirm with the judge that he was in a position to meet the IRD's demands.

The IRD had also prepared affidavits from Ross Gardiner and Adriaan Geerlofs supporting their position. It was the Adriaan Geerlofs' affidavit that caused me the greatest concern. In that affidavit he confirmed that the GST audit of Tannadyce was now "at an end". He went on to advise the court in this sworn document that assessments for $773,892-00 had been "issued". Of course, this was completely untrue.

To: PETER SIVERTSEN

COPY

Tannadyce Investments Ltd
David I Henderson

I am aware that DH is making noises about the March "agreement" with Ray Healey and myself to defer bankruptcy action being considered at the time subject to certain conditions being met.

As some background I was filling in for you during an absence at the time when ██████████████████████████ as he knew it was possible action would be taken to recover outstanding tax owed by him. The danger at the time was that he would focus on this action, as he is now, and not help Chris and Gibb progress the audit. At the time completion of the audit was the priority.

Also, at the time, it appeared to be still possible that Tannadyce **might** just be due for some level of refund as there were a considerable number of D/As outstanding which were likely to be eliminated or at least reduced if returns were filed. Suggesting to Ray H the he give DH some leeway with conditions was seen as a means of -

- focusing him back on the audit
- getting the overdue returns in
- using any credit arising from Tannadyce to offset debts in Henderson's own account and that of Omnivox ██████████████
  ██████████████

In the final analysis, when bankruptcy proceedings commenced -

- the overdue returns had not been furnished
- the audit had virtually been completed, and
- it was obvious that there was no credit available to be offset against other accounts.

Ross Gardiner
15/8/96

In court that morning Brian Palliser put up strong arguments as to why I shouldn't have to pay this money to the IRD. IRD staff solicitor Helen Sumner presented the Department's affidavits and opposed Mr Palliser. Master Venning noted that the IRD affidavits appeared to be "equivocal at best" and that there appeared to be a clear and binding agreement. Asked by Master Venning how much "Henderson owed to the Department," Mrs Sumner replied "nearly one million dollars". This, of course, was completely untrue. It was the first time that I had heard such a figure. But, as I was later to discover, it wasn't me that IRD was now claiming owed a million but rather Tannadyce. In the end Brian Palliser advised Master Venning that he was holding cleared funds to settle the personal IRD debt. Master Venning declared that there should be no order for costs, interest should be removed, and he made an order for me to pay just on $7,000 to the Department.

Some other lawyers acting for other personal creditors of mine were present in the court. One of those then sought substitution on the IRD bankruptcy petition. The hearing was set down for ten days time on 29 August. Substitution was granted to a company called Hurrell Holdings Ltd. They were claiming against me personally for a company debt. I did not have the resources to argue the matter properly.

The next day the *Christchurch Press* ran a large story on the business pages detailing the case. In particular, it highlighted the claim by the Department that I now owed them "nearly one million dollars". This caused me much difficulty. I still had a number of personal creditors with whom I was making arrangements to pay out over time. There is no doubt in my mind that I could have settled all my personal creditors had we had Tannadyce's refund from the IRD and the IRD off my back. I found that it is extremely difficult to convince anyone that you can pay them anything when IRD are claiming in the press that you owe them a million dollars. It is also the perception for the lay person that the IRD have priority for their debts in all cases. Although this is not always true, it is correct in the majority of cases. The story also ran that Friday in the national business weeklies.

All this caused me great distress and caused me great difficulty in generating further financial support. It concerned me how freely a member of the Department was willing to perjure himself in his affidavit so as to be sure to nail me at the hearing. Master Venning had noted that their affidavits were "at best equivocal". In reality, it was much worse than that. Firstly, Adriaan Geerlofs had sworn in his affidavit that "on 13 June 1996 the cur-

B 223/95

IN THE MATTER
of the Insolvency Act 1967

AND

IN THE MATTER of **DAVID IAN HENDERSON**

Debtor

EX PARTE   **THE COMMISSIONER
OF INLAND REVENUE**

Substituting Creditor

I, ADRIAAN STANLEY GEERLOFS of Christchurch, Area
Manager, Business Link, Inland Revenue Department,
swear:

1   THAT I am familiar with the proceedings currently
before this Court.

2   THAT as an Area Manager, I am responsible for the
tax investigation work undertaken by the Business Link
segment which includes the investigation of Tannadyce
Investments Limited, the company referred to in the
debtor's affidavit of 19 August 1996.

3   ON 13 June 1996 the current investigation of the
goods and services tax returns of Tannadyce Investments
Limited was completed and a letter of proposed
adjustment was issued to the debtor in his capacity as
the director of the company for his comments.

4   ON 10 July 1996 a letter was issued advising the
company of its objection rights and allowing an
extended objection period due to the absence overseas
of the investigator. Formal assessments have been
issued.

5   THE formal objection process is now available to the company and is being responded to by the solicitor for the debtor, Mr Brian Palliser.

6   THE GST audit on Tannadyce Investments Limited has concluded with assessments being issued for the unpaid tax and arrears of $773,982.00. The current debt has reached $924,341.00.

7   THERE are no tax credits available from Tannadyce Investments Limited to offset against the debtor's personal tax liability.

8   THE Department is considering further investigations for income tax of Tannadyce Investments Limited. However, to date, no further audits on the company have been commenced.

9   I believe that the debt owed by the debtor as verified in the affidavit of statements of claim by Mr Ray Healey, as filed with the Court, is true and correct and that the Department is under a statutory obligation to collect the outstanding tax owed.

10   I believe that the debtor cannot claim estoppel against the Commissioner in the proceedings for adjudication for bankruptcy where the debtor has failed to complete his statutory obligations in the payment of the debt owed.

SWORN at Christchurch   )
this   /9th day of   )
August 1996   )
Before me:)   ADRIAAN STANLEY GEERLOFS

A Solicitor of the
High Court of New Zealand
                G. J. WITHERS

rent investigation of the Goods and Services Tax returns of Tannadyce Investments Ltd was completed". Of course, it wasn't. As a senior IRD staff member actively engaged in this audit, Adriaan Geerlofs must have known that the audit was far from complete. Subsequently, Carson McNeill was to define completion of an IRD audit as that point when "an agreement is reached between the Department and a taxpayer or when a final determination is made by the court". I also took the time to ring other IRD officers around the country. They confirmed Mr McNeill's view, not Mr Geerlofs sworn statement to the Court. I also have many copies of letters from the Department, issued subsequently, referring to "an audit currently being undertaken" in respect of Tannadyce.

Mr Geerlofs also told the court that "formal assessments have been issued," and that "the current debt has reached $924,341". Not only had assessments not been issued, but I had been pleading with the Department for the past six weeks for them to provide me with those assessments. And, of course, this was the very first time that I had heard of the million-dollar debt being referred to.

The next day I challenged Adriaan Geerlofs about his affidavit and demanded copies of the assessments. He still couldn't provide them but assured me that he would look into it. Of course, this was entirely unsatisfactory. I then rang Peter Sivertsen. I demanded that he allow me to come in and pick up copies of the assessments that made up the million-dollar debt. He too refused this request. He told me he would look into it.

Later that day Adriaan Geerlofs phoned me with a lame excuse that technically speaking the assessments had been issued because they had been loaded onto the computer but due to computer difficulties they had not been printed off and sent to me. The next morning I went into the Department's Customer Service Centre on the first floor of their Cashel Street office. I took a paper number from the dispensing machine and waited with about twenty other taxpayers for my turn. After about 25 minutes my number was flashing and an IRD staff member was to see me. I innocently advised them that I was having some difficulty reconciling the company's GST position and asked if they would be so kind as to bring up the company's files on the screen and print them off for me. What was printed off was considerably different to what Adriaan Geerlofs had told the court and was now trying to tell me. Those computer records also showed that the files were being worked on as recently as 17 August, a couple of days before the bankruptcy hearing, where Adriaan Geerlofs advised the court, in his sworn testimony, that the matter was completed on 13 June. For the rest of the week, the Department continued to equivocate and was still unable to provide me with the assessments they had told the court were already issued.

What was worse, was that Chris Bond and Peter Sivertsen, in discussions with Brian Palliser, said that the Department would hold me personally liable for the million dollars they were claiming off Tannadyce. Their justification for this was that I was a Director of the company since its incorporation. They argued that I had been responsible for running up the million-dollar debt and that therefore if Tannadyce was ever put into liquidation, or if for any other reason it couldn't meet the million-dollar debt, they would pursue me personally for it.

I didn't want to go bankrupt. I had had financial difficulties several times in the last twenty years. Like every entrepreneur, I have made bad decisions, run myself short of cash, and been unable to meet commitments. I had been under financial pressure before and I had always worked my way back, ultimately meeting all my commitments. I knew fully the ramifications of bankruptcy. I would lose what little I had left. I would no longer be able to manage and run a business. And, most importantly, I would not be able to be the director and manager of Tannadyce Investments Ltd. There was no doubt that the Department knew that too. I had a few days to sort out an arrangement with the other petitioning creditor, Hurrell Holdings Ltd.

But I found it tremendously difficult for any one to take me seriously when it had become common news around town that I owed the IRD a million dollars. That difficulty, combined with the fact that I could see this audit going on forever, the Department continuing to dissimulate and use their enormous powers to harass me, weakened my resolve. For the first time in my life I felt beaten.

On Friday 29 August 1996 I was adjudicated bankrupt. For the first few days I took it hard. I didn't want to be a bankrupt. I wanted the freedom to work and to pay my bills. That was all beyond me now. I was broken. My ability to deal properly with the IRD was heavily circumscribed. I received great support from family and friends. But no one could really understand how I was now a bankrupt and at war with the IRD.

I was never in court that day. I had no desire to attend. Brian Palliser reported to me that the IRD were there in force taking notes and presumably scurrying off after the declaration had been made to report to their seniors.

It's hard to describe the sense of shame that I felt and the debilitating effect it had on me. Not only did it seem that I had screwed up my affairs so much that I was now bankrupt but I had, according to media reports, either cheated or screwed up on my taxes so significantly that I now owed the IRD a million dollars.

A few days after my bankruptcy I meet with the solicitor acting for the Official Assignee's office, Rob McDuff. Rob is a decent guy and we had had several pleasant exchanges over the years. He seemed as upset as I was that I had been adjudicated bankrupt. He recounted to me the day his staff solicitor had returned from court with the news. He told me that he didn't believe it and had assured his staff member that he must have got it wrong. Rob was aware that I had had financial problems in the past but that I had always worked through the difficulties and paid my bills. He was also aware that I was one of the few company directors who had personally paid a company's bills after it had gone into liquidation. He wanted to know my story and we had a very amiable discussion. He reminded me, though, that he was bound by statute and I would still have to comply with all the provisions of the Insolvency Act.

My life was now controlled by the office of the Official Assignee. Under the provisions of the Insolvency Act he was to become responsible for finalising all my financial affairs up to the date of the bankruptcy, taking off me any personal assets that I had and administering my financial position for the next three years. I hated it.

My secretary Tracey was by now my last remaining staff member. I had had to wind down all business activities and lay off all other staff in all the ventures I was associated with earlier that year. The cost to individuals and families was severe. I did what I could to help my former staff find new work but the experience was very traumatic for all of us.

Tracey had been extremely loyal. She had worked for long periods without pay. She had typed most of my letters to the Department from the very outset and was familiar with all the facts of the case. She knew that I was right and that I had been treated outrageously. But she had to be responsible for her own future and seek new work. She nonetheless came in unpaid many times to assist me and to help me out. I could not have asked for a better secretary.

As a bankrupt I was immediately removed as a director of Tannadyce Investments Ltd as well as other companies I was associated with. One of the first tasks that I had to attend to was to find a replacement director for

Tannadyce. If I didn't, the company could be forced into liquidation and the IRD audit would come to an end with the claim by the IRD against the company for a million dollars being sustained.

My whole attitude to the Department had now completely changed. It was now intensely personal. I felt that all their actions over the last 33 months had to amount either to malice or incompetence. Quite frankly, it didn't really matter which. There comes a time when incompetence unchecked by highly paid senior personnel ultimately becomes malice. I made a strong personal resolve that I would do whatever it takes to see the matter through to the end, for Tannadyce to receive its refund, for those responsible to be held to account, and for the Department to be cleaned up so that this type of treatment would never be experienced again by any other innocent taxpayer.

I approached several friends to become directors of Tannadyce. This was a poisoned chalice if ever there was one. People could see their lives disappearing in front of them as I pleaded my case. Imagine taking on a company that had no income, no assets, a million-dollar liability to the IRD, an audit from hell, with a bankrupt telling you it was no problem and that we were going to win. A young friend in Christchurch who had worked for me from time to time eventually succumbed and agreed to become a director on the condition that his name never be revealed publicly. This appeared to me to be pretty much an impossibility given the requirements of the Companies Act but it was better than any other offer that I had. I told him it was a deal and got him to sign an acknowledgement form on the spot. We were back in business. Tannadyce had a new director.

A week later, I suddenly thought of a business colleague of mine in Toronto, Canada. I immediately rang him in his office. I told him my plight. He had followed the case a little over the years but was horrified to learn of current developments. I knew that he had a healthy disrespect for malicious and vindictive public servants. He too agreed to be a director but with the caveat that his name never be made public either. Even ten thousand miles away, the fear of the IRD was strong.

I was now bankrupt. The IRD had destroyed me. They claimed in sworn statements to the court that all the assessments had been issued – they hadn't been. They told the court that I owed a million. I didn't. Gibb Lee was still on holiday. I have a month left to file objections. I wasn't about to give up.

Let's bankrupt Henderson again

The directors' first task was to instruct me to continue with all energy to deal with the issues relating to the audit and to work to bring it to a close. Both Brian Palliser and I advised the Department that I had been empowered by the directors with the responsibility for the audit and charged with bringing it to a close and that he was continuing as legal counsel for the company. The Department very reluctantly accepted this position. Peter Sivertsen kept on asserting that the only proper way to go forward was to work through Brian Palliser. This, of course, would be entirely impractical for the company, myself and Brian Palliser. It would also ultimately prove to be a lot more costly. Sivertsen continued to press his assertion for the next few weeks.

Ironically, on the same day that the directors charged me with completing the tax audit, I received a reply to a letter I had written to the Hon Peter Dunne who was now Minister of Revenue. Mr Dunne assured me that "the Government and Inland Revenue are doing what they can to reduce the compliance costs of small business". Dunne's assurance was cold comfort for me.

Finally, on 9 September 1996 I received the assessments that I had been advised two months ago were being issued. This was a full three weeks after Adriaan Geerlofs had told the court in sworn testimony that the assessments had been issued. The assessment showed the total debt now standing at $924,341-07. There was no explanation as to how these sums were arrived at. I now had only twenty-one days left to file my objections. The statutory period provided for under the Goods and Services Act is 60

 Inland Revenue
Te Tari Taake

Christchurch Service Centre

Charter House
165 Cashel Street
Private Bag
Christchurch
New Zealand

Telephone 03-379 8500
Facsimile 03-366 6654

6 September 1996

Attention Brian Palliser
Hill Lee and Scott
Barristers and Solicitors
P O Box 13-004
CHRISTCHURCH

Dear Sir

TANNADYCE INVESTMENTS LTD - IRD NUMBER: 56-427-031
OUR REFERENCE: CH/GST/CJB

Thank you for your letter of 20 August 1996.

Attached is a copy of our letter of 10 July 1996, the original of which was sent direct to your client. Also attached are copies of recent correspondence from your client, together with a copy of our letter of 13 June 1996, which accompanied the schedules of proposed adjustments.

Because of some specific difficulties with our computer system, it has not been possible to produce notices of assessment for all periods covered by the audit. In order to fully protect your client's objection rights, the following are to be treated as notices of assessment in terms of section 27 of the Goods and Services Tax Act 1985. The total outstanding tax includes default assessments for the periods May, July, September and November 1995, and January, March, and May 1996; these periods were not subject to audit.

Notices of assessment and statements of account for the periods May, July, September and November 1992, January, March, May, July, September and November 1993, January, March, May, July, September and November 1994 and January and March 1995 have previously been issued direct to your client.

PERIOD	ORIGINAL ASSESSMENT REVERSED	TAX NOW ASSESSED	PENALTY	REFUND TRANSFER PAYMENT	PERIOD BALANCE
Oct 91	(17,042.62)	11,226.65	62,831.75	*5,014.82	86,086.20
Nov 91	(44,046.96)	2,458.92	100,426.10		146,931.98
Jan 92	(49,549.55)	6,634.69	160,499.48		216,683.72
Mar 92	(3,999.36)	4,831.09	16,944.09		25,774.54
May 92	(33,355.03)	4,977.75	65,846.73	24,506.58	95,331.06
Jul 92	1,459.92	5,900.78	7,948.62	(1,459.94)	12,389.48
Sep 92	(194.70)	3,641.04	6,655.72	194.70	10,491.46
Nov 92	(1,228.71)	3,170.56	7,166.27	1,228.71	11,565.54
Jan 93	(6,495.14)	1,865.84	12,843.59	6,495.14	21,204.57
Mar 93	(3,106.25)	(1,310.04)	nil	1,310.04	nil
May 93	(25,013.67)	(31,949.30)	nil	31,949.30	nil
Jul 93	(130.66)	(4,397.06)	nil	4,397.06	nil

TANNADYCE INVESTMENTS LTD - IRD NUMBER: 56-427-031

Sep 93	(795.36)	20,346.03	23,348.63	795.36	44,490.02
Nov 93	(16,666.00)	33,055.56	48,294.90	14,121.72	95,472.18
Jan 94	(43,444.14)	3,883.85	3,702.79		7,586.64
Mar 94	1,196.89	1,176.86	143.57	(1,320.43)	nil
May 94	(1,187.79)	(1,135.82)	nil	1,135.82	nil
Jul 94	(4,737.59)	(2,487.35)	nil	2,487.35	nil
Sep 94	(3,104.04)	(2,028.31)	nil	2,028.31	nil
Nov 94	(1,874.55)	(1,918.47)	nil	1,918.47	nil
Jan 95	(1,966.84)	13,341.41	8,270.43	1,966.84	23,578.68
Mar 95	11,154.33	11,154.33	5,359.06		16,513.39
SUBTOTAL:	**$244,127.82**	**$82,439.01**	**$530,281.73**	**$96,769.85**	**$814,099.46**

The following are default assessments:

May 95	12,269.76	5,189.61	17,459.37
Jul 95	12,269.76	4,511.65	16,781.41
Sep 95	12,269.76	3,860.02	16,129.78
Nov 95	12,269.76	3,233.69	15,503.45
Jan 96	12,269.76	2,631.69	14,901.45
Mar 96	12,269.76	2,053.06	14,322.82
May 96	13,496.74	1,646.59	15,143.33

TOTALS:	**$244,127.82**	**$169,554.31**	**$553408.04**	**$96,769.85**	**$924,341.07**

(*$4,895.57 and $119.25 transferred to period May 1993 GST).

Please note that these assessments replace the printouts given to Mr Henderson during his visit to Inland Revenue on Monday, 26 August.

I note your comments "..the sequence in which the objection should be dealt". I remind you of the legislative requirements for objections, and that any objection should be full and complete. However, as this letter formally constitutes some of the relevant assessments, we will deal with the objection in accordance with our usual practice when you advise which of the various correspondence you want considered as the objection.

A significant amount of documentary material has previously been provided to Mr Henderson, on behalf of the company, to background the adjustments now incorporated in the assessments.

Would you confirm that you are continuing to act for Tannadyce Investments Ltd, or advise to whom future correspondence should be directed.

Yours faithfully

P Sivertsen
Area Manager
Technical and Legal Support Group

CB:AS

days. Once again, the Department was operating with contempt for the law.

I was now back fully determined to move ahead with all matters necessary to produce an equitable result. On 10 September 1996 I wrote to Chris Bond in respect to some inquiries he had been making for some further records relating to the associate companies of Tannadyce. I asked him to tell me specifically what information it was that he wanted by return fax and that I would endeavour to help. He never responded to that letter.

TANNADYCE INVESTMENTS LTD
1st Floor, Securities House, 221 Gloucester Street ,
P.O. Box 1066, Christchurch. New Zealand
Telephone: 64 3 351-8488   Facsimile: 64 3 351-5695

10 September 1996

Chris Bond
Inland Revenue Department
CHRISTCHURCH

By Fax: 03 366 6654

Dear Chris

John Ruane from the Commercial Affairs Office has contacted me in respect to Talic and Lapageria. I understand that you have advised him that as part of the ongoing Tannadyce audit you are now requiring some information in respect of Talic and Lapageria.

I would be happy to co-operate with you as best I can in this regard. Would you be so kind as to advise me by return fax specifically what information you are requiring in respect of those two companies and I will look at what we can provide you with.

In addition if you could perhaps tell me what it is exactly you are looking for, I may know of other information that you perhaps have not specifically requested that might provide a solution or answer to what you are requiring.

I look forward to your response.

Yours faithfully

Dave Henderson
Tannadyce Investments Ltd

Through the early part of September I continued to plead with all the senior staff at the IRD in Christchurch for them to provide me with the information that I was desperately seeking. As always, promises were made and broken.

Also on 10 September, I sent yet another letter to Adriaan Geerlofs encouraging him to provide me with explanations as to the make-up of the assessments I had just been issued with. As he had confidently told the Court in his sworn testimony that Tannadyce owed the Department nearly a million dollars, I believed that he would feel some obligation to explain the make-up of this debt. He never responded to that letter.

TANNADYCE INVESTMENTS LTD

1st Floor, Securities House, 221 Gloucester Street,
P.O. Box 1066, Christchurch. New Zealand
Telephone: 64 3 351-8488   Facsimile: 64 3 351-5695

10 September 1996

Adriaan Geerlofs
Christchurch Service Centre
P O Box 2871
Christchurch

Fax: 363 1519

Dear Sir

Subject: IRD Assessments

I have at long last received from the Department what purports to be Notices of Assessments.

We are endeavouring to have clarified what the situation is regarding objections given that the assessments we received in July purported to be the final assessments for the company.

I also note that there were no accompanying or support notes, advices, qualifications or explanations of any kind attached to these most recent assessments.

Given the significant amounts of money involved, the seriousness of the audit, and the tremendous delays to date I would have thought the least the Department could have done was to set out specifically and unequivocally what their position was in respect to these assessments and the basis on which they have established the transactions relating to the assessments. Perhaps you could care to explain why this has not occurred.

I note in your affidavit of the 19th of August that you said assessments had been issued for unpaid tax in arrears of $773,982. You go on to say that the current debt has reached $924,341. I note that the assessments we have received do in fact equate to the latter figure. Can you please explain how the former figure was made up.

You recently advised that there was specific difficulties with the computer system that have made it impossible to issue notices of assessments. I have advised you than on several occasions through August I was able to get printouts from your computer relating to the months in question. Can you explain what is going on here.

I look forward to your prompt response.

Yours faithfully

David Henderson
Tannadyce Investments Ltd

I worked diligently to file the company's formal objection. By 30 September I had filed objections to the million-dollar assessment to the best of my ability and limited resources. It was very clear to me that despite the continued assurances of Carson McNeill, Peter Sivertsen and Adriaan Geerlofs, the three most senior South Island IRD officers, I was not going to get a satifactory explanation of how the million dollars was made up.

Brian Palliser was still extremely confident that he could deal with the Department and bring the issues to a close. With my approval, he arranged to meet with Chris Bond and Peter Sivertsen on 1 October. At that meeting there were several implied threats. One of them related to allegations that I had personally received a salary in 1993 and 1994 from a company that I was a shareholder and director of. I had since resigned as a director and sold my shares. I had alerted the Department to my involvement in that company earlier in the year when I had filed my previous year's personal income tax return. I believed that I had filed that return exactly in accordance with my statutory requirements. Unbeknown to me, a short time after I filed that return, the company, Matol Botanical (NZ) Ltd, was audited by the IRD. That audit was described to me by Matol's accountant, a senior partner at Peat Marwick, as the most aggressive audit he had ever experienced.

When Chris Bond and Peter Sivertsen met with Brian Palliser they threatened that they would begin assessments against me for failing to file a salary from that company for two successive years. I knew it to be complete nonsense. But when you are a bankrupt, under investigation by the police for fraud, in battle with the IRD, then these types of comments are very intimidating. I complained to the Department and sought further information. That wasn't forthcoming. Instead, what I received via the Official Assignee's Office was notification that the IRD were starting a new audit against me personally. There was no prospect of them recovering one cent from this action. I was already bankrupt. They couldn't make me bankrupt twice. But they were doing it anyway. This new audit started a few weeks after the national business weekly, *The Independent*, ran an article suggesting that I was going to seek an annulment of my bankruptcy.

I was dumbstruck, how they could justify the resources for such an action when they had been repeatedly telling me that they didn't have the resources to deal properly and fully with the Tannadyce issues. The new audit was to proceed under the provisions of the new Departmental Disputes Resolution Process that was effective from 1 October 1996.

I was later to learn that mine was the first case in the South Island to proceed under this new process. The audit was to be headed by senior IRD investigator Keith Shand. I had several discussions with him over this personal audit. He would regularly complain to me about how poorly paid he was. I believed that the salary of $38,900 that he told me he was paid was way beyond anything he was worth. Keith was extremely agitated at every meeting and, like his colleagues, had a non-negotiable agenda to prove that I had evaded tax. The Department called on their pool of endless resources to support their actions on this audit. They prepared and filed with the Official Assignee a report totalling over one hundred pages to justify their proposed adjustments to my personal income tax returns. They filed this report with the Office of the Official Assignee who, given my status as a bankrupt, was responsible for dealing with it. Just to make things difficult, Keith Shand then advised me that he would not deal with me on my personal audit any more but rather would only deal with the Official Assignee.

My personal accounts had been prepared with significant input from Coopers and Lybrand. Richard Perrett, a tax specialist with that firm, had considered carefully certain transactions to ensure that I complied. He had even gone to great length to prepare an opinion for me on the one transaction that the Department now appeared to be focussing on. It made no difference to them that I produced this opinion and that Richard made himself available to discuss with the Department the legal propositions that he was relying on.

As the IRD well knew, the Official Assignee had no resources to deal with my personal audit. They don't have a budget or any inclination to deal with matters that have no possibility of a positive economic outcome. They wanted to roll over on the new assessment and accept the Department's position. Of course, the law is structured so that the IRD can make outrageous assessments and they are deemed to be valid unless opposed under formal objection procedures.

If the Official Assignee was to roll over on this, then the Department's position would automatically stand. I would have a further liability with the Department and I would have been deemed to have filed false tax returns. I knew what this would mean to a Department desperate to discredit me. I could have been prosecuted and sent to jail. I pleaded with the Official Assignee to allow me to deal with this matter at my own expense and in my own time. After much deliberation, he conceded on the condition that at all times I keep him fully appraised of my progress.

So here I was, with far fewer resources than I had several weeks earlier, a bankrupt, the Tannadyce audit going on interminably, and a new personal audit to deal with.

Meanwhile, Brian Palliser was still working feverishly with the Department to try and produce some resolution on the Tannadyce matter. He was given the opportunity to meet with Carson McNeill. At that meeting, much to my surprise, he elicited from McNeill an agreement for Brian and myself to meet with Peter Sivertsen and Gibb Lee to try and find a way forward.

We met on 6 October 1996. Sivertsen's own record of that meeting states that the principal purpose of the meeting was "ensuring that Henderson had a clear understanding of the reasons for the adjustments made by the Department". Gibb Lee once again went on to assert that his view on the nature of the relationship between the parties involved in the Station Village transaction was predicated on a number of letters and memos that he claimed were in his possession. Once again he could not produce those documents. Once again, he assured me that he would provide me with copies of them. To this day I have never received them. However, Sivertsen was once again happy to accept Gibb Lee's assertions in this regard.

Lee also started claiming that he did not now have all the records that

Keith Shand: Started a personal audit on me that was completely fruitless.

Kath Cook had delivered to the Department in May 1995. I was very concerned as this involved a substantial number of original invoices and statements. I also reaffirmed that I still had in my possession a number of documents that I believed might help deal with the misconceptions the Department had. I had told Peter Sivertsen of this in June that year. He had assured me then, and his own notes record this, that he would have staff visit me, inspect those documents, and report to him on their significance. Of course, that had not happened. I had restated to him and others, on several occasions, my offer to provide documentation and records, including our at length meeting on the 4th of July 1996. Once again, I reaffirmed my offer of co-operation in this regard. Also at that meeting, Brian Palliser and I pressed Peter Sivertsen and Gibb Lee as to whether they had ever had a legal opinion prepared to support the Department's position on their application of section 60. Gibb Lee advised that an in-house solicitor, Greg Pratt, had prepared such an opinion and that it supported fully the Department's position. Brian Palliser asked if the Department would be prepared to provide that opinion to him. They were unwilling to make that commitment. This was the third time I had been advised that a legal opinion on section 60 had been obtained.

Four days later, I was to track down and to speak on the phone with Greg Pratt in his office in Kilmore Street, at 2:15pm. He advised me, much to my alarm, that he had never provided an opinion. He said that he had just been supplied with a number of documents and agreements and he was "just this minute" starting work on preparing the opinion. This was twenty months after the IRD had laid their complaint with the police and just on 18 months after Mr Bond had told me that section 60 was the last remaining issue. I told him that he may not have all the documents to provide a complete opinion. He was unwilling to discuss this aspect with me and told me that if he needed anything further he would contact Gibb Lee.

When we had concluded our 6 October meeting, we all agreed to meet again more formally, this time with Carson McNeill, Adriaan Geerlofs and Chris Bond to try and thrash out all the issues. The Department insisted we agree to a stringent set of terms of reference before that meeting took place.

By this time, I was becoming something of an expert on the Goods and Services Tax Act. In particular, my attention was drawn to the provisions of section 31 of that Act. This section limits the Commissioner from making a re-assessment of a company for any period over four years old, unless the Commissioner has reason to believe that the taxpayer has "knowingly or fraudulently failed to make a full disclosure of all the material facts" relating to the return. Given that the Department had only issued its new assessments on 9 September 1996, it was my opinion that the Commissioner couldn't make a re-assessment for any period before 9 September 1992. That was unless he believed I had knowingly or fraudulently failed to make a full disclosure. Now the bulk of the million dollars the Department was now claiming related to the period before 9 September 1992. Virtually all the GST returns for that period had been completed by our Lower Hutt accountants Kendons. All those periods had also been audited by the Wellington office of the IRD.

I produced for Adriaan Geerlofs a copy of a 3-page brief of appointment that I had prepared and issued to a partner at Kendons giving him full and complete responsibility for all Tannadyce's accounting and administrative functions. The Kendon's partner was not only responsible for completing and filing all our GST returns but he even signed all the cheques to pay all the company's bills. The only involvement that I had with accountancy matters through that time was once a month approving for payment a schedule of accounts. My argument to the Department therefore was that there was no way that I or my staff could have "knowingly or fraudulently failed to make a full disclosure" of all the facts relating to our GST returns. We had nothing to do with those returns.

It seemed to me that this was a powerful argument. Brian Palliser concurred with me and satisfied himself that we had a strong legal position. Finally, after much pressing on this point, Adriaan Geerlofs wrote to Brian Palliser on 20 November 1996 setting out why the Department continued to feel justified in reopening these periods outside the four-year limitation. He stated that "the section 60 issue of agency between Tannadyce and the BNZ as mortgagee in possession being a contributing factor". He then went on to say "this information, along with the fact that records requested were not being supplied, was a reasonable decision that back year return periods be opened and available for re-assessment".

Of course, all records requested had been made available, and further offers to make other records available had never been taken up by the Department. The section 60 issue, as he was relating it "between Tannadyce and the BNZ, as mortgagee in possession", meant further refunds to Tannadyce – not liabilities. I was also aware that up to that time that they had never contacted Kendons. Adriaan Geerlofs then asserted that Mr Lee had had discussions with a Mr Calvert from Kendons. I learned that afternoon that Mr Calvert had been dead for twenty years. Some time later Mr Lee was then to change this advice and claim that he had spoken to a Mr Heywood. Of course, I phoned Mr Heywood at his office. He could not recall having any discussions with the IRD about Tannadyce. He said that if he had had any contact asking any meaningful questions he would have clearly remembered it.

I phoned back Gibb Lee and pressed him on his honesty on this issue. Finally, he acknowledged that contrary to all his claims, he hadn't actually spoken to any partners at Kendons. He said that he had gone to Lower Hutt to the address on the accountant's invoices that I had supplied him. On arrival at that address he found that the accountants had moved. He claimed to have then made contact with someone at the office by phone who said that they would look to see if they had any records in their office on Tannadyce. He had never bothered to talk with the partners or senior staff who had been directly involved with all of Tannadyce's financial affairs.

The IRD are continuing to mislead and ignore their legal obligations. I have another personal audit to deal with. I have little time to prepare an objection to the million-dollar GST claim, the basis of which IRD never explained.

IRD misleads the Ombudsman

It was now seven weeks since I had been adjudicated bankrupt. I had made virtually no progress on the Tannadyce audit and was making slow progress on my own personal audit. But I was not going away and I was using everything within my now extremely limited resources to maintain pressure on the Department. I had noticed a considerable change in the attitudes and behaviour of the IRD personnel involved. There was no question that they were becoming increasingly frustrated and annoyed that I had not just given up and gone away. Gibb Lee was becoming more contemptuous by the day. He even acknowledged in one phone conversation that he knowingly chose to be adversarial in dealing with me. He would regularly hang up on me if he could not answer my questions or deal with the issues I was raising.

Chris Bond would refuse to even talk to me and would direct me to Gibb Lee before hanging up. It seemed to me Peter Sivertsen still had no concept of the issues. On a number of occasions he would apologise to me for his behaviour on the phone and particularly his rudeness in shouting at me and hanging up in my ear. I was regularly being chastised by Carson McNeill for ringing his staff too often, for being rude, and in particular, for putting too much pressure on Peter Sivertsen. In one conversation Carson McNeill told me that I had put so much pressure on Peter Sivertsen that he "had to be attended to when he came off the phone". The implication was that I had no right to demand information or that the Department adhere to agreements and undertakings that it had made. The Department was continuing to employ every conceivable device and means to disenfranchise me.

In early August, before my bankruptcy, out of complete frustration at the Department's contempt for my Official Information requests, and as a

Office of the **Ombudsmen**

Nga Kaitiaki Mana Tangata

REF: W36735

19 November 1996

Mr D Henderson
Tannadyce Investments Ltd
P O Box 1066
CHRISTCHURCH

Dear Mr Henderson

I refer to my letter of 8 October 1996 in which I advised that I had notified the Inland Revenue Department of a complaint that the Inland Revenue Department had acted unreasonably in that it had withheld certain information requested of it. The information in question related to an investigation into GST transactions of Tannadyce Investments Ltd.

It has come to my attention that on 29 August 1996 you were adjudged a bankrupt. As an undischarged bankrupt you are not eligible to take part in the affairs of Tannadyce Investments Ltd. Nor, in terms of S.81 of the Tax Administration Act 1994, are you entitled to receive information related to the tax affairs of Tannadyce Investments Ltd and held by the Inland Revenue Department.

I have, therefore, discontinued my investigation into the complaint lodged by you on 21 August 1996 as the Chief Executive Officer of Tannadyce Investments Ltd. If and when you can provide me with evidence of your discharge from bankruptcy and your resumption of office in Tannadyce Investments Ltd, I will consider resuming my investigation.

Yours sincerely

Sir Brian Elwood
Chief Ombudsman

Level 14, Sun Microsystems House, 70 The Terrace, P.O. Box 10152, Wellington, New Zealand
Telephone (04) 473 9533, Facsimile (04) 471 2254, Answerphone - complaints 0800 802 602

last resort, I lodged a formal complaint with the Office of the Ombudsman. The Ombudsman's Office told me that the Chief Ombudsman Sir Brian Elwood would consider my complaint. The complaint was lodged on behalf of Tannadyce. Through September and October I co-operated with Sir Brian Elwood providing him with additional information to help him consider my complaint. In October he told me that he had called for a report from the Commissioner of Inland Revenue in respect of my complaint and that he would write to me once he had received that report and considered it.

Sir Brian Elwood: Chief Ombudsman, who refused to deal with me after I was adjudicated bankrupt.

I was to discover later that, instead of responding to my allegations, the IRD wrote to Sir Brian Elwood on 15 November 1996 to advise that I had been adjudicated bankrupt. They went on to say that as a consequence Henderson "is no longer eligible to be an officer of Tannadyce Investments Ltd and he must now be considered as essentially a member of the public". The Department advised Sir Brian that "Mr Henderson is no longer entitled to the information that he requests which relates to the GST investigation into Tannadyce".

On 19 November 1996 Sir Brian Elwood wrote to me care of the company repeating virtually verbatim the IRD's advice. He went on to say that as a consequence he had discontinued his investigation into the complaint lodged by me on behalf of Tannadyce and that once I could provide him with evidence of my discharge from bankruptcy he would consider resuming his investigation on my behalf.

I cannot tell you the sense of injustice that flowed over me on receiving the Ombudsman's letter. I had always held the Office of the Ombudsman in high regard. I saw it as a place of last resort where small people could seek assistance regarding injustices committed by government departments.

It concerned me that the Department's representations falsely claimed that the Department was no longer dealing with me and the Ombudsman's Office accepted this misrepresentation without question. I found it amazing that Sir Brian Elwood had never even bothered to ask me for my side of the story. Both Brian Palliser and I had been properly authorised by the company's Managing Director to deal with all the IRD issues. IRD had accepted that and were regularly, but reluctantly, dealing with both of us, and providing us with information. Once more I was completely disenfranchised and the process of gaining official information through the Official Information Act was blocked to me.

It was also interesting that one of the conditions set down by the Department for the meeting that they were proposing was that I was to agree not to make any more Official Information requests. I refused to agree to this demand because I thought it was wrong and unnecessary.

It was now clear there was nothing the IRD would not do to get me off the case – including declaring me a non-person.

More meetings, more stalling, more broken agreements

On 22 November 1996 at 2pm we started a new round of meetings with the Department. This time we were elevated to the fifth floor meeting room. Present at the meeting were Adriaan Geerlofs, Carson McNeill, Peter Sivertsen, Gibb Lee, Brian Palliser and myself. McNeill opened the meeting by explaining that he had very limited time. Once more I wanted to focus on the central issue: the application of section 60 and the reallocation by the Department of Tannadyce's expenditure. Carson McNeill set a new meeting to deal with this matter for the following Thursday at 2:15pm. The Department's own notes of the meeting record that they were to provide me at that time "a full and complete explanation of how they were applying section 60". Also, in the interim, Gibb Lee was to travel to Wellington and meet with the solicitors who acted for the BNZ.

Meanwhile, I provided other information and explanations relating to peripheral matters. It also appeared that the Department had lost a significant part of our records. They were now claiming that we had never delivered the large volume of records that had been provided to the Department in May 1995. Contrary to Departmental policy, Gordon Byatt had never issued a receipt when the records were delivered. The apparent loss of records was worrying me. I sought co-operation from the Department to address the matter and find a way of resolving it. Brian Palliser suggested that we have Kath Cook, who had delivered the documents to the Department, swear an affidavit setting out all the details in respect of the missing records. Peter Sivertsen gave us an assurance that if we were to do that then he would address the matter within the Department and seek a resolution. That affidavit was prepared, sworn and delivered to the Department. To this day, several years later, he has never responded to Kath's affidavit, nor addressed the issue of missing records.

We met on 28 November. This time we were in the IRD library. Carson McNeill could not attend. All the others who had been present at the previous Friday's meeting were in attendance. The Department had agreed to provide us with their complete explanation of their application of section 60. The Department's agenda provided for us to deal with a number of side issues first. Finally after an hour, we got to the matter of section 60. The Department didn't explain in any detail but simply advised that Mr Lee had met with the BNZ and that the BNZ agreed with the IRD stance. There was no further elucidation on this point.

I left the meeting and went back to my office to contact solicitors for the BNZ. In a long discussion with Justin Toebes, I discovered that Gibb Lee had in fact presented questions to Mr Toebes that would provide the answers Mr Lee wanted rather than provide an objective analysis of the reality of the transactions. Instead of BNZ agreeing with the Department, as the officers at the meeting had asserted, Justin Toebes acknowledged completely my interpretation of the relationship. He offered to write to me clarifying this very point. It's important to realise that if the Department was right, then not only would they establish the liability to Tannadyce of the million dollars which could never be paid, but the BNZ could justifiably claim back several hundred thousand dollars in GST. The result for the Department would be a net loss. I believed by this time that the financial outcome was of little interest to the Department. The only thing that mattered was beating Tannadyce and beating Henderson. I felt the senior IRD staff appeared quite willing to construct the facts to achieve this end.

There was another big tax story running in the papers at this time, The Winebox Inquiry. I hadn't been following it. It seemed too complicated and I had enough tax problems of my own. However, a press story on 28 November titled "IRD audit chief queries objectivity" caught my attention. The story referred to evidence given by Tony Bouzaid, the IRD's Director, Taxpayer Audit. I found what he said under oath quite amazing: "We train our people to carefully analyse the facts, gather the evidence, reach an initial conclusion, and ask a taxpayer for an explanation, and then make conclusions. What concerned me is that you had an official who was jumping to the end before he had passed the first go. I mean, tax investigations are really not much different to being a judge on a case. You make your judgements when you get to the end. It is a very dangerous situation for a tax department or an official to have a closed mind from the very start".

I caught Tony Bouzaid on his cellphone in a taxi as he drove from The Winebox Inquiry that evening. His testimony had been the most encouraging commentary that I had come across so far. I explained to him that I was experiencing just exactly what he had criticised. He told me he was too involved with The Winebox Inquiry and didn't want to know about my problems. I phoned him a few more times over the next couple of months as my case deteriorated. His mind proved every bit as closed as the ones I was battling in Christchurch. Eventually he instructed me to phone Brian Hutton, National Manager Operations Policy at National Office Wellington. Brian Hutton proved no use. Even at The Winebox Inquiry the IRD was saying one thing when their practice was the exact opposite.

On 3 December I met with Brian Palliser and Peter Sivertsen, this time in my office. Brian had insisted that I drag out of storage any and all records and documents that related in any way to Tannadyce and its associated companies. I had assembled in my office a massive amount of documentation. This included things such as daily bar receipts from a restaurant that an associated company, Talic Holdings Ltd, had owned and operated at Station Village. It included bakery flour usage records. I had a mountain of minutia.

Anything that could ever possibly be asked for was there. I showed all this to Peter Sivertsen. I told him that these records were available and that we would provide them to the Department. All I wanted was for the Department to explain to me the basis upon which they were applying section 60. Peter Sivertsen advised that he would need to go away and discuss this with Carson McNeill. I understand that he did and yet another meeting was set up for Thursday 5 December at 10:30am.

Tony Bouzaid: His winebox inquiry evidence outlined a standard of departmental behaviour not achieved in my case.

Adriaan Geerlofs could not attend but Chris Bond did. Also present were Gibb

Lee, Peter Sivertsen, Carson McNeill, Brian Palliser and myself. Brian raised the issue of the Department's complaint of fraud to the police which was still live. Brian got acknowledgement that most of the issues in the letter of complaint were no longer of any consequence and should be withdrawn. We could clearly show that the complaints were baseless. Sivertsen said that he was willing to consider this. I really pressed on him the importance personally of having the police complaint washed up, pointing out the debilitating effect it was having on me.

We then discussed the central issue of section 60. They explained that they thought that Tannadyce had acted as agent for the subsidiary companies that operated the businesses that Tannadyce had established at the Station Village. Gibb Lee made several statements about how he had reallocated expenditure based on who he thought the money had been spent on regardless of who the invoice was made out to. I asked him for a clear explanation as to what he used for his yardstick to measure what expenses should be allocated to which entity. He could not provide me with a meaningful answer. Carson McNeill declared that he would not tolerate any rearrangement involving the application of section 60 that would increase the Department's liability. This is the essence of the mind-set I was battling. It wasn't the law or reality that was driving this audit but simply the desire of IRD senior management to deny Tannadyce its refund.

I also questioned Gibb Lee on how he could reallocate expenditure based on studying invoices when he had been asserting in recent times that the Department had not received any invoices from us. The significance of that point appeared to go straight over his head.

At this meeting I made it very clear that I knew the case inside out and that I knew in my heart and my head that Tannadyce had completed its returns lawfully and was due a significant refund. I said that I would persist until the day that refund was repaid to us. The IRD staff present laughed in my face. The response of these senior staff to my heartfelt declaration of determination was to mock me. I was burning up inside.

The meeting ended with them agreeing to come to my office the following week to meet with myself and Brian Palliser to go through the records that I had. In particular, I intended to show Gibb Lee photocopies of our own records that I had obtained from the Department. Several of these photocopies have annotations on them in Mr Byatt's handwriting proving conclusively that the Department had the alleged missing records in their possession at some time. In return, I asked that Mr Lee bring with him an explanation of the Department's position on the records that were delivered by us in May 1995 and that the Department was asserting now were missing.

On Wednesday 11 December 1996 that meeting took place. Gibb Lee never brought the explanation that I had asked for. After some heated discussion, I agreed to allow him into my office to inspect my records.

Unbeknown to me, the day earlier Gibb Lee and Chris Bond had visited John Ruane who worked for both the Companies Office and the office of the Official Assignee. They were desperate to find out who the new Tannadyce director or directors were. They wanted to know why the Companies Office was not putting pressure on me to provide this information. John Ruane told me that they made several comments about concerns that I appeared to be still managing Tannadyce Investments Ltd. He told me to expect a letter in the next few days from the Companies Office addressing these issues.

On 18 December I complained to Carson McNeill about the actions of Gibb Lee and Chris Bond in making these complaints.

We met again in IRD's library on Friday 20 December at 2:30pm. Present were Gibb Lee, Chris Bond, Peter Sivertsen, Brian Palliser and me. Once more we began with side issues. The main focus was section 31 which prevents the Department from reopening periods more than four years old. Peter Sivertsen explained in some detail why he believed that the provisions of section 31 didn't apply and why the Department was justified in reopening periods going back more than four years. Among other things he said "the GST returns of Tannadyce were so substantially wrong in the 1991/92 period that the person who authorised them must have had knowledge that they were wrong". As I had explained to them innumerable times, it was Kendons who had prepared these returns. He was little interested in this and went on to assert that the Department had arrived at the view that it was me who had authorised Kendons to complete these returns so therefore it was me that must have had knowledge that they were wrong. He refused to explain why they were wrong.

The other issues of significance discussed at that meeting were that the Department advised that it was now commencing an action to recover what it believed was outstanding PAYE from Tannadyce. Peter Sivertsen undertook to prepare some more detail on this and to provide it to me.

I formally complained about Chris Bond and Gibb Lee's visit to the

Official Assignee and their complaints that I appeared to be managing the company. I also raised once more the issue of the Department's complaint to the police. I made it clear that I believed that the Department had an obligation to withdraw the letter of complaint. Sivertsen also undertook to look into this and advise me further.

On 23 December I received a letter from Peter Sivertsen. In that letter he confirmed that Gibb Lee was writing to John Ruane to retract some of the comments he had made. He also confirmed that Mr Lee would take up my offer to collect the balance of the records I held in my office. He also gave an unequivocal undertaking that those records would be returned to me within two weeks of being uplifted. I saw both these moves as progress. I was once more hopeful that we might be getting somewhere.

I arranged for Adriaan Geerlofs to come to my office on 6 January 1997 to pick the records up on Mr Lee's behalf. There were several boxes. I was providing them with every single document in my possession that related to Tannadyce and the Station Village Development. There were also some chequebooks and bank statements that were in possession of an accountant that I was to deliver up two days later. I discussed with Adriaan Geerlofs Gibb Lee's undertaking to return these to me in two weeks. I was very firm about having a specific date for the return of these records. My reason for this was simple. It appeared that the Department had lost records that we had delivered in May 1995. The longer matters dragged on the more chance there was of more records going missing. I told Adriaan that two weeks may not be long enough and that we could provide Mr Lee with a longer time period. In a written agreement, signed by Mr Geerlofs, he agreed to return all the records by 27 January 1997. I received just some of those records back over a year later. A good portion of them I have never seen to this day, despite constantly asking for them. Mr Geerlofs also undertook by 27 January to advise what issues had arisen from the Department's inspection of these records and what their further interest was, if any, in those records. He never did that either.

The same day I made a number of further Official Information requests about the other records the Department now claimed were missing. These information requests have never been responded to or even acknowledged.

All the while I was still involved with meetings and letters trying to resolve my ongoing personal audit.

On 28 January 1997 we met yet again. I understood that the purpose of this meeting was for the Department to set out for us any changes in their position as a consequence of the records I had supplied on 6 January. Little focus was put on that. It appeared that the Department had done little work on those records. There were some other significant issues discussed. I raised with Carson McNeill the fact that I was now dealing with a personal audit and a PAYE audit of Tannadyce. I appealed to him to enter into some

Inland Revenue
Te Tari Taake

Christchurch Service Centre

Charter House
165 Cashel Street
Private Bag
Christchurch
New Zealand

Facsimile 03-366 6654

23 December 1996

Mr D Henderson
Tannadyce Investments Ltd
P O Box 1066
CHRISTCHURCH

Dear Sir

Further to our meeting of 20 December 1996 and our discussions this morning, I advise as follows.

1   Mr Lee is preparing a description of what records are required for Tannadyce.

2   A letter has been issued to John Ruane of Commercial Affairs, pointing out the misunderstanding that occurred and withdrawing the letter of 18 December 1996.

3   Mr Lee undertakes to ensure that the records to Tannadyce, when uplifted, will be returned to you within two weeks.

4   Mr Lee will identify and advise how the PAYE outstanding for Tannadyce is made up.

5   I understand that you and Mr Geerlofs will arrange a mutually agreeable time for him to uplift the Talic and Lapageria records.

6   I have agreed with Mr Geerlofs that action on the additional matters listed in para 9(3)-(6) of my letter dated 19 December 1996 will be postponed until 28 February 1997.

7   In relation to the enquiries to be directed to Mr Wilson, Mr Geerlofs and I agreed that the ATO should proceed with their task of interviewing him.

     To attempt to talk to him on the telephone would offend protocol with ATO, and would be less satisfactory than an interview.

TANNADYCE INVESTMENTS LTD

8   Mr McNeill does not recall making a statement
insinulating that you had obstructed the department from
making contact with Mr Michael Wilson, and no such
insinuation is intended.

Yours faithfully

P. Sivertsen

P Sivertsen
Manager
Technical and Legal Support

YS

arrangement with me to defer these other audits until the Tannadyce GST audit was dealt with in full. After considerable discussion, and in the presence of my solicitor Brian Palliser, he gave me his personal undertaking that all the audits would be deferred until the Tannadyce GST matter was completely dealt with. We also discussed the complaint to the police. Sivertsen indicated that the Department was still looking at the issue.

Once more the matter of greatest significance was the Department's application of section 60. Once again, Carson McNeill agreed that by Wednesday 5 February the Department would provide their "specific, exact and unequivocal view of the basis of their application of section 60". I can remember talking with Peter Sivertsen after the meeting. He complained to me what a gruelling meeting it had been and how tired he was from it. The meeting was just over an hour long.

I looked forward to 5 February and to receiving this long-awaited information. We had also set down a time for another meeting on Monday 10 February so that the IRD explanation on section 60 could be discussed and debated in full. Instead of a "specific, exact and unequivocal view of the basis of their application of section 60", I received a one-page fax from Mr Bond with just six points on it. The fax did not even refer to the BNZ and made loose and irrelevant references to companies associated with Tannadyce. It stated that Tannadyce was not eligible to recover expenses that could be attributed to these associated companies. It went on to say "the onus of proof is on the taxpayer to prove otherwise. Therefore you are required to produce to the Commissioner prior to any further consideration of this matter documentary evidence which you would or could produce in any litigation in respect of this matter to support your case". Mr Bond went on to advise that "if such evidence is not received by the Commissioner by 21 February 1997 the Commissioner will assume that you do not hold the relevant evidence to establish your case and the matter will be considered as completed".

Once more I was shattered and disillusioned. The GST audit of Tannadyce had just celebrated its third birthday. We were no further ahead than the day we had begun. I was dealing with the most senior IRD officials in the South Island and they could not stick with the simplest of agreements or provide me with the most basic information.

Brian Palliser was a sensation. He would regularly drop what he was doing to assist me. I spent many nights at his house going over documents and the law and trying to find a way forward. I worked with Brian over the next ten days to prepare a full and complete statement of position setting out in great detail why we thought the Department was wrong in its application of section 60. As with so many of these other things we needn't have bothered. Our letter was never responded to.

The audit was now three years old. The onus of proof was upon me to prove I didn't owe a million dollars. I still didn't know the basis of IRD's claim. Records had now gone missing, additional records were provided, more agreements were being broken by senior IRD staff.

Rodney Hide rides in

T wo other very significant events happened in February that year. Firstly, I resolved to bring to the attention of senior IRD personnel in National Office, Wellington, my plight and some of the outrageous behaviour of the Christchurch senior staff. My first point of contact was Brian Hutton, National Manager, Operations Policy, who I had been directed to by Tony Bouzaid. My simple rationale was that someone like Brian Hutton should be very interested to learn if Departmental policy was being overtly breached. As time would show, no one in Head Office cared.

The other, and far more significant event, was that I managed to elicit the support of new ACT MP Rodney Hide. I had met Rodney several years earlier and we had built a friendship. When he was elected to Parliament in October 1996 I had contacted him to bring my ongoing tax problems to his attention. I was certain that he didn't have a full grasp of the case but I knew him well enough to know that if he got into it he would stick with it to the end.

As a new Member of Parliament he was very busy but in February 1997 he had given me his word that he would come to Christchurch and spend a couple of days with me to go through my files and to familiarise himself with the facts of the case. What I had told him to date, although only a tiny piece of the whole story, obviously troubled him. Early afternoon on Friday 14 February I heard a knock at the door and opened it to be greeted by the ever ebullient Rodney Hide exclaiming, "You are looking at an MP". This was a source of great amusement to both of us. I certainly needed cheering up. This was to be my last weekend in the house that had been my home for the past twelve years. It had just been sold at mortgagee sale.

All that afternoon and evening, and then for a good part of the next day, we pored through my extensive files and detailed records. Rodney was shocked. His own estimates were that the Department by that time would have spent close to a million dollars on prosecuting my case. He could not

Rodney Hide: Pondering a 'mountain' of tax legislation.

believe the blunders, errors, incompetence, and what appeared to be overt malice that characterised the Department's every step of the way over the previous three years.

Even though Rodney had only been in Parliament for a matter of months, he had an extraordinarily thorough grasp of the processes and personalities of government. He discussed with me in detail all our options. It was his view that the most productive approach would be an immediate letter directly to the Commissioner of Inland Revenue, Graham Holland. Rodney wrote to the Commissioner setting out a range of detailed questions concerning the Department's performance in respect of my audit.

Rodney is someone for whom I have tremendous respect. Rodney is highly intelligent with numerous degrees and great experience. For him to go through my files in detail and consider the positions carefully and confirm that he considered that I was in the right was a tremendous morale boost. In circumstances like these it's easy to get into self-doubt, no matter how right you are, and to start beating up and doubting yourself.

The other thing was that Rodney was quickly able to grasp the essence of the GST dispute and the law that governs it. Like Brian Palliser, he could not believe the legal and technical positions the Department were doggedly

Inland Revenue
Te Tari Taake

Christchurch Service Centre

Charter House
165 Cashel Street
Private Bag
Christchurch
New Zealand

Telephone 03-379 8500
Facsimile 03-366 6654

28 February 1997

Mr David Henderson
Tannadyce Investments Ltd
PO Box 1066
CHRISTCHURCH

Dear Mr Henderson

I refer to the volume of calls that you have made to various officers of IRD, including Adriaan Geerlofs, Peter Sivertsen, Chris Bond, Gibb Lee, and myself.

These calls have the effect of unreasonably obstructing those officers in the performance of their duties as well as frustrating their attempts to bring the audit and objection in respect of Tannadyce Investments Ltd to a conclusion.

I appreciate your concerns that you were seeking information to which you believe you were entitled. However, a log of these calls has shown that the volume and nature of your calls is unreasonable.

The officers concerned have obligations to other taxpayers, as I'm sure you are aware, and the extent of your telephone calls seriously impedes them from carrying out those obligations.

I am therefore restricting your calls to Tuesday and Thursday each week, between the hours of 9.00am and 10.00am. Messrs. Lee and Sivertsen will make themselves available to you at those times. Please do not contact them or other officers outside these times.

Yours faithfully

Carson McNeill
Service Centre Manager

c.c.   Mr Brian Palliser
        Hill, Lee and Scott
        PO Box 13004
        CHRISTCHURCH

holding on to. He left saying he would get on the case right away.

When Rodney left I had to turn my mind to the task of packing up my possessions and twelve years of my life. With the strain of the audit, and the general tasks of keeping myself alive, I had not been able to put a lot of effort into finding a place to rent. Everyone I had approached had rejected me as a tenant because I was now bankrupt. I even offered to pay months in advance but this still hadn't secured me a place to live. On the day that I had to be out of my home I had arranged for a removal van to come and collect my stuff. I left some friends who had arrived to help me load the van while I went into town still looking for a place to stay. About thirty minutes before the van was due to leave I was able to phone back to report that I had finally secured somewhere to go, an apartment that was vacant but on the market to be sold.

Through this period I was regularly phoning all the IRD officers involved and demanding their responses to earlier undertakings. Many of these calls were terminated by the Department hanging up in my ear. Letters were not being answered and Official Information requests were being ignored.

On 28 February I received the letter shown on the facing page from Carson McNeill: Of course, I protested and, in particular, the fact that the Department was pouring resources into other taxpayers whose audits would have been nowhere near as old as mine.

I thought this was irresponsible and extremely unfair. Despite hundreds of letters and hundreds of phone calls from me, and literally dozens of undertakings from the Department, I still had no further explanations as to why the Department had reallocated several million dollars of expenditure and created a debt for Tannadyce of a million dollars. I still did not have my records back. The police investigation was proceeding. It appeared that the only positive point that I had been able to negotiate was that Carson McNeill had assured me that all other further audits against Tannadyce and myself were on hold until after the completion of the Tannadyce GST audit.

However, and this time not to my surprise, from documentation I received it was obvious that my personal audit was continuing.

I received another agreement from the Department to have another meeting on Friday 28 February 1997. On the Monday before the proposed meeting Carson McNeill assured me that before close of business that day I would receive an agenda from the Department for that meeting. I didn't.

447

TECHNICAL AND LEGAL SUPPORT GROUP
CHRISTCHURCH SERVICE CENTRE

DATE   :   3 March 1997

RECORD OF DISCUSSION

FROM   :   Peter Sivertsen
                   Manager (TLSG)

SUBJECT   :   **DAVID HENDERSON**
                   FRIDAY, 28 FEBRUARY 1997, 4.15 PM

David wanted to work through the agenda for the meeting to take place on Tuesday, 4 March 1997.

1   Outcome of Records Check

David wants a full summary of the results of the records check and he wants the department to tell them what further interest it now has in those records. I explained that Gibb and Helen would probably work through the schedules with him, but that would take place subsequent to the meeting. They would make themselves available to give them the time that was needed to deal with these. ▓▓▓▓▓▓▓▓ ▓▓▓▓▓▓▓▓▓▓ He wanted more information at the meeting, given that it was five weeks since the records were delivered. I pointed out the records were not in order. He replied that the records were in reasonable order when delivered. He wants schedules to be placed before him on Tuesday.

2   Outcome of Consideration of Statements of Position

David went into detailed discussion about the agency. He wants a full explanation from Gibb of how section 60 applied, to the expenditure that he has disallowed. He wants Gibb to show how he constructs the adjustments in terms of section 60 of the Act. I tried to explain that Gibb may not be relying on section 60 but on other sections of the Act. ▓▓▓▓▓▓▓▓▓▓▓▓▓▓▓▓▓▓▓▓▓▓▓

3   Further Audits

▓▓▓▓▓▓▓ no discussion on this point.

4   Statement of Position on Management Fees From Tannadyce

David said bluntly he has not done it and will not be able to do it. He has been too busy dealing with IRD.

The same goes for number 6.

7   Outcome of Consideration of Complaint to the Police

David wants full details of the department consideration of this complaint. He insists that we must show reasonable grounds for laying the complaint. He wants it detailed out, where is the allegation of fraud in each case. He pointed out that Gibb had conceded that the BNZ leases were not an issue any more and this was an example.

RECORD OF DISCUSSION
DAVID HENDERSON, 28.02.97

SECTION 31

I agreed we would discuss this at the meeting.

OFFICIAL INFORMATION REQUEST

David insisted that there were a number of requests outstanding. I said I believed that they had all been responded to, but he would need to provide a list of those that he considered had not been dealt with.

David kept insisting I make commitments on each item, █████████████████████ ████████████████████ He said he would ring me next week.

The call ended at 4.55 pm. ████████████████████

P. Sivertsen

[Peter Sivertsen]
MANAGER
TECHNICAL AND LEGAL SUPPORT GROUP

On Wednesday I faxed McNeill to tell him that I was cancelling the meeting because I still had not got an agenda as he had promised. The next day I received the agenda. It contained no reference to the all-important section 60 issue. We set up the meeting for Tuesday 4 March.

On Friday 28 February at 4:15 I had a long discussion with Peter Sivertsen about the agenda. In particular, I explained how I still wanted a full explanation of how section 60 applied. Sivertsen seemed confused. He had attended many meetings over the previous ten months. He had written many letters and faxes advising me that section 60 was what the Department were relying on for their reallocation of the expenditure. Despite all that, he now told me that "Gibb Lee may not be relying on section 60 but on other sections of the Act". This observation was twenty-three months after Chris Bond had personally assured me that the last remaining issue to conclude the audit was the application of section 60. What could I say?

I asked for other minor matters to be included on the agenda like, where were the records that Adriaan Geerlofs had given me a written agreement to return six weeks earlier, what had the Department done in respect of their several assurances to revisit their letter of complaint to the police, and also, why had none of my Official Information requests been responded to? Peter Sivertsen saw all these as trivial but reluctantly agreed to include them on the agenda.

The meeting went ahead and, as Brian Palliser and I had specifically requested, the only personnel present were Carson McNeill and Peter Sivertsen. We were making a huge effort to try and appeal to McNeill in particular and to get him to realise that the Department had no substance to their case and that his auditors were leading him astray. I also wanted the opportunity to impress on McNeill that in my opinion Peter Sivertsen did not have a clue about what was going on even though he was Manager of the Technical and Legal Support Group for the South Island. As always, I tried to focus immediately on the application of section 60. I asked Sivertsen to explain specifically what documentation the Department were relying on to support their assertions that an agency relationship existed between the BNZ and Tannadyce and between Tannadyce and its associated companies. To Brian's and my horror Peter Sivertsen advised that there was no documentation but rather that the Department considered that there was an "implied agency". To this day I still do not know what that means. For the first time Carson McNeill looked mildly annoyed. Brian and I expressed our frustration and disappointment at this point. Sivertsen continued to stutter and stammer but at McNeill's direction he agreed to prepare and get to us further information. Of course, I referred to Gibb Lee's letter on 10 July the previous year where he had advised that I had already received full and specific detail relating to the Department's position on section 60. I explained that the time for games was up and that the Department really now had to provide their full and complete explanations. Carson McNeill insisted on this too. Once again, in the presence of Brian Palliser, he gave a firm and unequivocal undertaking. He agreed that Helen Sumner, IRD staff solicitor, would provide us with a full, complete and specific explanation to support the Department's position on section 60 in writing before the next meeting or the Department would, in writing, resile from applying section 60 and the reallocation of expenditure.

At the time, this seemed like a big breakthrough. Brian assured me that given the seriousness of the situation, and that McNeill was providing his personal undertaking, that I should be positive about this move. We briefly discussed the police complaint and McNeill and Sivertsen agreed to go through it and advise us promptly what, if any, complaints they were willing to withdraw. Once more, I left the meeting enthused.

Three days later on Friday 7 March I received a most bizarre letter from Carson McNeill. He referred to our previous meeting and said he had considered my "verbal argument that a global approach should be taken to

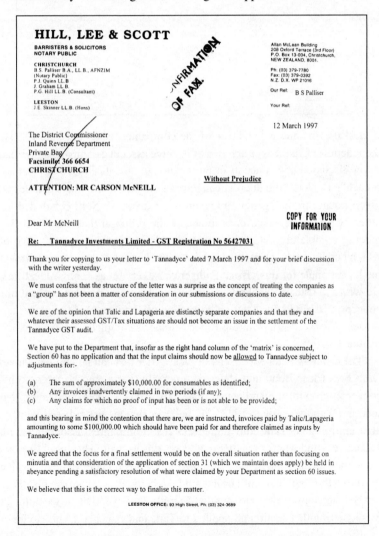

HILL, LEE & SCOTT

BARRISTERS & SOLICITORS
NOTARY PUBLIC

CHRISTCHURCH
B.S. Palliser B.A., LL.B., AFNZIM
(Notary Public)
P.J. Quinn LL.B.
J. Graham LL.B.
P.G. Hill LL.B. (Consultant)

LEESTON
J.E. Skinner LL.B. (Hons)

Allan McLean Building
208 Oxford Terrace (3rd Floor)
P.O. Box 13-004, Christchurch,
NEW ZEALAND, 8001.

Ph: (03) 379-7780
Fax: (03) 379-0392
N.Z. D.X. WP 21016

Our Ref: B S Palliser

Your Ref:

12 March 1997

The District Commissioner
Inland Revenue Department
Private Bag
Facsimile: 366 6654
CHRISTCHURCH

ATTENTION: MR CARSON McNEILL

Without Prejudice

Dear Mr McNeill

COPY FOR YOUR INFORMATION

Re: Tannadyce Investments Limited - GST Registration No 56427031

Thank you for copying to us your letter to 'Tannadyce' dated 7 March 1997 and for your brief discussion with the writer yesterday.

We must confess that the structure of the letter was a surprise as the concept of treating the companies as a "group" has not been a matter of consideration in our submissions or discussions to date.

We are of the opinion that Talic and Lapageria are distinctly separate companies and that they and whatever their assessed GST/Tax situations are should not become an issue in the settlement of the Tannadyce GST audit.

We have put to the Department that, insofar as the right hand column of the 'matrix' is concerned, Section 60 has no application and that the input claims should now be <u>allowed</u> to Tannadyce subject to adjustments for:-

(a)   The sum of approximately $10,000.00 for consumables as identified;
(b)   Any invoices inadvertently claimed in two periods (if any);
(c)   Any claims for which no proof of input has been or is not able to be provided;

and this bearing in mind the contention that there are, we are instructed, invoices paid by Talic/Lapageria amounting to some $100,000.00 which should have been paid for and therefore claimed as inputs by Tannadyce.

We agreed that the focus for a final settlement would be on the overall situation rather than focusing on minutia and that consideration of the application of section 31 (which we maintain does apply) be held in abeyance pending a satisfactory resolution of what were claimed by your Department as section 60 issues.

We believe that this is the correct way to finalise this matter.

LEESTON OFFICE: 93 High Street, Ph: (03) 324-3689

We will discuss the questions of Fringe Benefit Tax, Income Tax and PAYE as they relate to Tannadyce, with Mr Henderson and respond on those issues as soon as possible.

We are of the present view that such should be dealt with at the conclusion of the GST audit.

It may be helpful if your Mr McNeill and the writer were to meet as soon as possible to discuss your letter of 7 March and this reply.

Yours faithfully
HILL, LEE & SCOTT

per:

Mr B S Palliser
BSP:RWH

c.c.   D I Henderson Esq

overall income and expenditure of the companies as set out below". He then identified Tannadyce and two of its three associate companies. We had never discussed any concepts or put up any arguments about a "global approach". His letter did not relate in any way to the undertakings that he had given regarding the agency propositions. Carson McNeill concluded his letter by giving us seven days to accept the proposal that would involve redoing completely many years of accounts for three companies, two of which I no longer had any involvement with. I couldn't even begin to imagine his rationale for this. Brian Palliser was every bit as confused as I was. He wrote to Carson McNeill confirming that we had never discussed this concept, reasserted our position on section 60, and rejected the global approach. We were still awaiting Helen Sumner's complete and exact explanation.

The next day Peter Sivertsen rang me. After that call he sent a memo to Gibb Lee, Chris Bond and Helen Sumner. In that memo he refers to his conversation with me and stated that "DH wants a letter confirming that section 60 applies only to BNZ. He believes that we quoted section 60 as also applying to Talic and Lapegeria [the companies associated with Tannadyce] and wants the letter to address this as well. He would like this letter, the schedule and invoices tomorrow, but doesn't believe there is value in talking through them until he has studied them. Please confirm that these can be ready tomorrow". He says that I simply "believe" that the Department was asserting that section 60 applied to Talic and Lapegeria. Just to highlight how outrageous this was, consider a letter written to me six months earlier on 16 August 1996 from Peter Sivertsen. He says, "you quote me as alluding to 'entities' and 'various entities' that Tannadyce was acting as agent for without setting out specifically who these entities are. Yet, in my letter, when I refer to these entities and various entities, I have specifically named the companies of Talic and Lapegeria so that there should be no confusion". For at least six months the Department had been telling me that section 60 applies to Tannadyce's relationship with Talic and Lapegeria and now Peter Sivertsen is writing a memo questioning my "belief" that the Department is asserting this.

```
Fri  Mar 14, 1997   7:47 am   mailbox   standard   Page 1


  DATE      TIME          FROM              SUBJECT           CODES
 13/03/97  3:29 pm  Sivertsen Peter      re Henderson         [        ]

      To:  Lee Gibb,Sumner Helen,Bond Chris

      CC:  McNeill Carson


  Subject:  re Henderson              New [ ]      Codes:  [        ]
  Message:  I rang DH after talking with Carson.DH wants a letter confirming
            that S60 applies only to BNZ. He believes we quoted S60 as also
            applying to Talic and Lapegeria and wants the letter to address
            this as well. He would like this letter, the schedules and
            invoices tomorrow, but doesnt believe there is value in talking
            through them until he has studied them. Please confirm that
            these can be ready tomorrow.

  Priority:  Immediate      Delivery Acknowledge [ ]   View Acknowledge [*]

     From:  Sivertsen Peter      By:  10pps1@chca03      Attachment [*]
```

But it gets worse. The next day Brian Palliser received a letter from Carson McNeill. Enclosed with his letter were some new schedules. These schedules showed yet another complete reconstruction of the Tannadyce GST returns for the previous six years. There was no accompanying explanation, as McNeill had promised, as to the principles upon which the schedules had been constructed, other than the following confused statement. "In respect of the questions about section 60 of the GST Act, it is pointed out that agency is not created by the GST Act *per se,* but rather by the contractual arrangements between parties. The effect of section 60 is to negotiate (sic) the impacts of section 24 of the Act". Brian Palliser and I had no idea what this all meant. Carson McNeill concluded his letter by advising "the Commissioner must be mindful of the statutory requirements necessary to accommodate your proposal for a final seion (sic)". I could never recall

Inland Revenue
Te Tari Taake

Christchurch Service Centre
Charter House
165 Cashel Street
Private Bag
Christchurch
New Zealand

Telephone 03-379 8500
Facsimile 03-366 6654

14 March 1997

Hill Lee & Scott
Attention Brian Palliser
PO Box 13 004
CHRISTCHURCH

Dear Brian

Tannadyce Investments Ltd
Talic Holdings Ltd
Lapageria Holdings Ltd

Your letter 12 March 1997

IRD Number 56 427 031
Our Reference CH/GST/CJB

There are common issues to our discussions of 7 March, your letter and Mr Henderson's letter of 12 March.

Enclosed are amended adjustment schedules, which reflect the recent provision by you of records for Tannadyce, Talic and Lapageria. These adjustments are a reconstruction of the GST returns for those entities, and have been prepared without the benefit of your submissions on management fees. The schedules will form the basis of any future discussions.

The proposed discussion of the schedules, on a line by line basis, between Inland Revenue and Tannadyce can now be arranged. Mr Lee and a solicitor will be available between 24 and 26 March. It is expected that 10 hours will be sufficient for the discussions.

In respect of the questions about Section 60 of the GST Act, it is pointed out that agency is not created by the GST Act per se, but rather by the contractual arrangements between parties.

The effect of Section 60 is to negotiate the impacts of Section 24 of the Act, which would otherwise limit input claims to the nominee on the particular tax invoices.

The adjustment schedules show how individual tax invoices have been treated. Section 60 will impact particularly in those cases where the tax invoice nominee is different from the recipient of the goods or services, i.e the party to whom the input has been allowed. It is not appropriate at this stage to limit the applicability of Section 60 to Station Village inputs and outputs.

The input claim for the Stutz car has been disallowed, pending receipt of the underlying documentation to evidence Michael Wilson's debt to Tannadyce.

While it is agreed that Tannadyce, Talic and Lapageria are separate companies, it is appreciated that you wish to treat the complex development expenditure globally; the only way Inland Revenue can do

112

this is by grouping the entities. The Commissioner must be mindful of the statutory requirements necessary to accommodate your proposal for a final seion.

Yours sincerely

P. J. Swenbsen

for

C A McNeill
Service Centre Manager

cc Dave Henderson
Tannadyce Investments
PO Box 1066
CHRISTCHURCH

proposing a final or even a first "seion". Both Brian and I searched vainly through dictionaries trying to find a definition of "seion". I even rang an Islamic friend to see if he had come across the term. He hadn't. I asked him what the term was for a jihad against an out-of-favour taxpayer. He said Iran was too civilised to have one.

Despite several requests I never received any further explanation. Section 24 of the Goods and Services Tax Act sets out in detail what a tax invoice is. It has nothing whatsoever to do with section 60. The best that I could infer was that the Department was trying to justify how they were taking millions of dollars of properly prepared tax invoices made out to Tannadyce and arbitrarily assigning the GST benefit of those invoices to a third party.

It was now clear to me that the Department was completely out of control. The audit was 38 months old, it had cost me tens of thousands of dollars, and the Department hundreds of thousands of dollars. I was dealing with the Department's most senior South Island staff. It appeared that they were in it so far and so deep that to them there was no way out but just to keep digging holes in a vain hope that somehow I would die, give up, or just go away. Other than Rodney Hide, there was nowhere for me to turn for help. There is no independent party to complain to. The only glimmer of hope in Carson McNeill's letter was a suggestion that Gibb Lee and a solicitor would be available between 24 and 26 March to discuss with me the new set of schedules that had been prepared.

The good news was that I had an MP on board. The bad news was that the IRD was now just making the law up. More agreements and undertakings were broken by IRD's most senior staff.

Henderson declared unreasonable and frivolous

Meanwhile, Rodney Hide was working diligently in Wellington to move matters forward on a political level. His letter to the Commissioner seeking answers to a number of important points had been responded to by Carson McNeill who refused to answer any of the questions on the grounds of the secrecy provisions detailed in section 81 of the Tax Administration Act. This was despite Rodney's questions relating to the processing of my audit rather than my tax position. But what he did disclose were the times involved in GST audits. He said that 18 hours is typical for a one-period check, 150 hours for a full investigation, and 500 hours for a criminal fraud investigation. By our estimates, and later confirmed by the commissioner, the Department had spent over 2,000 hours by this time on the Tannadyce audit. Remember that senior officer Chris Bond had told me on 30 January 1996, over a year earlier, that there was approximately 40 hours remaining to conclude the Tannadyce audit. Mr McNeill assured Rodney that he had taken an active interest in the audit of Tannadyce. That was true. He went on to say that "a proposal to facilitate resolution of the audit is now with Mr Henderson". That was not true.

Rodney and I discussed this response in some depth. He was angry. He felt that this was a flip and irresponsible letter. But as had happened so many times before, the Department appeared to have successfully shut down another legitimate avenue of inquiry. Like me, Rodney is not one to give up. I went away and studied section 81 of the Tax Administration Act, an extensive section that is intended to prevent IRD officers passing out confidential taxpayer information. It certainly isn't intended to stop legitimate questioning by an interested and properly authorised third party. It suddenly occurred to me that under the Act, Tannadyce could formally appoint Rodney Hide as an agent. As this agent Rodney would be fully entitled to receive answers to every question that he might ask that might relate to Tannadyce. I ran this by Brian Palliser who told me that while it was a novel approach it was entirely legitimate and would place no unnecessary liabilities on Rodney.

I put the proposal to Rodney and he loved it. He agreed that he would check it out professionally and come back to me. He did and declared, "Let's do it". He said that no MP had ever taken this approach before. I discussed this with Tannadyce's director in Toronto who was by now the sole director. The other local director had resigned at my suggestion because it had become apparent that eventually we would have to make public who the directors of Tannadyce were. I was extremely anxious that should he ever be identified he could become the subject of attacks from the Department. The Toronto director immediately agreed and executed a document confirming Rodney's appointment as an agent of the company.

On 25 March 1997 Rodney wrote to Carson McNeill confirming that he had become an agent of Tannadyce and demanding immediate answers to the questions that he had asked a month earlier.

Minister Bill Birch was later to imply repeatedly that there was something improper about Rodney's involvement. In a letter to Rodney he darkly suggested that "there could be justification for concern about conflict of public and private obligation". In another letter he suggested that Rodney's actions were prejudicing his duty as an MP and putting "the interests of the company ahead of any other obligation undertaken as an MP to the wider voting public or the nation". This was all nonsense clearly designed to unsettle Rodney and put him off balance. Rodney, in my view, was the only one carrying out the proper duties of an MP. As well as being smart, Rodney is tough. He stuck to his guns to get my audit concluded and to hold the IRD to account for their actions. Bill Birch's threats didn't worry him.

In the meantime, I continued to write to Brian Hutton (National Manager, Operations Policy) in Wellington. I continued to place before him hard evidence that charged inappropriate and unlawful behaviour by the Department. I offered to come to Wellington at my own expense to provide him with further evidence to support my allegations.

On 1 April 1997, an appropriate day for such a letter, he wrote to me. He said "I do not intend to meet with you to discuss this investigation, because as I have had explained to you on several occasions the Christchurch Service Centre has the ultimate responsibility for dealing with your investigation. However I would be happy to receive any written suggestions that you may have on how you believe Inland Revenue could improve on its published policies in relation to investigations".

TANNADYCE INVESTMENTS LTD

P.O. Box 1066, Christchurch. New Zealand
Telephone: 64 3 377 1383   Facsimile: 64 3 377 1390

March 24, 1997

Peter Siversten
Manager
Technical and Legal Support Group
Inland Revenue Department
Christchurch

Fax: 363 1519

Dear Peter

I refer to recent schedules provided to us by you.

Pursuant to the provisions of the Official Information Act please provide us with the following information

A. Pursuant to what section of the GST Act has each adjustment been made?

B. What information (in its entirety) is the Department relying on to support such adjustments?

Yours sincerely

Dave Henderson
Tannadyce Investments Ltd

Copies: Brian Palliser
Brian Hutton

I wrote back to him the same day. I pleaded with him to direct me to someone at National Office with whom I could meet to discuss my concerns to try and solve the issue. On 8 April in a long phone conversation, Brian Hutton explained that there was nothing that he or anyone in Wellington could do in respect of the Tannadyce audit or in regard to the allegations that I had been making about the improper behaviour of officers in the Southern Region. I wrote to him that day and, in response to his earlier offer, suggested that this policy should change. He has never responded to my letter.

All the while I was still beavering away desperately trying to get the promised explanation as to the Department's application of section 60. Peter Sivertsen had promised me that Gibb Lee and a solicitor would be available between 24 and 26 March to explain line by line the reallocation schedules. On Friday 21 March, Mr Sivertsen wrote to me saying I was to contact either Gibb Lee or Helen Sumner and for them set up a time to meet with me the following week. I immediately phoned Gibb Lee but he was not available. I then phoned Helen Sumner who went into a long dissertation about how I was never to phone her and that she did not want to speak to me and slammed the phone down. I phoned Peter Sivertsen. He too was unavailable so I set out these events in a fax.

On Monday 24 March 1997 Helen Sumner wrote a long letter to Brian Palliser saying that Peter Sivertsen had not forewarned her of the meeting. I wrote back to her asking her to provide me with an agenda for our proposed meeting. Also, out of complete frustration, I lodged an Official Information request requiring the Department to provide me with copies of all the information they had in their possession to support their position on section 60 and the reallocation of expenditure.

On Wednesday 26 March at midday, Peter Sivertsen faxed me. He said that my requests under the Official Information Act were unreasonable and frivolous. He said that the only time available for Mrs Sumner and Mr Lee to meet with me and to discuss the new schedules was between 9am and midday the next day. This was Easter week and the next day was the last working day of the week. I rang Brian Palliser to check whether he was free. He couldn't make it. I rang Peter Sivertsen. He was extremely irate. He would not allow a meeting to proceed at any other time other than the one he had specified. As Brian could not be available, and as we had only three hours when the Department itself had identified in earlier letters that ten hours was necessary to explain the schedules, I declined the invitation.

Inland Revenue
Te Tari Taake

Christchurch Service Centre
165 Cashel Street
PO Box 2871
Christchurch
New Zealand

Telephone 03-363 1845
Facsimile 03-366 6654

26 March 1997

Attention: Mr David Henderson
Tannadyce Investments Ltd
P O Box 1066
CHRISTCHURCH

Dear Sir

TANNADYCE INVESTMENTS LTD
OBJECTION

The department is in receipt of your six faxes dated 24 and 25 March 1997; four addressed to Mr Sivertsen, one to Mr Geerlofs and one to Mrs Sumner.

The department considers your continued demands under the Official Information Act and response to the department's attempt to resolve your objection to the department's assessment issued on or about 10 July 1996 as unreasonable and frivolous.

The opportunity is available to you to meet with Mrs Sumner and Mr Lee on Thursday, 27 March 1997 between 9.00 am and 12.00 pm to discuss the schedules forwarded to you in the department's letter of 12 March 1997.

If you wish to prepare an agenda you can forward it to Mr Lee or Mrs Sumner prior to this meeting.

The Commissioner is in a position to issue amended assessments on the information provided.   You are reminded that the burden of proof rests on you under section 18 of the Taxation Review Authority Act 1997 to show why the Commissioner's assessments   are incorrect and by how much.

If you wish to take the opportunity to meet on Thursday, 27 March 1997, between 9.00 am and 12.00 pm, please telephone Mr Sivertsen and leave a message on his answer phone advising that you will be attending at the department.

On your arrival please ask the receptionist to advise Mr Lee, who will escort you to the meeting room.

Yours faithfully

Peter Sivertsen

Peter Sivertsen
Manager
Technical and Legal Support Group

The Department from that point on continually refused to ever meet with me or to provide explanations as to their bizarre reallocations contained in their schedules.

National Office refused to deal with or help me. Now Christchurch too was refusing to meet me. It was up to me to prove the IRD wrong but they would not explain how the debt was made up.

The Problem Resolution Service has a problem

I t was clear that I wasn't going to get the information that I required. I was keen to seek any way forward. One day in early April I spotted a brochure on display at IRD's public counter titled "Problem Resolution Service". It seemed to me that this was a brochure I should be reading. The brochure begins by advising that "most people's dealings with Inland Revenue are trouble free, but sometimes there are problems. Because it's important that all our customers are treated fairly Inland Revenue has a Problem Resolution Service. Each Inland Revenue Office has a Problem Resolution Officer, who is an experienced senior staff member. This officer will undertake to resolve your problem quickly and fairly and will aim to find a solution within five working days". This was the person I was looking for. It went on to confirm that the Service can help with long delays over GST refunds.

As you can imagine, I immediately rang the Christchurch office to put me in touch with their Problem Resolution Officer. Oops, another problem. The IRD receptionist frankly informed me that such a person did not exist. I then rang IRD Wellington. I spoke to Alison Williams. She assured me that the Problem Resolution Service was alive and well and that it should be operating in Christchurch. After some research, she was able to provide me with a contact number in Christchurch but she also offered to work for me through the Wellington office to solve any difficulties that I might have. She confirmed that indeed the Department would find a solution in five working days as promised. I thanked her for her help and suggested to her that I would first proceed with the woman she had put me in touch with in Christchurch.

Yet another problem. The woman I was to contact only worked part-time. She was not going to be there until some time the following week, no one knew when. She appeared to have taken glide-time to hitherto uncharted limits. I kicked up a fuss and I was put onto a Mrs Admiral. She told me that she knew a little bit about the Problem Resolution Service but that she could not deal with a corporate complaint. After putting me on hold for several minutes, she told me that I would need to speak to Steven Hayes. I dutifully contacted Steven Hayes. He enthusiastically told me that he was "resurrecting the Problem Resolution Service". I took the time to explain to him the nature of my problem and the specific people in the office that I was dealing with. He explained to me that he had a problem: Peter Sivertsen was his boss. I respectfully suggested that this should make no difference. Our discussion continued with me pressing him to resolve my problems. It finally ended when he became irate and slammed the phone down in my ear because I had kept pushing him to take up my case. Who do I turn to? I now have a problem with the Problem Resolution Officer.

I invoked a thirty-minute cooling down period for his benefit and phoned him back. We had a reasonably amicable discussion in which he explained to me emphatically that the Problem Resolution Service was not available to myself or Tannadyce. He refused to explain why and, once more, hung up. Not to be deterred I phoned back Alison Williams in Wellington. She was unavailable and I was put on to Ngaire Blong. She confirmed with me that the Problem Resolution Service was definitely available to myself and Tannadyce.

Several days later I made contact again with Alison Williams. She told me that she was not authorised to speak to me any more regarding my problems. It had taken the same time frame as the Department promotes that it can solve a taxpayer's problem to discuss and deny me access to the Service.

The so-called Problem Resolution Service was defunct. Its services were specifically denied me. I had no more ready options available.

"It's important we don't deal with Henderson anymore"

- Peter Sivertson, Senior IRD Officer

In November the previous year the Department's incorrect representations had resulted in the Ombudsman ending his investigation into my complaints about the Department's refusal to reply to my Official Information requests. I had been pursuing this matter aggressively with the Ombudsman both directly and with the assistance of a solicitor at Russell McVeagh in Auckland, Julian Long. The Ombudsman continued to maintain that he had not been misled by the Department. He also steadfastly refused to consider my evidence on the fact that the Department had been advised that a new director had been appointed to Tannadyce and that this director had fully authorised me to deal with the IRD matters.

It appeared that the IRD were desperate to find out who the director of Tannadyce was. I did not believe that the name was important to them. The fact that Brian Palliser, as solicitor for the company, had confirmed with them that a new director had been appointed and that both he and I were authorised to represent the company was sufficient. Sir Brian Elwood was also pressing me hard to try and find out who the Director of the company was. I now have a one-inch file of letters between the two of us dealing with the matter.

On 17 April I managed to identify and track down the IRD staff member responsible for liaising with the Office of the Ombudsman. His name was Dave Elwood, no relation to Sir Brian. I set out for him some of the difficulties I was having, particularly in respect of Official Information requests. He told me that Christchurch had said that neither I, nor Brian Palliser, had ever told Christchurch that we had authority to deal with the company's affairs. Christchurch had also told him that the Department was not having any dealings with me and indeed hadn't since my bankruptcy, in August the previous year. I told him that was an absolute lie. I then went to the considerable trouble of providing him with hard evidence that the Department had been dealing extensively with me. I sent him copies of letters and minutes of meetings. He undertook to put this to Chris Bond and come back to me. He claimed later that Bond was now asserting that the only reason that they were dealing with me was because I held some of Tannadyce's records and the only way they could get access to them was through me. This too was completely untrue. Once again, I hoped that by providing hard evidence to a senior IRD official at National Office that I might cause some investigation into my audit. But that wasn't to happen.

Dave Elwood's boss at National Office was Paul Matson. He was officially National Manager, Strategic Business Relationships. Over the next few months I worked with him as well providing him with numerous copies of documents and correspondence establishing improper behaviour by the IRD in Christchurch. Like everyone else in National Office, he didn't want to know.

It was also about then that the audit took a nasty turn. At the end of April the Department started laying complaints to the Office of the Official Assignee alleging that I had been managing Tannadyce in contravention of the provisions of the Insolvency Act. On 5 May 1997, Peter Sivertsen spoke at some length to Ken Derby of the Official Assignee's office. Ken told him that the IRD did not need an authority from their office to deal with me. That was not good enough for Sivertsen. He was desperate to find some angle to exclude me from IRD dealings over Tannadyce matters. He made

18/4/97

174

HENDERSON DAVE & TANNADYCE INVESTMENTS

History

Henderson David is a Taxpayer in ChCh. He was the director of a number of
companies many of which are or have been subject to IRD investigations.
One of these companies is TANNADYCE INVESTMENTS LTD. An overview of
this coy is included as appendix 1.

The company has been under almost constant investigation from March 1993.

Although Gibb Lee, Chris Bond, Peter Sivertsen, Ross Gardiner, Peter Boerlage,
Phillipa Foulds Adriaan Geerlofs and Carson McNeil have all been involved with this
case, GIBB LEE, CHRIS BOND and PETER SIVERTSEN are the primaries
involved.

OPINION

Issues

Information Provided to the Ombudsman :

Henderson complained to the Ombudsman in October 1996 regarding IRD acting
unreasonably in withholding information he had requested under the OIA.
Christchurch (Chris Bond TLSG.)informed the SBR unit that Henderson is a Bankrupt
August 1996) therefore cannot have access to info re Tannadyce.

It is now apparent that Christchurch may still have been discussing TANNADYCE
with Henderson. Henderson raised this with the Ombudsman via letter and with me
via telephone on 17/4/97. Mr Henderson provided evidence of this inconsistent
approach in the form of letters from IRD inviting him to meetings at which
Tannadyce business was to be discussed and minutes from those meetings.

Information regarding the Ombudsman investigation

123

This apparent inconsistency was raised with Chris Bond who indicated that the extent of the discussion was that Henderson had the records for Tannadyce and he was the only one that knew what Tannadyce did as per s 16 TAA.

OPINION OF IRD STAFF WITHHELD.

Detail re Ombudsman Investigation

&

OPINION OF IRD staff.

Peter also indicated that he had a meeting with the Insolvency Manager at commercial Affairs that afternoon. The purpose of this meeting was to explore options for identifying who the new director of Tannadyce is.

Things to clarify:

What was the outcome of Peter S's meeting with Commercial Affairs?
Is Christchurch still planning to discuss Tannadyce assessments with Henderson?
What is Christchurch planning to do next?

Note 1. In reviewing the file I note that a coy secretary is listed (Karen Cook [OPINION OF IRD STAFF.] that the new assessments should be sent to the Coy secretary.

Note 2. I have undertaken to respond to Henderson ASAP to his complaint of apparent inconsistencies in CHCH's dealings with him. I would appreciate the issues above being resolved urgently prior to my communicating further with Mr Henderson.

it clear to Ken Derby that it was "quite critical" for the Department to "cease any involvement with Henderson". These comments are recorded in his own notes of that conversation.

The Official Assignee took the matter up with me. I provided him with a lengthy explanation and evidence that I was properly authorised to deal with the Tannadyce matters relating to the GST audit. On 12 May 1997 Sivertsen advised that as I was now a bankrupt it was considered "that your

Inland Revenue
Te Tari Taake

Christchurch Service Centre

165 Cashel Street
PO Box 2871
Christchurch
New Zealand
Telephone 03-363 1845
Facsimile 03-366 6654

12 May 1997

Mr David I Henderson
P O Box 1066
CHRISTCHURCH

Dear Sir

TANNADYCE INVESTMENTS LIMITED
IRD NUMBER: 56-427-031
OUR REFERENCE: CH/GST/CJB

Following your assistance during the audit of the above company, the material aspects of the audit are now complete.

As a consequence of your bankruptcy, it is noted that you have been required to resign as a trustee of Impolat Trust (the shareholder in the auditee).

Under the Companies Act and the Insolvency Act you are not able to directly or indirectly manage a company. It is therefore considered that your involvement with the tax affairs of Tannadyce Investments Limited is no longer appropriate.

The Tax Administration Act specifically prevents the Department from communicating or disclosing any tax information to persons not authorised to receive that information.

As a consequence, the Department will no longer be able to communicate with you in the above matter.

Yours faithfully

[signature]

[Peter Sivertsen]
MANAGER
TECHNICAL AND LEGAL SUPPORT GROUP

involvement with the tax affairs of Tannadyce Investments Ltd is no longer appropriate".

Once more, the Department was desperately employing every device and trick available to try and exclude me to railroad through their bizarre assessments. I protested all this vociferously with Carson McNeill. He was not interested in my concerns. A few days later McNeill wrote to me and advised that from that point on the Department would "deal only with the company's directors on current and future tax issues". He concluded that letter by stating "further correspondence on this issue will not be entered into by the Department".

This was serious. No longer could I, Brian Palliser or any other professional person represent Tannadyce and deal with the tax issues. The Department would from that time be willing only to deal with a director who by this time they had been advised lived in Toronto. This was on an audit that was clearly out of control. This demand would put financial demands on Tannadyce way beyond anything it had. It would also be clear to the Department that the director in Toronto would have no knowledge of all the detail involved with the audit or everything that had been going on in the last forty months of the audit. It was clearly a ploy by the Department to try once more to bring the audit to a close on their terms and to bury forever what was fast becoming an extremely embarrassing affair.

I sent this letter to Rodney Hide. He was outraged. What especially upset him was that it was now mid-May and he still had not received from the Department answers to the questions he had asked at the end of February. I remember him telling me, "What's the point of being an MP if you can't get answers to simple questions to Departments you're supposed to be overseeing?" Clearly, their contempt extended to elected representatives voted into Parliament by us to hold them to account.

Rodney Hide wrote to the Minister Bill Birch setting out his views on how outrageous the Department's actions were. He told Birch that his view of Carson McNeill's letter was that it was "one that would make the Revenue Minister of Zaire proud". He went on to suggest that in his view this new and outrageous requirement was in breach of the Bill of Rights, the Human Rights Act, and particularly, the provisions of section 6 of the Tax Administration Act.

Section 6 of the Tax Administration Act is interesting. In all the hundreds of thousands of pages of tax law and legislation this tiny little section is the only formal requirement directing the behaviour of the Minister, the Commissioner and thousands of staff to whom he delegates his authority. In lay terms what this section says is that everyone who has responsibility under the Tax Acts must at all times use their best endeavours to maintain the integrity of the tax system. It goes on to define the integrity of the tax system as including, in part, the public's perception of that integrity. Certainly my perception of the integrity of the tax system was dented. I could not think of an IRD official in the last three-and-a-half years of this nightmare who at any time had done anything that would come close to being construed as using their best endeavours to promote the integrity of the tax system. I

Inland Revenue
Te Tari Taake

IR 22010

Christchurch Service Centre
165 Cashel Street
PO Box 2871
Christchurch
New Zealand

Telephone 03-363 1845
Facsimile 03-366 6654

14 May 1997

Mr David Henderson
P O Box 1066
CHRISTCHURCH

Dear Sir

RE: EMPLOYEE AUTHORISATION - TANNADYCE INVESTMENTS LIMITED

I refer to your letters of 13 May 1997.

The Department has considered your status as a bankrupt and I refer to my letter of 12 May 1997 advising the Department's position in respect of its ability to deal further with you on the Company's tax affairs.

If the Company's directors wish to involve you in the Company's tax affairs, then that is between you and the directors, however the Department will deal only with the Company's directors on current and future tax issues. This includes any information concerning the Department's dealings with third parties concerning Tannadyce.

Further correspondence on this issue will not be entered into by the Department.

Yours faithfully

C A McNeill
Service Centre Manager

was left to conclude that either the actions that I had experienced were the norm or that the Department treated this piece of legislation with as much contempt as the other legislation they were supposed to be bound by.

It was Rodney's considered view that Bill Birch – who had as much responsibility under the statute as, say, Peter Sivertsen – would be a little more concerned and might move to investigate the matter a little more thoroughly. As it transpired Mr Birch never responded to Rodney's letter. Eventually, Birch did respond to other letters from Rodney relating to my audit. In one of these letters he advised Rodney that "the Commissioner also assures me that his Department is committed to treating all people in a fair and equal manner, and that there has been no campaign of harassment directed at Mr Henderson. Because of the secrecy provisions contained in the Tax Administration Act 1994, Inland Revenue is no longer able to disclose information regarding Tannadyce Investments Ltd to Mr Henderson". However, the preceding pages clearly indicate that I had been harassed for several years . Clearly, the Department was working vigorously at all levels.

Meanwhile, I was working equally vigorously to try and somehow get around the impossible position I found myself in. On 15 May 1997 at 9:18am I braved a phone call to Carson McNeill. He was unwilling to deal with me. He was emphatic that he would not move from his earlier position and that I had no authority to act for the company. I put up some persuasive arguments and he countered all of these by asserting that he was relying on advice from the Official Assignee's office. Finally, he admitted that he had had that advice in a letter from Ken Derby from the Official Assignee's office. I told him that I had spoken to Ken Derby and he had given me a quite different story. Carson McNeill ended the call asserting that I was wrong. At 9:26am I spoke again to Ken Derby. I relayed to him the fine detail of my discussion with Carson McNeill. Derby rejected all McNeill's claims. He then said that he would speak to McNeill and come back to me.

Subsequently, I got a letter from Robin McDuff, solicitor for the Official Assignee. Mr McDuff confirmed that the Official Assignee was satisfied that my present employment with Tannadyce Investments Ltd did not contravene the provisions of the Insolvency Act as asserted by the Department. He went on to confirm that I did not require the consent of the Official Assignee to work for Tannadyce. Craig Richards, also from the Official Assignee's Office, wrote to Carson McNeill confirming Mr McDuff's position and suggesting that everything that he had seen showed that I was the only person the Department should be dealing with in respect of resolving the Tannadyce GST audit. None of this fazed the Department. They remained intransigent. Brian Palliser also vainly appealed to them.

Finally, the Department came back with a proposal. If we were to detail formally the name and address of the director of Tannadyce and to file this information in the Companies Office, something we had deliberately not done, then they would consider dealing with me again. It is my firm belief that the Department didn't believe that there was such a director. This was despite confirmation from my solicitor and the Official Assignee's office that this director existed and had authorised me to deal with the IRD on Tannadyce's audit. They were hoping to catch me out. I discussed this with

Bob Shaddick & family: Served with notices from IRD, 10,000 miles away in Toronto.

my friend in Toronto. He had concerns but I assured him that the chances of the New Zealand Department of Inland Revenue beating up on him in Toronto were nil. Bob Shaddick agreed for me to disclose his identity and home address. I have no doubt now that the staff at IRD Christchurch would have been phoning Revenue Canada that night to verify Shaddick's existence and probably to obtain information on him.

By this time there were still over thirty Official Information requests outstanding. These requests were vital for me to try and identify the Department's thinking and, in the absence of co-operation from them, the basis for their re-allocation of all Tannadyce's expenditure. I was continuing to deal with people at National Office responsible for Official Information requests. I was also receiving no co-operation from Sir Brian Elwood, the Chief Ombudsman.

On 21 May 1997, I spoke to Dave Elwood in National Office. I told him that there were two critical outstanding Official Information requests. These were (1) the basis of their application of section 60; and, (2) the issue of the missing documents supplied by us in May 1995. He subsequently advised that he had sent a memo to Carson McNeill requesting that this information be made immediately available to me. It never was.

In May Rodney received a response from Peter Sivertsen to his February letter. Sivertsen advised that the Department did not accept his legal status to receive information concerning Tannadyce. he concluded the letter by saying "I can assure you that the Department has at all times acted in a professional manner and the delay in responding to you is a reflection of the complexities which surround these matters".

Brian Palliser met with Carson McNeill in late May trying to break the deadlock over them not dealing with me. At that meeting, McNeill undertook to get back to Brian with further proposals. He never did. But eventually the Department would be forced to concede and go back to dealing with me.

On 26 May Bill Birch, in a letter, advised Rodney that new assessments had been issued. This was supposedly a complete new set to those issued on 6 September the previous year. On the same day, as Bill Birch gave this assurance, Chris Bond wrote to Brian McDiarmid, who by this time had taken over from Brian Hutton as National Manager, Operations Policy. In that internal memo Mr Bond advised Mr McDermott that "the assessments had not yet been issued". I was disgusted and felt myself to be a victim of a campaign of deliberate misinformation.

Despite the fact that we had met the IRD's requirements by providing the details of the director of Tannadyce, Bob Shaddick, the Department continued to exert pressure on the Office of the Official Assignee. In particular, the Department seemed very concerned with the letter of 26 May by Craig Richards of the Official Assignee's Office where he had written that not only was I free to deal with them but indeed I was the only person they should be dealing with. On 27 May Helen Sumner spent an hour on the phone with Craig Richards discussing that letter and promoting the Department's position. On 28 May Carson McNeill wrote to Craig Richards declaring, "the Department is concerned that the New Zealand Insolvency Service is allowing Mr Henderson, as a bankrupt, and the previous sole shareholder/director of a small private company, Tannadyce Investments Ltd, to act in a liaison role, as an employee, in respect of the company's tax affairs. Due to the nature and structure of this company, there is little distinction, if any, between a liaison role as an employee and management undertaken by Mr Henderson. In reality, there appears to be little change from his previous role as director in the company". On 29 May Helen Sumner and Peter Sivertsen personally delivered that letter to Craig Richards. They asked if they could meet with him, which he agreed to. They had him read the letter and then spent a considerable amount of time seemingly desperately trying to sell him on the merits of Mr McNeill's complaints. It was clear that all their efforts in bankrupting me had not produced the desired results.

What was particularly frustrating about the Department's continued pressure on the Office of Official Assignee to have me excluded was that publicly the Department was continuing to assert that they were trying to bring the matter to a close as quickly as possible.

Throughout this entire period I had continued to plead with the Department to withdraw their fraud complaint against me. The Department had given me many assurances that they would consider my pleas. Although I had plenty to occupy my mind the fact that I was under investigation for fraud was still very debilitating. Finally, the Department revealed that they were in possession of a letter from the police, dated October the previous year, where the police had formally notified the Department that they had discontinued the investigation as there was no evidence of any fraud. I was naturally delighted. But I wish I had been told about the case being abandoned seven months earlier. I had Brian Palliser follow up with the police to find out why I had never been notified. He received from the police a copy of the letter that had allegedly been sent to me around that time. It was addressed to me at 217 Fendalton Road; not only had I never lived at this address, but the address did not exist. The address that the police had executed their search warrant on was 2/127 Fendalton Road. Nevertheless, I was overwhelmingly pleased that this particular nasty side of the audit was now over.

The IRD is now dodging the probings of a determined MP. They are working hard to push me right out of the case. They are making further complaints to the Office of the Official Assignee. But the two-year fraud investigation is over – it had all been nonsense.

IRD purge Henderson's files

My personal audit was proceeding. This was despite Carson McNeill's personal undertaking to my lawyer in January that this audit would not proceed until the Tannadyce audit was complete. I was presented with a weighty tome from the Department setting out in great detail all their legal and technical arguments as to why I had improperly completed my tax returns and was due to pay the Department a whole lot more tax. I had given careful consideration to their propositions. I realised that to respond properly and fully would require a great deal of work and cost. I did not have the time, money or energy to turn to it. I appealed once again to Carson McNeill. He assured me that he had given instructions for the matter not to proceed. I told him it sure as hell was proceeding. He said that he would look into it and make sure that it stopped. It didn't stop.

The matter was proceeding under a new Disputes Resolution Process. Under that process my case was now proceeding to internal adjudication with the IRD Adjudications Unit in Wellington. The Department had prepared their case. It was now up to me to file a complete and full response. In the end I resolved that as I did not have the resources I would prepare a short political statement which I eventually sent off the day before the deadline to file. Just to show how out-of-control the Department is, some weeks later I received a ruling from the Adjudications Unit in Wellington in my favour. Despite the tens of thousands of dollars that the IRD in Christchurch had spent preparing a very detailed case, and despite me not having the resources and time to present a proper case, the Adjudications Section found in my favour. I no longer owed the Department any more money and it was accepted that I had correctly filed my personal income tax returns. That audit was over. I was vindicated. But the matter gets even crazier.

On 9 June Carson McNeill advised me that his undertaking still stood and that the personal audit was not proceeding. This was the same day that I received the adjudication from National Office rejecting the Department's assessment from the very audit that he was supposedly deferring. McNeill appeared to have no idea where matters were at.

It didn't matter. I now had the police out of the way. My personal audit was out of the way. The Department's complaints to the Official Assignee's Office had come to nought. I felt I was making some progress. The insanity of all this was that the Tannadyce GST audit at any point in the last three years could have been concluded in a few days. But at least now I knew from experience that that was not about to happen.

After discussion with Rodney Hide we agreed that I would write a letter to Bill Birch setting out my allegations in respect of the audit to date. On 16 June I wrote to Mr Birch stating my belief that his senior IRD staff had lied, cheated, broken the law, and broken innumerable agreements. I said that I had hard evidence in the way of letters and audio tapes (I had taken to taping phone conversations and meetings with the IRD) to support my allegations. Naively, I thought this would concern him and that I would receive a response. It would be many weeks before I heard back.

The next day Rodney wrote to Bill Birch still seeking an answer to a letter he had written a month earlier. The same day Rodney wrote again to Peter Sivertsen expressing his frustration that he still had not received answers to questions that he had asked on 21 February. He demanded an immediate response.

In mid June I received the new assessments that the Department had been promising for the last two months and which Birch had told Rodney had been issued some weeks earlier. These assessments set new standards in artistic licence. However, they were accompanied this time by a letter from Peter Sivertsen. The letter explained how virtually all of my earlier objections had been rejected, but new assessments had been created – arriving at virtually the same figure. The new assessments were so insane that they even referred to allocations of expenditure to an entity that did not even exist. I subsequently asked for clarification and explanation. To this day I have no idea what the letter really means or how the assessments were arrived at. I was completely lost. I discussed it with Brian Palliser. He couldn't make any sense of the letter or the assessments either.

I went back to Carson McNeill. He claimed that he understood it fully and that he was comfortable that it was all correct. But he would not explain it to me. Nor would he provide staff to go over it with me. He did agree to meet with me on 3 July and to have Helen Sumner present for her to describe for me how I was to proceed to file objections to this new set of assessments. That meeting was postponed at Carson McNeill's request.

On 9 July at 8:30am we finally met. The meeting started with Helen Sumner establishing her ground rules. Central to her position was that "the Department did not accept Mr Henderson's authority to make decisions on behalf of the company as to any action it wished to take in law". I endeavoured at this meeting to raise several serious issues and concerns that I had. McNeill seemed determined to close down all debate. I reminded him that I still had not received the company's records back. I also reminded them that I had a written agreement from Adriaan Geerlofs to return those documents by 24 January, some six months earlier. McNeill undertook to investigate that matter and reply to me within ten days. He never did. He also refused to give me an undertaking that no records would be destroyed. McNeill and Helen Sumner both made it clear that to date we had not put up any decent arguments to show why the reallocation of expenditure should not proceed. Unfortunately, all I had been able to put up in that regard was the exact reality of what had transpired. I was a bit puzzled as to what more I could provide. The meeting concluded with McNeill advising me that he was "not going to shift one iota from the fact that assessments have been issued and that Tannadyce must now formally object to those". I had already objected to the Department's assessments 10 months earlier, but now, because the Department had issued new assessments totalling an almost identical figure, I had to completely re-do our objections. McNeill went on to say that he had personally satisfied himself that the assessments were all correct and that they would stand in court. However, despite this certainty, he would not explain to me how the Department had arrived at their position.

During this period an even more bizarre process was being played out. Finally, after innumerable complaints to the Ombudsman and IRD's National Office, the IRD in Christchurch agreed to open up their files. They arranged for Dave Elwood to supervise. He explained to me that there were some 15

Eastlight ringbinders involved. He would fly to Christchurch, go through the ringbinders purging the files, identifying what information would be available to me in full, in part, or completely withheld. He said he would undertake this task over several days in a three-week period. He offered to keep me informed as to his progress. The arrangement was that once he had been though the files they would be made available to me at the IRD's offices. I could identify documents that I needed and the Department would copy them for me. Apart from the fact that this seemed like overkill, and that meaningful and significant documents would be withheld, I agreed to it.

True to his word, Dave Elwood rang me every day to report progress. It was slow. After three days of progress reports I learnt, much to my horror, that he was flying to Christchurch from Wellington every morning and returning to Wellington each evening. He estimated that this would need to continue for the next two weeks. I was horrified that this was the way my tax dollars were being spent. I told him so. That was the least of his worries. What worried him most was that work was piling up on his desk back in Wellington.

I made him a proposal. It was simple. I would forgo all my Official Information requests, and the right to go through my purged files, if the Department would meet in full two requests that they had never, ever responded to. One, provide me with all the information that supported their application of section 60 and the reallocation of expenditure. Two, provide me with all information relating to the receipt of the large number of records delivered to them in May 1995 which now appeared to be lost. Dave Elwood was genuinely enthused by this prospect of a short cut. But his Christchurch colleagues did not share his enthusiasm, despite me being fully entitled to receive this information. Christchurch did not agree and Elwood was committed to commuting daily from Wellington.

Over the next couple of months that process was to be completed but not without some fun and games. I was to make appointments to visit the Department's office in Cashel Street where a meeting room had been specifically set aside to hold my files and to provide me with space to inspect them. An IRD officer would sit reading a newspaper for the two or three hours that I was there to ensure that I did not abscond with anything. On more than one occasion the Department would not front for the appointments at the specified time and I would have to return home having made a wasted trip.

It was also clear to me that a large number of documents, including internal memos and letters to third parties, had been withheld. However, there were many interesting documents that I copied, some of which I have already referred to.

On one occasion when I turned up to inspect my records I asked Peter Sivertsen to identify his response to a very important Official Information request that I had made six months earlier. He had constantly asserted that he had made a lawful and proper response to this request. But rather than simply dig out the response and show it to me, he appeared to me to become extremely overwrought.

Back in Wellington Rodney Hide was keeping up pressure on the Department and the Minister's office. On 28 July he finally received a response to his letter to the Commissioner of 21 February, five months before. The letter from Carson McNeill was riddled with dissimulation. For example, the Department was telling Rodney that the audit had been completed in May 1996. In his sworn testimony to the court Adriaan Geerlofs said it had been completed in June 1996. However, given that we had only received assessments a few weeks earlier, it was clear that the audit was far from completed even in May 1997. McNeill advised Rodney that assessments were issued in July 1996. They were in fact issued in September 1996. He went on to claim that the entire audit process had "been undertaken in accordance with IRD policy" and that Tannadyce had "been accorded the same respect provided to all taxpayers".

I was continuing to try and catch the attention of someone at National Office to get them to review the whole affair independently. I had continued writing to Brian McDiarmid endeavouring to get him to address some of the more serious breaches of policy that had occurred. He had asked me to fax to him on 24 July copies of unanswered letters to his predecessor Brian Hutton. He undertook to respond to me by Tuesday 29 July. He didn't.

I still had not received a response to my 16 June letter to Bill Birch. That letter contained an Official Information request and the statutory time period for responding had lapsed. I wrote to Mr Birch on 3 August chasing him up. A few days later I received a response. He denied me the information that I had sought, advised me that he could not get involved with my case, that the administration of the Inland Revenue Department was the "complete responsibility of the Commissioner", and that he had referred a copy of my letter to the Commissioner's office "for comment and direct reply". It had taken the Minister six weeks just to pass the buck.

I had won against the IRD's personal audit – and the huge effort they had put in – with just a one-page political statement. I had got some information about my audit. But Bill Birch had washed his hands of my case.

"That's
a lot of
crap"

– George Gray, Group Manager Customer Services

I never received the Commissioner's promised reply. What I did receive a few days later was a letter from Brian McDiarmid. He told me that "due to the current situation of your case, and to expedite its finalisation, I am formally advising you that National Office personal (sic) will, from the date of this letter, cease to enter into any further discussion/correspondence with you over any matter relating to this case". My response was obvious. I immediately phoned him. Contrary to his policy laid out in his letter, he took my call.

In a rather candid conversation he made a number of rather remarkable observations. He told me that National Office never gets involved in individual cases. He confirmed that he had looked at all the materials in the Tannadyce audit and that he was aware of exactly where everything was at. He said that he accepted that Peter Sivertsen had made an error in applying section 60 and that he himself didn't understand fully the basis of the reallocation of expenditure that the Department was doggedly adhering to. I brought up the example of a building contractor Ashley Sparks that Tannadyce had used on the Station Village complex. He told me that the Department had gone to this builder and that this builder, along with several other contractors, had told the Department that, while they invoiced Tannadyce and were paid by Tannadyce, they believed that they were doing the work for some other third party. He said that this was the basis for the reallocation. He acknowledged that the Department had a lot of problems with the Tannadyce audit and that the investigation should have been completed a long time ago. He also advised that there were a lot of other taxpayers

Inland Revenue
Te Tari Taake

OPERATIONS POLICY

National Office

Plaza Chambers
107 Manners Street
PO Box 2198
Wellington
New Zealand

Telephone 04-472 1032
Facsimile 04-802 6100

7 August 1997

Mr David Henderson
C/- Tannadyce Investments Ltd
P O Box 1066
CHRISTCHURCH

Dear Sir,

I refer to your letter faxed to me dated 31 July 1997.

I must point out to you that Service Centre Managers are responsible for all aspects of work carried out in their areas, broadly and in relation to specific tasks.

I have been advised that the questions you continue to raise have been answered in the past by either National Office or Christchurch Service Centre personal. I am also informed that your case is now at the stage of NOPA's having been issued.

Due to the current situation of your case, and to expedite it's finalisation, I am formally advising you that National Office personal will, from the date of this letter, cease to enter into any further discussion/correspondence with you over any matter relating to this case. Should you continue to insist on writing to National Office your correspondence will be forwarded to the Christchurch Service Centre for action.

Yours sincerely

Brian McDiarmid
National Advisor Investigations policy
National Office

having problems like mine. All this from the National Adviser, Investigations Policy. He told me that Carson McNeill had taken full responsibility for the conduct of the audit.

Of course, McNeill was breaking agreements and not even beginning to accept responsibilities in my audit. I had been asking him for months who his boss was. All IRD written policy says that if you are not happy with a performance of a staff member, you should speak to their manager. McNeill consistently refused to tell me who his manager was. Brian McDiarmid candidly told me that it was George Gray, Group Manager, Customer Services. I phoned him. George Gray was rude and dismissive. His greatest concern was how I had got his work phone number. He refused to believe that his staff were performing as badly as I was telling him. He had no interest in my evidence supporting my allegations. He then demanded that I "stop using this number from now on. I do not want you calling this number". He went on to say, "Well, you know, I am actually not going to talk to you anymore. You should talk to Mr Carson McNeill. I have to go now". And he hung up.

Here is George Gray, Group Manager, Customer Services, thumbing his

nose at the soothing words of the Revenue Minister Bill Birch who declared in Parliament that when a taxpayer receives unfair treatment the taxpayer should "contact the officer's team leader or manager. The team leader or manager will endeavour to resolve the taxpayer's complaint".

Out of complete desperation I was to phone George Gray a few weeks later, pleading once more for his assistance. Once again, he didn't want to know me. This call, made shortly after Carson McNeill had gone overseas for an extended period, typifies the attitude of IRD's Head Office to my plight.

George Gray: Without checking my evidence, told me I was talking 'crap'.

GRAY: *Hello.*

HENDERSON: *George?*

GRAY: *Yes.*

HENDERSON: *Hi, this is Dave Henderson from Christchurch.*

GRAY: *Dave, how are you?*

HENDERSON: *I'm fine, and you?*

GRAY: *Busy week.*

HENDERSON: *Is it? It is for me too. Before Carson left to go overseas, he rang me and said that Helen Sumner was in charge of all my affairs and I was to communicate with Helen, and that Helen was answerable to Katrina Williams.*

GRAY: *Yes, Katrina is acting Service Centre Manager, that's right.*

HENDERSON: *Right. And so therefore, she's in charge of the whole of the Service Centre, correct?*

GRAY: *She is.*

HENDERSON: *Now subsequently ... um ... I've had a real difficulty getting hold of Helen, I've got some important matters that need to be dealt with ... um ... Katrina has spoken with me, but said that she has nothing to do with it, and is not interested in it.*

GRAY: *No ... well she won't be able to get up to speed on it, that's absolutely right.*

HENDERSON: *I understand that, and I ...*

GRAY: *... to the extent of making sure that you are able to get hold of the person who is carrying the ...*

HENDERSON: *Correct.*

GRAY: *... position at the moment.*

HENDERSON: *And I said that to her, I said "Katrina, I understand. I don't expect you to understand the case. I just want some action, that's all. Um ... then what's happened, is I finally spoke to Helen Sumner yesterday, I've been ... Katrina's been assuring me for two weeks that she'll get Helen to phone me, Helen's never phoned me ... I've phoned and caught her yesterday, I asked her to clarify whether she was in charge of the audit or not because in our first conversation, the day after Carson left, she told me she wasn't.*

GRAY: *Well I ... I don't think she's in charge of the audit, what she is, is a person with some legal training who is handling these affairs for Carson while he's away.*

HENDERSON: *So who is in charge of the audit then George?*

GRAY: *Well, you know, I mean I don't have those items and issues for you, ah, Dave, I'm afraid. I think, as we spoke last time, this is not something that is going to be handled on a line item by me.*

HENDERSON: *Yeah, no, I don't want it to. You've got to understand, I've had seventeen people now, the Department's asked me to deal with.*

GRAY: *Yeah, I don't want to go through all this Dave, we have quite different points of view on what's happened and that's where it's going to stop at the moment, so I don't have the time nor will be bothered going right through the process. Helen is the person that will interface with you as far as I'm aware. She's not looking ... ah ... or ... nor is she the auditor or the audit manager.*

HENDERSON: *Well that's different to what she told me. George, she told me that Adriaan Geerloffs is now handling the objection.*

GRAY: *Well, Adriaan Geerloffs is the Area Manager of Business Link, he is ... ah ... the most senior person there, in ... with ... with investigative experience. Look, the audit is at the stage of either going to the courts because we don't have agreement between the two parties, and ... and ... that's what we really should be looking at.*

HENDERSON: *No, that's not correct George. I got served with a Section 17 notice last week.*

GRAY: *Well, that's to provide for more information.*

HENDERSON: *Well therefore it can't be in a position where it's going to the courts, can it?*

GRAY: *Well ... you know, I don't know issues with the case, Dave.*

HENDERSON: *And I don't expect you to George.*

GRAY: *I'm not going to go through this nonsense again where I hang up on you, because I ... I'm not talking through that.*

HENDERSON: *Well George, please understand, I'm on my knees asking for some help here.*

GRAY: *No, I disagree with that entirely ... the ... the ... the process that you go through is one that you have elected to go through ...*

HENDERSON: *Not at all ...*

GRAY: *The people that you can talk to is Helen Sumner in connection with the legal parts of the case, Adriaan Geerloffs is the senior Audit Manager in Christchurch.*

HENDERSON: *But everyone passes the buck ... they say ...*

GRAY: That's a lot of crap! I ... I don't agree with the way that you have summed up this issue, and ... and we really need to have that decided firstly in the courts on the tax matter, ah, secondly the way in which the administration does its business can be investigated quite separately.

HENDERSON: By whom?

GRAY: Nothing to do with you, actually.

HENDERSON: Well, it's everything to do with me, actually George, I'm the aggrieved party here my friend.

GRAY: Well, I don't think you are.

HENDERSON: You don't think I'm aggrieved?

GRAY: Not at all.

HENDERSON: And you're not interested in it?

GRAY: Well ... I'm not interested in talking to you on the phone about it. No, not at all.

HENDERSON: Well, what are you interested in doing about it?

GRAY: Look, you know, what I do or don't do is actually nothing to do with you, if you want to talk ...

HENDERSON: Well, in respect of my affairs, I'm sure it is.

GRAY: Oh look, do we have to go through this again?

HENDERSON: No George, I have some serious ...

GRAY: Goodbye. (Hangs up)

I never bothered appealing to George Gray or anyone else at National Office ever again.

In the latest assessments issued by the Department one of the few things that I could understand was that the Department was still reallocating half-a-million dollars of Tannadyce expenditure to a company called Wertha Enterprises. This despite very clear objections and submissions to the Department a year earlier about how insane this was. This company had never traded and the reallocation of expenditure from Tannadyce to it related mostly to a period before the company was even incorporated. I arranged for Buddle Findlay in Wellington, who had incorporated the company, to confirm all these facts for me. I received a letter from them the next day which I forwarded to the Department, but to no avail.

I was busy through the early part of August completing formal objections that were due for filing by the 18 August. Once more Carson McNeill promised to explain to me Peter Sivertsen's confused letter that had now accompanied the assessments. He never did.

With no resources, and virtually no understanding of the basis of the assessments, I filed an eight-page letter of objection. I was feeling really embattled. However, the filing of the objection meant that the matter was still alive and that I hadn't lost. I also had to specify whether I wanted the matter heard through that Taxation Review Authority or the High Court. On legal advice from Brian Palliser the company chose to have the matter heard in the High Court. One of the determining factors for this was that the company could bring an action against the Department and its staff simultaneously with our objection being heard. This would be a costly process but I would cross that bridge when I came to it.

Brian McDiarmid's advice on the phone on 8 August was troubling me. It was the first time that I had received any meaningful advice as to the basis of the Department's reallocation. The information that the Department had met with contractors involved with the Station Village project and that these contractors believed that they were doing the work for a third party really bothered me. In early September I flew to Wellington and met with the principal building contractor, Ashley Sparks. I carefully explained what the Department was saying. He rejected everything that Brian McDiarmid had said. He did confirm that Gibb Lee had visited him earlier that year and had questioned him over his dealings with Tannadyce. He made it very clear to Gibb Lee that he was contracted by Tannadyce, that he invoiced Tannadyce, and that he received all his payments from Tannadyce. He immediately had his secretary prepare a letter confirming that position.

I also meet with Gary Lavan. He had been the manager at the BNZ who handled our accounts and with whom we had negotiated the Station Village transactions. He had been pivotal in all of Tannadyce's dealings over the Station Village. The IRD had never approached him. He set out in a four-page letter the exact nature of the relationship between BNZ and Tannadyce. In particular, he made it very clear that the BNZ had no interest in the businesses created by Tannadyce in that shopping complex. These clarifications were of no interest to the Department.

Finally, McDiarmid at National Office accepted that IRD's application of section 60 was in error – but refused to help. They had no interest in my complaints against the staff that they were responsible for. This was contrary to policy and the soothing words of the IRD's complaint process.

Massive fines, demands for cash

With National Office refusing to consider my complaints or involve themselves in resolving the audit I was faced with the fact that I must deal with Carson McNeill. It seemed that the only way forward would involve expensive and significant litigation. I was very keen to avoid that.

Carson McNeill had assured me that he was now personally responsible for my audit, and that he had personally satisfied himself that all the assessments were correct. On 9 September, in a personal, very frank, three-page letter, I appealed to Carson McNeill's decency. I sought from him guidelines as to how we might move forward without the expense of litigation. I simply and very frankly set out my intentions: "Our motives then are quite simple and straightforward: we want to get to the end of the investigation and establish reality and the correct and lawful tax position. We want to show that the propositions being promoted by the Department to increase liabilities are absurd and unfounded. We want to understand why the Department have treated us this way. We want to ensure that neither ourselves nor any other business person will ever be treated this way again".

I pleaded with him to deal with the issue of our missing records and to provide us with guidelines for moving the audit forward. I concluded this letter with the following appeal: "I would also like to restate my proposals to you on the phone last week; given our respective aspirations why can't we meet, agree on where our aspirations are common, set out an entire agenda involving common aims and individual aims, and tie each party to a timetable, agreed actions and a code of conduct to wrap all this up. Surely this would suit your ends? Please let me have your thoughts on this. We would be willing to compromise in an effort to put together such a programme. If there is anything else in any regard that you would like us to consider or do then please set this out for us to look at. Please also feel free to phone the writer at any time to discuss this letter or any of the issues that flow from it".

Carson McNeill never phoned me to discuss my letter. In fact, he has never responded to it in any way. I didn't know what else I could say or do to extend goodwill and genuinely seek a way forward. I had been frank and open and had really shown my vulnerability. I had copied the letter to Brian McDiarmid at the Commissioner's office. If there was any goodness in the Department now was the time for it to be displayed. What was to follow over the next three weeks was to stun me.

On 15 September, Mr Bond served formal section 17 notices on myself, Bob Shaddick in Toronto, Michael Wilson in Sydney, and two people in Christchurch. These notices demanded a number of documents and information from Tannadyce but in particular they demanded transcripts of telephone calls between myself and IRD staff. I had made the Department aware that I was taping my phone calls to hold them to account. These notices threatened myself and the others with fines up to $25,000 for not complying within 14 days. This was a nasty twist. It seems that the Department was getting more and more vicious. I discussed this new development with Brian Palliser. He told me that the matter was now extremely serious and it was time to seek specialist help. I asked Brian to provide a formal opinion of his position.

In Brian's letter he said that it was a matter of utmost urgency that I get help from someone with marked expertise in tax law. He confirmed that it was his opinion that the section 17 notices were a clear abuse of procedures and that he could only conclude that the Department held a hidden agenda or that there was a massive degree of incompetence.

I had had previous dealings with the law firm Russell McVeagh in Auckland. I had always been impressed with Geoff Clews (now a specialist tax barrister) from that firm. With the agreement of friends and family who were helping me financially, I made contact with him and briefed him as best I could on the phone. It was his view that the section 17 notices were illegal and should be contested. What had endeared Geoff to me were several reports of him displaying an aggressive approach to bureaucratic dogmatism and entrenched IRD attitudes. Regardless of the reports, I also found

Inland Revenue
Te Tari Taake

15 September 1997

IR 220/10

Christchurch Service Centre

Charter House
165 Cashel Street
Private Bag
Christchurch
New Zealand

Facsimile 03-366 6654
Telephone 03-363 1000

Mr David I Henderson
P O Box 1066
CHRISTCHURCH

Dear Sir

TANNADYCE INVESTMENTS LTD - IRD NUMBER: 56-427-031
OUR REFERENCE: CH/GST/CJB

Take notice that I, Christopher John Bond, Technical Adviser, Technical and Legal Support, Christchurch, being duly authorised by the Commissioner of Inland Revenue, pursuant to the provisions of Section 7 of the Tax Administration Act 1994, DO HEREBY REQUIRE you to furnish in writing or produce for inspection, pursuant to the provisions of Section 17 of the Tax Administration Act 1994 (a copy of which is enclosed), within 14 days after and inclusive of the date of this notice, the following information, **not already supplied**, which I consider necessary or relevant for the purposes relating to the administration or enforcement of the Goods and Services Tax Act 1985, and which may be in your possession or under your control, namely:

All originals or, if originals not held, copies of -

1   books,
2   records,
3   minutes,
4   memoranda,
5   transcripts and schedules of telephone calls between company representatives and Inland Revenue staff,
6   correspondence,
7   debentures,
8   mortgages,
9   statements of claim,
10 directions or instructions to act,
11 Deeds of Trust, secret trust, and/or Arrangement,
12 Agreements for sale and purchase of land, goods, or businesses, including stock and/ or chattels,
13 copies of missing invoices identified on the adjustment schedules.
14 or any other items not already disclosed, which may be produced as evidence.

I point out that failure to produce the information and/or books and/or documents within the 14 days stated above could render you liable for prosecution under Section 143A of the Tax Administration Act 1994, and on conviction to a fine not exceeding $25,000 for a first conviction.

If no records are held, I require a written response within the time specified above.

Dated at Christchurch this 15th day of September, 1997.

Yours faithfully

C J Bond
Technical Advisor
Technical and Legal Support Group

147

a different side to Geoff. He turned out to be one of the most careful and measured advisors I have ever dealt with. Geoff Clews is a very sharp and very professional top-class barrister. It was good having him on board.

On 16 September Brian Palliser received a notice from Chris Bond. This notice confirmed that we had lodged our objection, that we had requested that our case be heard in the High Court and that we had until 17 November to file what is called a "points of objection" notice and that if we did not file that notice by that date we would forfeit our right to have our objection heard. Of greatest concern in this letter was a demand that within ten days we pay to the Commissioner the sum of $138,551.07. The Department was demanding that we pay this money before we could proceed with our objection to the million-dollar debt they had manufactured. Mr Bond charitably suggested "if the company is unable to make payment, the Commissioner can consider taking security over assets that the company may own".

A few days after Geoff Clews weighed in, the Department upped the stakes even more dramatically. On 30 September the IRD issued a statutory demand against Tannadyce for $175,760.72. To this day I have little idea how they justified this figure. Despite the Department's several observations that the company had made losses, they were also now asserting an income tax debt. I figured that the only way to deal with this was to show, through our records, that we had indeed made losses.

Geoff Clews: Specialist Tax Barrister – without peer.

I had a problem here: the Department held all our records. They refused to hand them back. Out of desperation, and on the advice of a solicitor, I went to the police to lodge a complaint of conversion in relation to these records.

After much debate, the duty officer at the Christchurch central police station called down a sergeant from upstairs. He had little sympathy and almost fell about laughing when I told him the nature of my complaint. He enthusiastically explained that laying

NOTICE OF STATUTORY DEMAND

TO: **TANNADYCE INVESTMENTS LIMITED,** a duly incorporated company having its registered office at Suite 58, 224 Cashel Street, CHRISTCHURCH, 8001.

TAKE NOTICE that the COMMISSIONER OF INLAND REVENUE at Wellington HEREBY DEMANDS payment from you in the sum of $175,760.72 being:

$133,101.67	Goods and services tax assessments and penalties thereon under the Goods and Services Tax Act 1985
$24,651.64	PAYE tax deductions assessments and penalties thereon under the Income Tax Act 1976 and the Tax Administration Act 1994
$1,014.90	FBT tax deductions assessments and penalties thereon under the Income Tax Act 1976 and the the Tax Administration Act 1994.
$15,570.84	Income tax assessments and penalties thereon under the Income Tax Act 1976 and the Tax Administration Act 1994
$1,421.67	Accident Compensation premiums and penalties thereon under the Accident Rehabilitation and Compensation Insurance Act 1992
<u>$175,760.72</u>	**TOTAL**

FURTHER TAKE NOTICE that if within fifteen working days after the date of service upon you of this notice you neglect to:

*   pay the said sum; or
*   enter into a compromise under Part XIV of the Companies Act 1993; or
*   otherwise compound with the Commissioner; or
*   give a charge over your property to secure payment of the debt to the reasonable satisfaction of the COMMISSIONER OF INLAND REVENUE

then the Commissioner may petition the High Court of New Zealand for an order that **TANNADYCE INVESTMENTS LIMITED** be put into liquidation.

The address at which payment should be made or to which enquiries should be addressed is the office of the Inland Revenue Department at 165 Cashel Street, P O Box 2871, Christchurch, Attention: Chris Bond.

DATED at Christchurch this 30th day of September. 1997.

Team Leader
BusinessLink

a complaint would be a waste of time, the IRD had far more powers than the police.

The significance of the statutory demand was that Tannadyce, under the Companies Act, had 15 days to pay this sum failing which the Department could then petition the High Court for an order that Tannadyce be put into liquidation. The effect of that would be that the GST audit would be ended in the Department's favour. Given the way tax law is structured, where in effect a taxpayer is guilty until proven innocent, the court is obliged to accept any assessment the Department makes in a winding-up action like this no matter how ridiculous or fantastic that claim might be. I met with Geoff Clews in Auckland to try and put together a strategy to counter these extremely aggressive actions from the IRD.

In the space of two weeks the Department had issued section 17 notices, later acknowledged to be improper, threatening fines up to $125,000, had demanded we pay $138,551.02 before our objection could be heard and issued a statutory notice demanding $175,760.72. It wasn't a good month.

Meanwhile, Rodney Hide was gaining the Minister's attention. He was confident he could get an inquiry. I brought Rodney up to speed with the latest actions by the Department. He understood the urgency of the situation and the need to bring further pressure on Bill Birch immediately.

We were racing against time. We had been served with three separate documents all running on a short fuse. I again packed up all my files in a large kit bag and headed up to meet with Geoff Clews. We were searching for a novel way to try and sting the Department back as hard as they were hitting us. It was not going to be easy. Geoff discussed a range of options, the most attractive of which was to bring actions for damages personally against several of the key IRD personnel. It was going to be a massive task involving putting together several detailed separate statements of claim. I was fully aware of the consequences of allowing the Department to succeed with any one of the actions they had underway.

Then on 10 October 1997 we achieved the breakthrough we were looking for. Bill Birch agreed to meet Rodney the following Thursday at 4pm. On the Tuesday before that meeting Rodney prepared a detailed letter setting out a large number of our concerns. It didn't pull any punches. Rodney had the Minister's attention and he wanted to keep it. The meeting took place in Bill Birch's office with the Commissioner Graham Holland and several of the Minister's IRD staff present.

It was all over in about 40 minutes. I can remember clearly receiving Rodney's enthusiastic call as soon as he had got back to his office. He had pulled it off. The Commissioner had agreed, seemingly under pressure from the Minister, to hold an internal review of the conduct of the audit. This was to start immediately and was to be wrapped up within four weeks. The Commissioner was to appoint a very senior officer from National Office who had had no prior contact with the audit to conduct the review.

Rodney noted a number of interesting points that had arisen at the meeting. The Commissioner had advised the Minister that all outstanding Official Information requests had been met and further that Tannadyce and myself had never attempted to bring the matter to the attention of the Commissioner's office. Both these assertions were wrong. This was of little consequence now that we had the prospect of an internal inquiry. But the Commissioner's comments did prove that the Minister wasn't getting objective advice.

Peter Barrand: I found his report to the Minister was inaccurate and misleading.

I was later to discover that in advance of that meeting, Peter Barrand, IRD's General Manager, Operations, had prepared a report for the Minister. I found this report inaccurate and misleading. Amongst other things, Mr Barrand referred to my allegations of improper behaviour by his staff. He advised the Minister that the Department was endeavouring to investigate these and that it had written to me on 15 September seeking full details, and that no reply had been received by me. No such letter was ever sent to me by the Department.

The day after the meeting with Rodney and the Minister I received a letter from Chris Bond reminding me that I had not complied with the terms of his section 17 notice and that I was now liable for prosecution and a potential fine of $25,000. That day I also received a Notice of Statutory Demand for $164,445-57 for another company that the Department knew I was associated with. This company, like Tannadyce, had not traded for a number of years. The Department was very aware of this. It didn't matter. They were out now to bust me quick.

The IRD were using the law to force me to hand over tape transcripts of their conversations with me and were making huge and fanciful financial claims against me. They were moving against me hard. But we had a review under way at last.

IRD confirm million dollar debt as fanciful

At about 5pm on Friday 17 October I received a call from the Commissioner. He told me that he was appointing a Mr Max Carr, National Manager Corporates, to undertake the review. He confirmed with me the terms of reference of the inquiry that had been already relayed to me by Rodney. Not only was there to be a review of the Tannadyce audits but also those of myself and associated companies.

In answer to a written question, the Minister admitted to Rodney that the Department to this point had spent 2,200 hours, excluding management time, auditing Tannadyce. Rodney's estimate of a million-dollar audit was close to the mark. And it still wasn't over. We all had a long way to go yet.

On 20 October Max Carr commenced his review. He contacted Geoff Clews in Auckland, with whom he had dealt many times previously. He asked that all communication with me be channelled through Geoff Clews. This was obviously going to be an extremely expensive process. Geoff Clews is not cheap. But I was not about to do anything that would obstruct the review. I also asked Geoff Clews as a matter of urgency to ask the Department to withdraw the statutory demands and section 17 notices. Mr Carr agreed on the condition that we paid an amount of approximately $25,000 to the Department. I refused. I had had a personal undertaking from Carson McNeill that no further action on these matters would proceed until the Tannadyce GST audit was complete. This undertaking had been given in the presence of Brian Palliser at a meeting in January 1997. Mr McNeill was now denying that he had ever given such an undertaking.

Unfortunately for Carson McNeill, he had repeated his undertaking to me in a taped phone conversation in June. I was intransigent that we would not pay the Department any money. It was morally wrong. I believed the Department owed us. Besides, we had no cash.

Max Carr would not withdraw the notices. Geoff Clews was forced to make further representations to the Department. I found all this quite stunning. There was absolutely no prejudice to the Department in withdrawing the notices. It would have been a wonderful demonstration of goodwill and a great way to get the review under way. But here they were incurring us extra cost as we argued back and forth with our lawyers.

On Thursday 30 October Mr Carr set up a meeting with Brian Palliser in Christchurch. Brian Palliser made his views of the whole affair very clear. He told him of the broken agreements, the fact that his own letters had gone unanswered and the outrageous treatment that I had received. He explained that as a senior solicitor with thirty-plus years experience he had never witnessed an abuse of power by a government department of this magnitude. He managed to convince Max Carr that I did not have horns sticking out the top of my head. Max agreed he would meet with me. Brian rang me and I stopped what I was doing and drove immediately to Brian's office. I found Max Carr to be a pleasant and professional person. He was clearly labouring under a heavy load of preconceived notions about me. As the meeting went on I could see that he was fast changing his opinion. He offered to deal direct with me rather than the cumbersome and expensive process of working through Geoff Clews in Auckland. Before we concluded the meeting he made one important request of me – that I would not tape his phone calls. He had clearly been stirred up by Christchurch staff. I found this request to be a little unusual because I couldn't imagine what he would say to me that would ever embarrass him. I said that I would agree to his request on one condition: that at all times he would be open and straight with me. I concluded the meeting by trying to finalise the outstanding statutory demands and section 17 notices. He said he would consider it and get back to me.

Max had arranged to meet with Rodney on Monday 3 November. I worked with Rodney over the weekend providing him with information and explaining key areas of difficulty to him so that he was fully prepared for the meeting. Max Carr had wanted from Rodney the evidence of the many serious allegations Rodney had made in his letter to Bill Birch. I suspected

Max Carr: Wasn't game to criticise his peers.

that the Commissioner did not accept Rodney's allegations and believed that he could embarrass him. However, Rodney doesn't make allegations he can't back up. By the time Monday arrived he had all the evidence he needed prepared and laid out in a letter to Carr.

The meeting went extremely smoothly with Rodney reporting that Max Carr appeared already to have a handle on the key technical issues involved in the audit. In particular, and of great interest to me, he had told Rodney that he believed that the Department was wrong in its application of section 60. After all I had been through, this was like being told I had just won lotto.

Max Carr then set up a meeting with myself and Geoff Clews at the offices of Russell McVeagh in Auckland. That meeting took place on 10 November at 9am. Also there was Angela Satterthwaite, the Commissioner's personal legal counsel. The meeting was very productive. It was clear that Max Carr had an open mind and was not approaching the issue with any bias. In particular, it was clear that we were going to be able to resolve quickly the issue of section 60 and the reallocation of expenditure. Max Carr was perplexed as to exactly where the Department stood on the matter and when I set out for him the position that we had agreed upon with the Department in April 1995 he freely accepted that logic and rationale. The other issues by comparison were minor and suddenly they all seemed capable of quick and final resolution. We discussed the issue of the outstanding section 17 and statutory demand notices. Max Carr said that he had already instructed Christchurch that they were to be withdrawn and that the very next day letters would be sent to the recipients of all the section 17 notices in Toronto, Sydney and Christchurch formally withdrawing them. In respect of the statutory demands he gave an undertaking that they would stand but that no further action would be taken in respect of them without the Department providing us seven days notice of their intention.

Geoff Clews had quickly grasped all the technical and legal issues and was able to put up solid argument to support our position. It was costing me but it was worth it. I had to pass the hat once again around my friends and my family. The meeting ended with all parties having a clear course of action to move forward. Over the next few days Geoff Clews set out in writing detailed arguments to support the propositions we had raised at the meeting.

The next day we didn't get the letters withdrawing the section 17 notices as Max Carr had promised. Instead, yet another section 17 was served on a company in Christchurch in respect of its dealings with Tannadyce. That notice was issued by Chris Bond. Geoff Clews raised this with Max Carr who was extremely embarrassed and personally apologised to me. Eventually this new notice was withdrawn along with the others. Max was clearly having trouble with the Christchurch office.

Tannadyce was still under a tight timetable to file a "Points of Objection" notice following on from the objection we had filed against the million-dollar assessment on 17 August. Max Carr had not been prepared to do anything about this and it even appeared that there was no basis for the Department to negotiate an extension of time. This notice was a very important document. It was to spell out all the arguments that we relied on to support our objection to the Department's absurd assessments. Here we were being told that it looked like we had been right all along but that we still had to file detailed notices arguing why the Department was wrong in respect of propositions, details of which they had failed to provide us. I would also have to involve Geoff Clews. I would have to work extensively over the next twelve days to get this notice prepared and filed.

Ms Angela Satterthwaite: Graham Holland's personal legal counsel.

On Monday November 17 I completed our Points of Objection notice. This had to be couriered to Wellington to arrive that day. The front pages of it were required by law to be a standard document that the Department held with blank spaces to be completed by the taxpayer and to be attached to the taxpayer's presentation. In the morning I visited the Christchurch IRD office to get the standard form. After an hour of searching the Department had to admit they held none of the necessary forms. After another hour's negotiating the Department finally agreed to accept our Points of Objection notice without the standard form attached.

On Friday 14 November, Christchurch Show Day, I met with Max Carr in my flat. Max had divided his review of the Tannadyce GST audit into two sections: the technical issues and the relationship issues. Our meeting focused mainly on the relationship issues. Max had no idea of what had gone on. To do the review properly I would have had to set out for him the entire contents of this book so far. Max Carr was offering me this day and perhaps one other day to set out for him all that had happened. It was really an impossible task. I had to focus on what I thought were the key allegations. I had to distil those down to their essence and present Max Carr with my evidence.

I gave it my best shot during the day and ended up covering a huge amount of ground. It was clear to me that Max was battling to take it all in. It was also clear that he was shocked by my allegations and the significant amount of evidence I had to support them. Over that weekend I prepared a letter to send to Max highlighting some of the key allegations and reminding him what I had set out for him. A few days later I sent him another 14-page letter highlighting further allegations.

I met with Max again on Thursday morning 27 November. Once more we traversed my allegations and I was able to advance more evidence. On Tuesday 9 December Max Carr, Geoff Clews and myself once more met in Auckland. This was nearly four weeks past the date the Commissioner had set Max Carr to complete his review. At the meeting Max Carr presented the first of two reports he was to prepare setting out his findings. He also provided me with a letter from the Commissioner. That letter was an apology from the Commissioner for the time taken to reach this stage of the audit. It also confirmed my full and complete co-operation with Mr Carr, thanked me for that, and provided me with a number of undertakings to deal urgently with outstanding issues like the missing records. I did not read the report at the meeting, but focused on dealing with all the little issues. It appeared to me that Max Carr was recommending that the Department would concede to our point of view on the greater number of issues.

On the way home in the plane that night I took time to read Max Carr's fifty-page report. It had one significant finding. It was to do with the Department's application of section 60 and the reallocation of expenditure that had produced the million dollar debt. Max said "I have found this to be the most confusing part of the investigation to date and have not sighted a clear indication from the Department as to which costs do and which costs do not come within the scope of section 60 as they would seek to apply it". He went on "it is difficult to ascertain from the reading of the correspondence and files the periods in time and the basis of our views as to the various applications of section 60. However, I am quite clear that we now contend that section 60 only applies to the BNZ/Tannadyce relationship in so far as it relates to rental activity costs. We now accept without reservation that it does not apply to the structural cost issue or to any of the fit-out costs of the bakery, brewery and restaurant". He stated that "I think that this particular issue has caused the greatest frustration and anxiety on the part of the taxpayer and having read practically all the correspondence, I have been at a loss to understand exactly what our position was in respect of the application of section 60 at any one point of time". He concluded by stating that "whatever our views have been in the past they are now history, but they cannot be dismissed simply as that as they have caused a lot of frustration and anxiety for over twelve months".

Of course, ultimately they were to be dismissed as simply as that.

But at that point I cannot express to you the overwhelming sense of relief I experienced as I flew home to Christchurch that night. The audit was approaching its fourth anniversary. I had been working on it full time for two years. I was bankrupt and my life was in tatters. I had been plead-ing for three years for the Department to explain to me their reason for reallocating enormous amounts of expenditure which ultimately resulted in the Department negating Tannadyce's refund and assessing it for a million dollars. And here was the Department finally accepting that I was right all along.

I couldn't help but reflect on how out of control the Department was and how woefully lacking it was in checks and balances. Any of these people: Carson McNeill, Peter Sivertsen, Adriaan Geerlofs, Chris Bond or Gibb Lee could have bought the audit to a conclusion years earlier. Even the people at National Office that I had made contact with: Brian Hutton, Brian McDiarmid, Dave Elwood, Paul Matson, George Gray had been presented with enough hard evidence to know that something was wrong. At any time any one of them could have spoken up and taken some simple actions to have brought the matter to a close and to have saved me months of hardship and cost. I also couldn't help but reflect on the thousands of small businesspeople who through the years must have suffered similar treatment but who didn't have my perseverance and energy or access to a Rodney Hide who had been so pivotal in bringing about this review. I knew that they would have given up and been forced to walk away from their businesses, their dreams, their aspirations, and in some cases, as I was tragically to learn, even their lives.

I vowed at that moment not just to win for myself and collect my refund but not to rest until this rot and contempt in the Department was rooted out and some semblance of civility, professionalism and respect was introduced into our most powerful and feared department of state. I wanted to turn my experience into a win not just for myself but for small businesspeople everywhere. I couldn't bear the thought of anyone else having to endure what I had had to go through.

The next morning I phoned both Rodney Hide and Brian Palliser to share with them the findings of Max Carr's report. Rodney was ecstatic. He had come to the same conclusion as I had. "Now we start the fight to put it right," he declared.

But my own personal fight was still far from over.

The audit had now been going for three years. The Commissioner had apologised for the delays. The IRD had accepted that the million dollar debt was incorrect. I still had to get my refund.

"I'm embarrassed to be an IRD employee"

– Max Carr, National Manager Corporates

Before Max Carr had commenced his investigation I had taken time to inquire from someone who knew him as to whether he was up to the job of conducting a robust internal review of his peers. My contact told me that he believed Max Carr was basically an honest and fair person but might be reluctant to criticize colleagues when under pressure within his Department. That observation appeared to be accurate as I read his report. He had confronted the million-dollar debt and properly dealt with it. But the rest of his report did not even closely square with the observations he had candidly made with me in our meetings. His review was particularly critical of me in one key respect: that I had written too many letters and had made too many phone calls to the Department. The Department were ultimately to come to level this allegation repeatedly against me and to use it to try and justify the length of time taken to complete the audit. In the first two years of the audit I wrote 37 letters to the Department. Virtually all of these were in response to the Department's demands. Max Carr would later privately acknowledge that this was not an excessive amount of contact with the Department. I readily accept that from early 1996 on I dramatically increased the number of letters and faxes sent to the Department. But I believe that I did that with great justification given the circumstances.

Max Carr's report into the IRD behaviour was really a whitewash. He didn't report accurately on what his Department had done to me. He didn't report admissions he had made to me that I thought were significant. But over the next few days both Geoff Clews and I worked to provide Max Carr with the information we had undertaken to provide. Max Carr produced an additional addendum to his report making several technical changes all in our favour. He had also undertaken to collect from Christchurch a considerable amount of information and provide that to me. This did not come through in the next few days as he had promised. I was to later find out that he was again having difficulties with the Christchurch office when it came to providing simple answers and explanations.

Max Carr and I were to meet again on 15 December to discuss the relationship issues further and for me to present more evidence. Once again we met at my flat and I started working my way through a long list of my allegations. Max Carr was becoming more and more outraged as I provided him with the detail of what had gone on. At one stage expressing great anger he told me "I'm embarrassed to be an IRD employee". His most stunning and candid observation was that if he had been doing the audit he could have got through it in four weeks.

It was clear that we had little prospect of getting though my entire agenda. In fact, as it transpired, we covered less than half the items that I wanted to bring to his attention. He assured me that what I had told him was of considerable significance. He had agreed to file a further report on his investigation into these further relationship allegations. He told me that in this further report he was going to be "a lot harder on the staff in Christchurch". As a consequence of this assurance – and because he was really battling to take everything in – I agreed not to present the rest of my allegations. I was disappointed that he didn't want to hear and investigate the whole story. His second report would ultimately prove to be as timid as his first and, once more, his unwillingness to criticise his colleagues would hold sway. We concluded the meeting with him acknowledging that he still had a considerable amount of information to provide to me.

On Friday 19 December Max couriered to me the information that he had promised urgent delivery of since 9 December. This information related to a number of claims, largely for small amounts that Gibb Lee and Chris Bond were declaring that we had claimed twice for. It related to GST periods in 1991 and 1992 where accountants acting for Tannadyce had inadvertently claimed twice for a small number of expense items in successive GST returns. The amounts weren't great but the issue for some reason perplexed me. I spent the weekend going through old correspondence files. What I discovered stunned me. When these returns were filed, back in 1991 and 1992, each return had been audited by the Wellington IRD office. In completing those audits the IRD investigator had identified every single one of these double claims. He had made adjustments, brought it to the attention of our accountants, and reduced our refunds accordingly. During the entire four years of this audit neither Messrs Bond, Lee, Sivertsen or any one of the IRD officers involved, had ever bothered to check with the IRD auditor in Wellington or to inspect his records or files.

First thing on Monday morning I bought all this to the attention of Max Carr. I faxed him through the documents I held. He was in his own words "extremely angry". Christmas and the holiday period were fast approaching. On Tuesday 23 December I appealed to his decency. I pleaded with him to bring the audit to a close. I told him I would be willing to compromise on some yet unresolved issues even if it would cost us. He asked me to leave it with him and that he would call me back in an hour. At 10:57am he phoned and advised that he had the Commissioner's permission to do a deal and reach a global settlement. He reiterated how embarrassed he had been about the material I had shown him the day before. We discussed the principles of how a settlement might work. In particular, I conceded on a transaction of $137,000 that I had believed did not involve GST. I was trying to extend some goodwill to him and I was willing to make a considerable compromise just to bring it all to an end.

That afternoon, through a number of phone calls, we reached conclusion on all the remaining issues. By the evening of 23 December 1997 Max Carr and I had both agreed on and signed a principles of settlement agreement. The intention was that this agreement settled all the technical issues between myself and the Department right up until that time. It was a settlement that could have been reached just as quickly any time in the preceding four years. Max Carr insisted that Tannadyce could not claim back any of the GST on expenses that it had occurred in fighting the IRD. There were by now tens of thousands of dollars in legal bills, travel and other professional services. He explained that the reason for this was that fighting the IRD was not part of our "taxable activity". This ruling by the Department has probably cost the company over $20,000.

I made it very clear to Max Carr, and in an accompanying letter to the Department, that I reserved all of Tannadyce's rights in respect of the relationship issues of this audit. I kept in mind the advice that I had had that I could sue the Department and officers personally. Max Carr was leaving on holiday until 7 January. He would provide Christchurch with a copy of this agreement and would ask them to commence work preparing schedules to ascertain the exact refund position. He agreed to come to Christchurch on 8 January 1998 to help finalise the settlement.

Max Carr was still to complete and file his final report of his review of the Tannadyce GST audit. I worked over the Christmas and New Year period preparing evidence and submissions to support my allegations to him. On 8 January we met in the lobby of the Park Royal in Christchurch. He presented me with a schedule that was a draft assessment that had restored all our GST returns from 1993 and 1994 virtually to their original figure. It provided for the adjustments that we had agreed upon and the compromises that we had made. It indicated a refund due to Tannadyce of some $60,000. This was not far from what Kath Cook had originally identified four years earlier. There was a small amount of PAYE still owing by Tannadyce that I had refused to pay a number of years earlier when the Department was withholding our refunds. That had to be calculated and the Department was suggesting that there was Fringe Benefit Tax also owing on a car the company owned. Max Carr acknowledged that the company had appeared to have made income tax losses over the entire period and so the matter of income tax was not to be an issue. He advised me that he was now going to pass the matter back over to Christchurch to prepare final formal assessments and conclude the matter with me. I pleaded with him not to do this. But he assured me that Christchurch had a responsibility to deal with the matter properly and responsibly.

There was one final issue that Max Carr and I had agreed to deal with. It related to some outstanding returns that the Department was alleging for companies associated with myself and income tax returns for Tannadyce. We agreed to meet in February to resolve that issue.

As we wrapped up our meeting Max Carr gingerly inquired as to what I was going to do now. I told him I had a strong determination to see the Department cleaned up so that my experience would never be visited on any other taxpayer. I also wanted compensation for what I had been through. Max Carr thought about this for a moment, and then he leaned forward in his chair, and said to me, "Do you know what your problem is Dave? You need to learn forgiveness and grace".

Max Carr had set out the basis of our tax assessment – but I had to go back to Christchurch for the refund still owing.

IRD eventually pay up – four years too late

The next day, Friday 9 January, I was to work with Carson McNeill to complete the assessments and to pick up our refund cheque. Unfortunately it didn't prove that easy. Just after 11am that day McNeill phoned me to advise that he had completed the calculations and that we now owed the Department approximately $9,000. I was floored by their effrontery. Once more they were working assiduously to erase our refund. At my insistence he explained to me the calculations that had occurred. What he had done was to take the small amount of PAYE owing, add penalties and interest, which blew it up to $70,000. He then did a straight line deduction from the GST refund that was now over four years old that Max Carr had identified to arrive at a debit position of just over $9,000.

I rang Max Carr. He instantly could see how wrong this was. He asked me to leave it with him. I agreed to meet with Carson McNeill that afternoon at which time he would have redone the calculations removing all the PAYE penalties. This was entirely equitable because if we had had our GST refunds all those years before we would have had the money to pay the PAYE at the time it was due.

When I met with Carson McNeill that afternoon he had not done a thing. It appeared that his staff had gone home early and the recalculations had not occurred. McNeill was clearly under pressure from Head Office to get the matter concluded but despite that he still did not have the authority over his staff to demand that this matter be dealt with. I berated him for his failure and threatened to ring Max Carr once more. He asked me not to and as a concession undertook to come to work the next day, Saturday, and to complete the calculation himself. He was clearly unhappy with this arrangement and even had the gall to tell me that I would be ruining his weekend. His weekend! He and his colleagues had just ruined four years of my life.

Our conversation drifted onto other matters. I was keen to get some things off my chest. I told him that apart from the continual broken agreements one of the most repugnant aspects of his behaviour in this audit was his baseless complaints to the Official Assignee. He claimed that he had made these complaints at the insistence of Ombudsman, Sir Brian Elwood. According to McNeill, it was the Ombudsman who had pushed these complaints. This admission annoyed me. The Ombudsman had been the person I had been going to for help. Sir Brian Elwood subsequently advised me in a letter that he was "unaware of any basis for Mr McNeill's reported comments".

The next day we had several conversations as he and his staff worked to complete their recalculations and present me with further assessments. Late in the day I received via the fax the fruits of their work. This time we owed IRD $14,007. They were obviously working hard. They had come up with a FBT bill that with penalties blew away our GST refund. The Fringe Benefit bill was twice the value of the car concerned. I rang Max Carr. We agreed no FBT was due. Max agreed to ring McNeill and confirm this with him. McNeill phoned me back a short time later to say that they would be working Sunday and would have a new assessment out for me on Monday.

Monday was to be a big day. First thing Monday morning Carson McNeill, for the first time, acknowledged to me that Tannadyce was indeed due a refund. He told me that there would be interest due Tannadyce on the monies owed over the past several years. He went on to explain the complex formula that Treasury had established for the Department to calculate the rates of interest it is to pay taxpayers on outstanding refunds. I guessed no matter how it was calculated that the amount would be insignificant. After some negotiation and discussion we settled on an interest rate of 8.5 percent. McNeill then agreed for me to meet in his office late that afternoon to pick up the cheque.

When I arrived at his office at 4pm he presented me with what was supposedly his final statement. Something seemed wrong. Determined to the end to cut us short McNeill had only calculated interest up until mid

1995. Even at the death the games continued. I rejected his schedule and the cheque that he had prepared. Away he went again to do the figures. About 30 minutes later he appeared with a final schedule for me to approve. I accepted it. Ten minutes later he appeared with the cheque for $65,000.12. It was then that I insisted that the cheque be made out to cash. He was adamant that this was not possible and could not imagine why I could not bank the cheque into an account. I very politely explained that we didn't have a bank account and hadn't for some time. The reason was simple. The Department had taken to emptying my own personal bank accounts, without ever telling me. As far as I was concerned they were stealing money from me. I had closed all my and Tannadyce's accounts as an act of self defence. It's a terrible feeling to get your bank statement, with your hard earned cash supposedly safe in it, to find that the IRD have entered your account and cleaned it out. There is nothing you can do about such an invasion.

McNeill made some frantic calls to Head Office to get clearance to instruct the bank to cash the cheque for me. I walked outside the Department at 5:20 that evening. I was clutching a cheque for $65,000. It was worth much more than that to me. My first call was to Rodney Hide. He had kept in touch all through the shilly-shallying over the weekend. He was over the moon. He asked me for a favour. I said anything. He wanted me to make a colour photocopy enlargement of the cheque and have it laminated and sent up to him. It was the very least I could do. That cheque hangs on the wall of Rodney Hide's parliamentary office. He has it there as a proud trophy celebrating a grand battle. I understand from others he enjoys telling the story of the day the IRD finally had to pay out a cash cheque to Dave Henderson and to Tannadyce. He's very proud of it. Rodney says it serves as a constant symbol of everything that is wrong with the IRD.

I also rang Brian Palliser and Geoff Clews. We shared the relief and the joy. It had been a long campaign. I am sure it was the hardest $65,000 any of us had ever earned. I estimated that in hard cash alone it had cost me more than three times that. And this was for a refund that was simply our due.

The next morning, after some difficulty, I cashed the cheque at the Westpac bank in Hereford Street. The next day I left for the United States and ultimately the Bahamas and banked the money into an account in Nassau truly safe at long last from New Zealand's IRD. I wasn't looking for a tax haven – I was looking for an IRD haven. McNeill had given me an undertaking that if I opened a bank account in New Zealand the IRD wouldn't

Inland Revenue Department

Westpac Banking Corporation
NEW ZEALAND GOVERNMENT BRANCH WELLINGTON NZ

	Thousands	Hundreds	Tens	Units	Cents
Pay the sum of	*Sixty five*				/2

Date	To the order of		Amount in figures
12/1 /98	*Tannadyca Investments Ltd*		$ 65000 /2

Not negotiable
Account Payee only

Inland Revenue Department Crown Payments Account - Refunds

Exempt Cheque Duty

⑈9759260 ⑈030049⑈ 0001100⑈28 ⑈

move to sweep it clean. As you can imagine, somehow I didn't trust his warm assurances. Even as I stood in the queue at the Bank in the Main Street in Nassau I found myself looking over my shoulder. I was half expecting to see Peter Sivertsen in dreadlocks, Adriaan Geerlofs in his thongs slopping along the street, or Gibb Lee as percussionist in the reggae band playing on the opposite street corner.

After four hard years I had the refund. Better than that, it was banked safe and secure well away from our clearly out-of-control IRD.

"I'd rather deal with the Mongrel Mob"

– 'Holmes Show', Febuary 1998

B efore I left for the Bahamas I had asked Carson McNeill to meet with me in two weeks time to discuss how we would deal with the media. After all the difficulties that the IRD had put me through, and all the negative publicity that I had received, I deemed it extremely important that we jointly produced a very positive press statement clearing my name. I also wanted my records back. I wanted too to discuss with Carson McNeill whether the Department would be willing to make some compensation for everything that I had been through and the massive costs I had incurred. I needed to know what assurances they would give me that they would be changing their procedures so as to ensure no other taxpayer would have to endure what I had been through. On 2 February I rang Carson McNeill to set up the meeting. He refused to meet me. I reported that outcome to Rodney Hide who by now was extremely determined to clean up the Department.

Rodney had already approached the Holmes Show and explained to them the facts of my case. They were very interested. Rodney was focusing on just the key facts of the case – the four week audit that had turned into a four year beat-up and the manufacturing of a one-million dollar liability. Carson McNeill's refusal to meet was all the motivation that I needed to agree to appear on Holmes. I agreed to give the Holmes Show Max Carr's report to confirm the key facts of the case.

The following week the Holmes Show contacted the Department seeking their comment. I was immediately rung by Carson McNeill desperate to hold the meeting that the week before he had refused. I told him it was too late. I was completely and utterly sick of his stupid games.

By this time Max Carr had completed and provided a copy of his final report. Contrary to all his assurances at our meeting on 15 December it was bland and equivocal. He had not been "a lot harder" on the staff in Christchurch in this report, as he assured me he would at our meeting on 15 December 1997. I sensed that the Department believed that by paying us our refund the matter was at an end. Clearly they hadn't and weren't interested in learning a thing. But it was far from over.

On the week commencing 9 February I completed an interview with the Holmes Show. The two people producing the item – Jackie Maher and Mary-Anne Ahern – worked extremely hard to understand the case. It made me humble that TV reporters took more time to understand the issues than the National Office of the Department ever had. They also were anxious to allow the Inland Revenue to put their side of the story. The Department kept on asserting that the secrecy provisions of the Tax Administration Act precluded them from being free to discuss the matter on TV. To assist the Department I arranged for Bob Shaddick to fax from Toronto a full release for the Department in respect of any legal obligations they might have to withhold comment on the Tannadyce case. The Department never picked up on the opportunity.

The Holmes Show did a great job in objectively summarising the case. They had understood a very complex history and boiled it down to its essence. I said on the show that I would rather deal with the Mongrel Mob than the IRD. The Commissioner exchanged faxes with Holmes and finally faxed a statement that he "was continuing to communicate with Mr Henderson over unresolved issues". The Commissioner's office had just weeks before stated that they would have nothing further to do with me or the issues surrounding the audit. This was an outright lie. All I had had from National Office were two one-page letters from David Woodnorth, the IRD's Corporate Legal Adviser. He had desperately tried to kill the Holmes Show. He had told me that "formal processes are available to taxpayers who may wish to chal- lenge or question the conduct of Inland Revenue". He had gone on to pro- pose that "any allegations against Inland Revenue and its staff will be fully addressed, but only in the appropriate forum". The Holmes Show wasn't appropriate – the IRD didn't control it.

I had had enough. From now on "The Henderson Case" was to be de- bated in lots of forums that the IRD would no doubt deem inappropriate and that they certainly didn't control.

Still I was encouraged by the idea that the Commissioner might move to deal with me responsibly and enter into discussion with me. On 18 February I spoke to him. He wanted to send David Woodnorth to Christchurch to meet with me. I asked him what the agenda would be. He said it was to identify my concerns and hear my claims that there were still unresolved issues. I suggested that if David Woodnorth was to phone me and confirm the agenda then I would meet with him. I was by this time well used to the games he and his department played. Woodnorth phoned later that afternoon but would not commit himself as to the purpose of his trip. He was equivocal. Over the previous week he had hung up on me on couple of occasions and refused to take my calls because I had been frank enough to confirm that I was taping him. In typical IRD fashion he was unwilling to be held to account for what he was saying. There was no agenda, no commitments and no meeting.

On Tuesday 17 February, the day after the Holmes show ran, the *Christchurch Press* told the story. The banner headline ran across the front page of the business section: "Henderson triumphs in $1m tax row". They quoted me in a grab saying, "It is one thing to pay taxes but another to be completely beaten up in the process of paying those taxes".

On 18 February Rodney Hide took the case to Parliament's Debating Chamber. He asked the Minister of Revenue Mr Bill Birch whether IRD had treated Dave Henderson in a fair and equal manner like all other taxpayers. Bill Birch replied that it was not proper for him to comment on the affairs of an individual taxpayer. But he did say it was his responsibility to require the Department to treat all taxpayers on a "fair and equal basis". He went on to say that he also required of the Department that "wherever it becomes aware that any taxpayer may not have been treated fairly and equally to enquire into the matter urgently, diligently, and, where necessary, on an independent basis". He said that "if unfairness is shown to have occurred [that he and the Department had a responsibility] to ensure that the matter is remedied in full and that all practicable steps are taken, without delay, to avoid any recurrence".

We saw this as a great opportunity. The Minister had set out for us his personal standards that he demanded of the IRD and what he would do if they fell short.

The week of the Holmes Show I was contacted by Simon Carr of the *National Business Review* who was keen to do a large piece on my story for his column that Friday. This was extremely significant for me. A couple of

Simon Carr: A fearless journalist who now, sadly, resides in his native England.

years earlier I had had contact with another NBR journalist over another story. In providing comment for that story I had got into a discussion about my problems with the IRD. The journalist was fascinated by the story but was unwilling to write it up. He said that no journalist would ever take on the IRD. They were simply too scared that the IRD would aggressively audit them.

Simon Carr wasn't scared. Here was an Englishman of the old stock, the type who had sailed out in sailing ships in arduous conditions to conquer the world. The IRD didn't bother him. He also knew a good story when he heard one. He shared my and Rodney Hide's enthusiasm to see the IRD held to account for their actions.

Simon's story ran on Friday 20 February in his column on the inside cover of the *National Business Review*. It was headed in bold type "IRD appoints itself Judge, Jury, Jailer". He didn't pull any punches. Simon jumped straight in with a description of the key players from Christchurch.

"Inland Revenue staff appears to be the product of some unusually rigorous affirmative action programme. You ask around and find that they're either under 5'5" or over 6'8"; one of them is dressed like a flatting victim in unwashed clothes two-sizes too small; another's a member of the Natural Law party who believes in yogic flying; here's a chap with coke-bottle-bottom glasses with (I forget which) two hearing aids and a speech impediment or two speech impediments and a hearing aid; here's one wearing gold chains who does an over-excited line in sexual harassment and handcuff bondage".

Simon went on to describe "Hendo's" case that he was about to make infamous in business circles throughout New Zealand:

"The four-year saga is a black morality tale exemplifying (in roughly alphabetical order) the sins of bullying, cowardice, cruelty, deception, harassment, lying, sloth, vindictiveness and a generally obnoxious attitude".

NBR 17 April 1998

Minister demands more dirt on IRD

But aren't 72 allegations about Inland Revenue's behaviour enough?

We remember the relief, do we not, when we heard Bill Birch agreed to investigate David Henderson's complaints against the tax department personally. ("Hendo" had a $65,000 GST claim turned into a $1 million demand and was driven into bankruptcy by the department's officials. Only after four years and political interve- tion at the highest level was the claim fi- admitted and paid.)

The Minister of Revenue declare Parliament that, as soon as he rece evidence of treatment that wasn' equal, he would swing into acti

This statement, coming a Hendo's first offer to provi detailing the astonishing t received, wasn't promp welcome. New Zealar fixer was on the cas

Simon Ca

The minister asked for a comprehensive list of charges with which he would immediately confront the commissioner. This most powerful of public servants would be required, within 14 days, to answer each charge in full. His responses would be put - of the Crown Law Office to deter- ...er the questions had been ... issue had been evaded. ...this information, Mr ... er there was ... pro-

After eight days, it was discovered Mr Birch had not sent the document to the commissioner. He had not done anything with it at all. He had read it and written back to Hendo saying he wanted more charges, more evidence.

He wants every single delinquency detailed. He wants the charge list to be declared to be full and final (which is difficult because as days pass, new charges accumulate).

"For pete's sake, isn't it enough?" Hendo asks. "I've given them 72 precisely-framed charges, with times, dates, places. Isn't that enough to determine whether ...e is grounds for a judicial inquiry?" ...ested readers may decide for ...hen we publish the 72 ... in ***The National Busi-***

February 27

INSIDE COVER

Simon Carr

The National Business Review

Tar shows through IRD scandal whitewash

On learning that David Henderson was proposing legal action, the Commissioner of Inland Revenue has instructed the Crown Law Office to "vigorously defend Inland Revenue and its employees against all of the serious allegations which have been made".

Does that include, you have to wonder, the serious allegations that the Inland Revenue has already admitted to?

The story so far: David Henderson applied for a GST refund as a result of which IRD landed him with a $1 million liability which it refused to explain and forced him into bankruptcy.

A report on this monstrous episode was prepared by the department's top gun over a period of three months and was not ... whitewash absolutely everythin...

While the terms of ... addressed and wh... breaches of ... mislea...

fraud that the department laid with the police were mischievous).

IRD auditor Geerlofs swore an affidavit that Hendo's audit was complete. But "subsequent actions, ongoing queries, further correspondence and ultimately the issue of Section 17 notices give a fairly clear indication that our audit was by no means complete" (love that "fairly clear").

How was the $1 million ... structed? "I have found th... confusing part of th... and have not ... the dep...

Taxpayers fund awful writing

The only reason I bought Keith Hill's novel *blue kisser* (Flamingo, $19.95) was because it acknowledged the assistance of a grant from Creative New Zealand.

What is it Keith Hill has to say th... such significance that taxpaye... sidise its saying? The bo... written in a tradi... the cover ...

th me cons Hend "I u suggest t take the v racy is par complaint o

IRD appoints itself judge, jury, jailor

Inland Revenue's staff appears to be the product of some unusually rigorous affirmative action programme. You ask around and find that they're either under 5'5" or over 6'8"; one of them is dressed like a flatting victim in unwashed clothes two sizes too small; another's a member of the Natural Law party who believes in yogic flying; here's a chap in coke-bottle-bottom glasses with (I forget which) two hearing aids and a speech impediment or two speech impediments and a hearing aid; here's one wearing gold chains who does an over-excited line in sexual harassment and handcuff bondage.

But let's start with the story in a nutshell.

David Henderson, a Christchurch businessman, applied for a GST refund of $70,000. The department converted his claim for a refund to a million dollar liability, and forced him into bankruptcy.

The four-year saga is a black morality tale exemplifying (in roughly alphabetical order) the sins of: Bullying, cowardice, cruelty, deception, harassment, lying, sloth, vindictiveness and a generally obnoxious attitude.

Hendo had a claim for $70,000 but, when his company moved to Christchurch, it met with stiff resistance. The department's auditor sought a meeting with their financial officer.

What was said is disputed by both parties although the auditor has agreed he has a tendency to say things like: " Hold out your hands – nice small wrists, you'll only need small handcuffs."

Because of his concerns about the way the meeting was conducted by the department, Henderson felt it appropriate to remonstrate with the authorities. As he did so, the complaints machinery swung into action.

They began an auditing procedure that turned him upside down and when they couldn't find anything underneath they turned him inside out.

The initial investigation was estimated at 40 hours – but the finishing line was an ever-receding mirage. Ever more issues arose, ever more documents were sought, ever more files were demanded. As one audit closed another opened, month after month, year after year. Boxloads of schedules and records were delivered to the department; no receipts were issued and most of the material was lost.

Oh, and just to keep Hendo occupied with some running ...

... affairs to produce this astonishing sum. Unfailingly they refused to tell him.

So, here is one of the foundation stones of the IRD's culture – a bureaucratic culture that is alien to the rest of New Zealand's. In this Kafkaesque world you are guilty until you can prove yourself innocent.

Christchurch IRD boss Carson McNeill affirmed he has personally satisfied himself the assessment is correct and that it will stand up in court.

On the department's track record for veracity the case for disbelieving this is obvious. Its record is a scandal.

> In the Kafkaesque world of IRD you are guilty until you can prove yourself innocent

Its officials say assessments have been issued but they don't arrive. They say proceedings won't be issued, then they are issued. They promise information, it never comes. They say they will offer an explanation of how the $1 million liability is made up, it never happens. They say they will not proceed with a personal audit – almost immediately a 100-page audit is produced and goes to adjudication (thrown out, incidentally).

... private time is out.

When finally he is backed into admitting that he is McNeill's boss, he will say only two things: Direct all your complaints to McNeill and stop using this telephone number.

Oh, how the department hates being taped.

When the department's lawyer learned Hendo was taping his recent call he did his scone: "It's completely unethical to telephone a conversation!"(sic).

However, before that particular tape was switched off, the lawyer did reveal the only good thing to have come out of the sorry story: Senior careers are on the line.

But let's be clear – so far no liability has been publicly accepted by the department. It's true that they abruptly withdrew the $1 million claim and gave Hendo a cheque for the GST refund but the only way you can see who might be to blame is by looking for the people covered in whitewash.

Who's responsible? Boss Carson McNeill in Christchurch? George Gray in Wellington? The commissioner for Inland Revenue himself?

No, probably not the commissioner. As recent events have turned out, the commissioner doesn't appear to be in control at all. Hendo wrote to him earlier this week saying, rather tartly, he may feel, "Either your undertaking has no value or [the] Christchurch office is not 'within your control'."

The fact is that the undertakings of the commissioner himself have been no more reliable than those of his underlings.

Things only improved for Hendo when MP Rodney Hide swung into the action like the SAS breaking into a siege house.

Rodney, it's worth saying, is one of the most formidable opponents in politics. He is clever, he is highly-educated and he has a brain like a wrecking ball.

His sponsorship brought the issue to a head and began the still-continuing process of bringing some natural justice – and indeed some legal justice into the situation.

Forthcoming action includes: Hendo suing IRD and its officers severally and collectively for a familiar million.

He is setting up an organisation called Taxbusters (Who you going to call? Taxbusters!). Finance Minister Bill Birch has indicated in Parliament he will launch an independent inquiry. And a flood of calls has gone into the Act office with cases as bad or worse than Hendo's.

The department's position is: "David Henderson is being treated no differently from any other taxpayer." Imagine that.

It's no wonder they have to collect so much tax – they need it for all the buck-passing they do.

The National Business Review • March

IRD: It's our job to be really, really nasty

A London friend of mine once succumbed to pressure and put up some social goat for the Garrick Club.

When he was blackballed, the poor wretch asked so plaintively, "Were there many black balls in the urn?" that my friend searched for the gentlest way to break the news.

"Well," he said, "you know what caviar looks like...?"

I need an equivalent image to answer the question, "Is there much more mucky stuff to come out about Inland Revenue?" Because yes, you see, there are troughs of it, there are trenches of it.

First, the familiar summary. Christchurch businessman makes GST claim.

Four years later he has been continuously audited, forced into bankruptcy and landed with an unexplained IRD liability of $1 million. Political pressure is applied and, when the rock is lifted, sights stranger than we are used to in our cosy democracy come to light.

Now, because there are constitutional issues to deal with, it is vital we don't get diverted by trivial issues (I'll return to them next week, in a story about the commissioner and the handcuffs).

But – settle down at the back – the secret circulars referred to on the front page reveal that the department is effectively a law unto itself. That's not a metaphor, that's a fact.

You can be arbitrarily assessed for a tax liability and the department is actually obliged by its secret circulars to withhold all material evidence supporting the assessments.

Tax lawyer Bruce Grierson says: "Get the picture of a person in a concrete cell, with a bare light bulb, and an official telling them they're an enemy of the state, but not in what way. The charge is never made – only the penalty. That's what it is to be prosecuted by the IRD."

While the Bill of Rights, the Official Information Act and the Privacy Act are all framed to protect the citizen from the arbitrary power of the state, the IRD views its founding legislation as taking precedence.

You can't budge the massive department (as Alliance Party leader Jim Anderton confessed to a group of small businessmen – there was so little point in his trying to gain satisfaction for them from the department he wouldn't even try to do).

IRD is known to be the most powerful department in the state's apparatus.

The commissioner has more pure power in his person than the SIS, the police force and the Resource Management Act put together.

By virtue of the Tax Administration Act, he has "full and free access to all lands, buildings and places" with no need of a search warrant.

Every one of his assessments is assumed to be correct and taxpayers have to pay more or less on demand. If you dispute the amount the commissioner wants, you still have to pay half of it within 30 days while the matter goes to court.

But still you are never allowed to find out why you have been sent the commissioner's bill.

And if you dispute the sum, the burden of proof lies with you, the taxpayer, to show it isn't so.

In America, it was proposed to reverse this burden of proof. When Senate hearings revealed how the IRS treated taxpayers, the Democrats withdrew their opposition to the bill and it passed through the Senate unanimously.

That sounds fair. And I bet the IRD – even while its officials are spitting tacks at these stories being published – will have to agree that it's fair. After all, they say that's what their job is.

orth- se to ... et to now and ent tter ss- is ith aff ... ss ie in

Simon concluded his description of the case:

It's no wonder they have to collect so much tax – they need it for all the buck-passing they do.

All this and more in pole position in New Zealand's leading business weekly. Simon also said that I was considering suing IRD and its officers severally and collectively for a "familiar million".

The article caused an immediate response. At one o'clock that Friday afternoon I received a fax from the Commissioner. He referred to Simon's reference to possible legal proceedings. He advised that he had instructed the Crown Law Office to act on his behalf and that they were vigorously to defend the Inland Revenue Department and its employees against the serious allegations that had been made.

Year Five had got off to a good start. I had the refund. The million dollar debt was cancelled. And the IRD were beginning to be held to public account for their outrageous behaviour and contempt.

"I don't think this will be the end of the negative coverage"

– Graham Holland, Commissioner of Inland Revenue

Also at this time Rodney was busily determining the next political course of action. He had decided to write to new Prime Minister Jenny Shipley and demand that the government hold a full judicial inquiry into my case. It was his belief that should such an inquiry take place that the public and politicians would be so outraged that significant reform would have to occur within the IRD.

At that time I did not really grasp the full significance of his demand for a judicial inquiry. I accepted his judgement and agreed to help in any way I could. I was also mindful of Bill Birch's advice to the House and it seemed to me that such an inquiry was the only way of properly meeting his professed standards.

Back in November Max Carr had given me his personal undertaking that no action would be taken in respect of the statutory demands for very large sums issued against both Tannadyce and an associate company. In respect of the associate company the demand for $164,445.57 related to default assessments for GST returns that I had not filed for that company.

The company had not traded for a number of years and in March 1996 I had made this point to senior IRD staff and had further advised them that if and when it traded in the future I would tell them. That made little difference. When Max Carr gave me his undertaking that no further action would proceed without me first being given seven days notice I also agreed with him to file properly the nil returns confirming that the company had not traded. I had done this before the end of November.

Unbeknown to me, on 12 December 1997, and contrary to our agreement, the IRD filed in the High Court in Christchurch a raft of documentation to support their application to liquidate the company. A hearing date was set for Monday 16 February 1998 at 10am. We were never notified of this hearing date. To support the application Colin Barry, an IRD officer in Christchurch, swore an affidavit confirming that the $164,445.55 was owing and that there were no outstanding objections to this debt. Once more, a senior IRD officer had seriously misled the Court.

The matter was ultimately settled by the Department seeking leave of the Court to withdraw their action. Their withdrawal was admission that this debt didn't exist either. The withdrawal was as big a surprise to me as receiving the notice initially. By this time the Tannadyce matter had been settled and I suspect the Department was starting to scrutinise their actions as they related to me a little more closely. I never got to the bottom of it. I rang Colin Barry who said he was under instructions not to talk to me and slammed the phone down on me. Max Carr subsequently acknowledged that his undertaking had been broken by the Christchurch office and he apologised for that.

The IRD's attempt to liquidate this company highlights again how incredibly careless and casual the Department is about extremely important agreements. It highlights too how freely IRD officers spend money and how casual they are about the massive responsibility imposed on them by the "guilty until proven innocent" nature of our tax laws.

I also became aware of another bizarre IRD process. From January 1998 on, the Department had all my and Tannadyce's mail from the Department directed to Gibb Lee at their own box number, PO Box 2871 Christchurch. It appears that they would then sift through it, decide what I should receive and should not receive, and twink out their address and write in my name and box number. The upside of all this is that the masses of mail we had previously received quickly dried up. The downside was that later that year the Department would accuse me of not dealing with returns that we had never received. I have on several occasions asked the Department to explain why they were diverting my mail but no one has ever explained it to me. The only reason that I can come up with is that their computer is so out of control that the only way the IRD have of controlling the letters it generates is to convert a taxpayer's address to their own dead drop allowing them to sift through the mail. It seems crazy but I can think of no other explanation.

On 27 February the *National Business Review* published a Letter to the Editor from the Commissioner of Inland Revenue, Graham Holland, where he rejected "totally" all the allegations made by Simon Carr the week before. Things were getting crazier. Several of the allegations made by Simon Carr had been accepted by the Commissioner and his confirmation of that was set out in a letter he wrote to me on 9 December the year before. The Commissioner was now rejecting everything, including Max Carr's negative findings about the Department.

I couldn't help but reflect on Mr Birch's answer to Rodney Hide's question in the House. He had said in part that "if unfairness is shown to have occurred [then he and the Department had a responsibility] to ensure that the matter is remedied in full and that all practicable steps are taken, without delay, to avoid any recurrence".

The Commissioner's letter was confirmation of my fears: the Department had learnt nothing, was not interested in learning anything, had no desire to address the matter, change their procedures, and remedy the matter in full. I found it repugnant.

Simon Carr ran the story again in his column that same week. He focused on the million-dollar claim and how after four years the Department could not even explain to Max Carr the basis on which they had assessed it.

As a consequence of the media coverage Rodney Hide's phone was running hot. I too was receiving a large number of calls from taxpayers who had suffered similar treatment as my own. Their stories were gut-wrenching: outrageous assessments, massive penalties, no one to communicate with, rude and abusive treatment, interminable audits, massive legal costs, and in lots of cases, bankruptcies and company liquidations. I felt angry but extremely powerless. I guess on reflection it just hardened my resolve to hold the Department accountable in my own case.

Simon Carr also received a number of calls from accountants and tax-

Graham Holland: Commissioner of IRD since 1995.

payers. He started to follow up some of their cases. In the 6 March edition of the *National Business Review* under the banner heading "IRD: It's our job to be really, really nasty" he highlighted some more of the realities of how out of control the IRD was. He quoted tax lawyer Bruce Grierson, "Get the picture of a person in a concrete cell, with a bare lightbulb, and an official telling them they are an enemy of the state, but not in what way. The charge is never made – only the penalty. That's what it is to be prosecuted by the IRD".

The following week the Commissioner had another letter in the *National Business Review*. It was yet another attempt to discredit me by implying that there was something unique about my audit and that it had undisclosed features that justified the Department's actions over the last four years. "While this audit was not without difficulty, there were contributing factors, which I cannot discuss in detail", the Commissioner pontificated He went on to assure the public that "I have full confidence in all my staff who have worked on this case and that, despite an extensive review, there is no evidence of anything improper in how the case was managed".

The following week, Graham Holland reprinted his letter and referred to the Holmes Show and Simon Carr's articles in his regular column in IRD's staff newsletter *Revenews*. He told his staff that "our secrecy provisions, which are properly there for the protection of taxpayers and society, have on this occasion not helped us as they have prevented full and open debate on the facts". He went on to assure staff that "we have, however, been very actively managing the issue with the taxpayer, his advisers and the media". This was simply untrue. He concluded his column by declaring that "I don't think this will be the end of the negative coverage".

The clear implication was that there was another side to the story that the Commissioner knew and which if told would exonerate him and his department. This is nonsense. Bob Shaddick had faxed to the Commissioner from Toronto a release removing any obligations that he might have under the secrecy provisions of the Tax Administration Act. We had publicly authorised him to speak freely about the tax position of Tannadyce. I did the same. It was the Commissioner's choice not to have "full and open debate on the facts". I was very disappointed that the Commissioner would now imply that he was in possession of facts that would somehow justify his and his department's behaviour.

I was very aware that there was a campaign to smear my character and to discredit me. People were reporting stories about me from all over the country. One that particularly hurt came right from the Minister's office. Bill Birch's Senior Private Secretary, Paul Stocks, told Rodney's secretary Val Wilde that "there was another side to this story" and implied that this justified the Department's actions. He was reported to have said that Henderson "had been bankrupt several times before". This was a straight lie. I had him write to me and apologise for his remarks. He assured me that he would not initiate any more discussions about my affairs. It was clear that widely defamatory statements were being made about me in an attempt to justify somehow the treatment that I was receiving. I can only assume they were originating from a whispering campaign out of the IRD.

Max Carr and I had agreed at the end of December that we would meet early in the year to go over what the Department alleged were a number of outstanding returns relating to Tannadyce Investments and associated companies. Through February, after the Holmes and *National Business Review* stories, Max Carr and I had a number of telephone conversations. He was very circumspect but expressed to me a clear concern for the way the Commissioner was handling the matter. We finally agreed to meet on 4 March. He was to come to Christchurch and meet me at my flat.

In a phone conversation that preceded the meeting he asked if we could have a decent off-the-record conversation when we met. Clearly there were things that were troubling him. In December 1997, after Max Carr had filed his first report to the Commissioner, it became apparent to me that he was telling me one thing and the Commissioner another. I had then resorted to taping phone calls and meetings with him.

It was clear to me that the Commissioner had invoked a lot of fear into his "independent" investigator. There was certainly enough fear that he was now only willing to make these previously candid observations in an off-the-record conversation. Max is a very senior public servant and committed

Christian. He had often promoted his Christianity as a means of establishing his integrity. He is someone who the Commissioner subsequently described to the Minister as "a senior Departmental Manager of unquestionable integrity". I knew it was going to be tough as a discredited bankrupt pitting my word against his. I believed that if it wasn't for these indisputable tape recordings I would have gone crazy in the face of the overt dissimulation that was to follow. I also believed that the Commissioner would use my allegations to discredit me further. Without any evidence, he would have succeeded.

On Wednesday 4 March I picked Max Carr up from the airport at 12:30pm. We drove straight to my home and held the meeting. We began with a general conversation and reflected on some of the audit issues. Max Carr told me that he was wrong to have asked for an off-the-record conversation and that he felt that it was inappropriate for him to be discussing these issues when the Commissioner had put the matter into the hands of the Crown Law Office. I accepted his position but I expressed my frustration that he had made observations to me personally that he had not made formally to the Commissioner in his report. That fact combined with the Commissioner publicly rejecting all my allegations led me to the conclusion that nothing was going to change within the Department.

As the conversation went on Max became more anxious to express his true feelings. In a carefully worded statement he made it plain that he was not happy with the Commissioner's behaviour but, because he was the Commissioner, Max Carr had to accept it. On several occasions he asked if he could go off-the-record. I said that was fine as I was keen to get a decent understanding of what was really going on at the highest level of the Department. In those off-the-record conversations he reaffirmed key and very significant conclusions from his review. These conclusions never appeared in his report to the Commissioner: "I would have thought that if I was doing this investigation and we had started off in the very early days, just you and I, I think I could have got through it in four weeks". "I think one of the biggest issues was that we didn't talk to you, we didn't listen with an unbiased mind". After he made this remark he said flippantly that "if I read in the press that Henderson said that Max Carr said that they were biased, Henderson's dead". "This is off-the-record – I am sorry it happened all like this, I wish I had been involved, you know, two weeks after it started – I am sure I could have done a far better job. But all that means nothing now". And much more. He also recognised the desperate need for an independent Tax Ombudsman to investigate complaints like mine. "I have often talked about an Ombudsman for taxpayers too, because that's the job that I would like. Quite seriously, that is a job I would enjoy".

I liked Max Carr. I had been very grateful for his involvement. I had once described him as "a diamond in a dust bowl". He thought that was great. He had stopped the nonsense where many other National Office staff had not even bothered to try. But I became very disappointed with his failure to tell the Commissioner and the public the truth of what had really gone on in my audit and how poorly the Department had performed. It was my belief that until that truth came out the Department would continue to beat up on taxpayers. I told Max Carr that his failure to present his conclusions honestly and unequivocally meant that he was now a part of the problem. I drove him to the airport disappointed in him and angry with the IRD culture that he represented.

On 9 March, Bill Birch wrote to Rodney Hide regarding his request to Jenny Shipley for a judicial inquiry. Bill Birch appeared to be treating the matter seriously. He advised that he was giving the Commissioner 14 days to report on a number of matters relating to the Tannadyce audit. He then said that on the receipt of that report he would refer it to the Crown Law Office as to whether it satisfactorily addressed all the significant residual issues. He told Rodney that on the basis of that opinion the government would be in a position to determine whether my case would need immediate judicial inquiry.

On the face of it this appeared to be a most promising development. But what was played out over the next few months was a frightening demonstration of how out-of-control the Department is, how it completely lacks accountability, and how its senior staff will distort the truth to protect their positions.

The IRD's PR machine was pumped up to counter my claim. There was also an underground campaign against me. But I wasn't to be deterred now. Nor was Rodney.

Tapes catch out IRD National Manager Corporates

On 16 March Bill Birch wrote to me saying that he had changed his mind and that he had put on hold his request for the Commissioner to respond to a number of points. He was now asking me to prepare "a single, comprehensive, consolidated statement of your complaints against IRD, which I can regard as final. I will then be in a position to check off any responses by IRD against that master list". He continued "on receipt of that advice from you I will immediately forward it to him [the Commissioner] and ask him to complete his report in 14 days". He assured me that the report from the Commissioner was "not in any way an inquiry into your behaviour or affairs".

The Minister had done a 180-degree turn-about. The onus was once more on me. The IRD were no longer having to provide an explanation of their audit. Instead, I was having to restate my complaints which the IRD would receive and respond to.

It turns out the IRD have a hefty presence in the Minister's office and play a key role in managing difficult cases like mine. The IRD operate a Ministerial Services Unit headed up by an IRD staff member responsible for dealing with all matters between the Minister and the IRD. IRD staff member Margaret Denny works out of the Minister's office and liaises directly with the unit. I felt I was not dealing with the Minister but simply with IRD staff in his office.

Bill Birch did have staff who were not IRD but they did not seem motivated to fix and resolve problems like mine. One of Parliament's top-priced spin doctors is Bevan Burgess. He works now for Birch after having worked for Roger Douglas in the 1980s. Instead of writing speeches, he got bogged down trying not to write letters to me and trying not to answer my questions. He told Rodney that he didn't mind – he was getting paid and he reckoned the government had a lot more resources and patience than Dave Henderson and Rodney Hide. It was this uncaring and cynical attitude that Rodney and I were constantly up against. It's very disappointing especially when you have been a taxpayer paying their wages all these years and, then when you are in trouble, they fail to help and then make light of it.

I was disappointed that I now again had to do all the work and restate my case but my commitment to having matters properly aired meant that I decided to co-operate fully. For the next two weeks I worked night and day and on 31 March faxed to Bill Birch a 35-page letter setting out 75 significant allegations. I spent a long time working with Geoff Clews to ensure that this report was complete and adequately presented. These were serious matters: breaches of the Tax Administration Act, breaches of the Official Information Act, misleading the Ombudsman, breaches of IRD code of conduct, broken agreements. I concluded my letter by advising the Minister

Ministerial Services Unit members. (From left). Moira Thompson, Tim Te Huki, Margaret Denny and David Belchamber. Absent was Beverly Pearce.

that "I do not make any of my allegations lightly. I hold many hours of taped telephone conversations with Departmental officers and many records and files to support all my claims and allegations". This was the first time that I had formally complained about the nature of the Carr report. To be fair to the Minister I went to some trouble to set out what Geoff Clews and I believed a "robust investigation" should have covered.

It had taken me, with no resources, 14 days to prepare all this. The Minister had assured me in his letter on 16 March that he would have the Commissioner respond within 14 days of receiving my report. Eight days later on 8 April I received another letter from Bill Birch. He complained that my 31 March letter was incomplete as I had not certified that my letter included "everything significant enough to warrant investigation". There was a further exchange of correspondence about the completeness of my complaint. Finally, on 27 April the Minister confirmed my letter of complaint was complete and could proceed to the Commissioner for his response.

By mid-May Rodney and I were becoming impatient that there was still no response to my complaint. Rodney had regularly been sending written

---

Question for Written Answer No 04117
For Answer on Wednesday 13 May 1998

Rodney Hide to the Minister of Revenue:

> Did senior Inland Revenue Department officer Mr Max Carr admit that the Tannadyce audit could have been completed in four weeks instead of 206 weeks and then fail to mention this key fact in his report into the case as alleged in the *National Business Review*, of 24 April 1998?

Rt Hon W F Birch [Minister of Revenue] replied:

> Mr Carr made no such comment. This issue is raised numerous times in Mr Henderson's letter dated 31 March 1998 and other correspondence, and will be responded to in full in the Commissioner of Inland Revenue's report to me due 29 May 1998.

Approved:

---

questions to the Minister regarding the operation of the IRD. A great game developed where they tried not to answer questions and Rodney tried to put questions that were hard for the Department and the Minister to dodge. We decided to put to the Minister a number of questions relating to key allegations that I had made in my 31 March report and which I had solid evidence to support. The Minister has to respond to a written Parliamentary question in five working days.

For example, on Wednesday 6 May 1998 Rodney lodged Question for Written Answer Number 4117. "Did senior Inland Revenue Officer Mr Max Carr admit that the Tannadyce audit could have been completed in four weeks instead of 206 weeks and then fail to mention this key fact in his report into the case as alleged in the *National Business Review*, of 24 April 1998?"

Five working days later the Minister Bill Birch replied: "Mr Carr made no such comment. This issue is raised numerous times in Mr Henderson's letter dated 31 March 1998 and other correspondence and will be responded to in full in the Commissioner of Inland Revenue's report to me due 29 May 1998".

IRD's dissimulation had just infected Parliament. Both Rodney and I battled to grasp their level of contemptuous behaviour. In making this remark the Department, through their Minister, was telling the world that I was a liar. The Commissioner and his staff put great emphasis on their integrity. In all their dealings they seize the high moral ground proclaiming how honest and upright they are. They have to their advantage the fact that ordinary New Zealanders want to believe that government is honest. Accordingly, in circumstances like this, the benefit of the doubt flows to the IRD and against the taxpayer. IRD's level of contempt and their disregard for the truth was such that they were willing to state absolutely and unequivocally to their Minister and to Parliament that "Mr Carr made no such comment".

In reality, Mr Carr made that comment to me not once but several times on several different occasions including at our 4 March meeting.

The day before the Commissioner's report was due, Rodney was again pestering Bill Birch in Parliament. The sting was in his supplementary where Rodney read out what Max Carr had actually said at our 4 March meeting. He was reading from the transcript of the tape I had taken.

Hansard number 43, 1998. May 28th 1998.

Audits—Inland Revenue Department

4. RODNEY HIDE (ACT NZ) to the **Minister of Revenue** : Although he has stated that senior Inland Revenue Department officer Max Carr made no comment to "admit that the Tannadyce audit could have been completed in 4 weeks instead of 206 weeks", has he been advised if Mr Carr did comment to Mr Henderson on how long the audit should have taken; if so, what was that comment?

Rt Hon. BILL BIRCH (Minister of Revenue): I have not been advised of any comments made by Mr Carr as to how long the Tannadyce audit should have taken.

Rodney Hide: How does the Minister reconcile his original answer with the transcript of a tape that has Mr Max Carr telling Mr Henderson: "I would have thought, if I were doing this investigation, if we had started off in the very early days, just you and I, I think I could have got through it in 4 weeks", and does the Minister not now agree that his written answer has misled the House, and what, if anything, does the Minister intend to do about it?

Rt Hon. BILL BIRCH: No.

Mark Peck: Is the Minister perhaps just a little bit concerned that his future coalition partner ACT seems more intent on personally attacking a member of his department, than on attacking Government policy, which I would concede does include the efficiency of the Inland Revenue Department?

Rt Hon. BILL BIRCH: The member can draw his own conclusions about the motives of the member who has raised the question, but I can assure him that we do not regard him as a future coalition partner.

Rodney Hide: I seek leave to table the transcript of the tape between Mr Max Carr and Mr Henderson, which contradicts the Minister's statement.

Document, by leave, laid on the table of the House.

It was a shame Rodney could only get to ask just one supplementary question and that Labour's Mark Peck and National's Bill Birch would simply use the opportunity to poke fun at a new MP trying to hold the most powerful department of state to account. But Rodney wasn't bothered by these other MPs. He declared to me that hard work and truth would show them all up. I hoped he was right. My experience with the MPs that I had approached hadn't been great. I had met with New Zealand First's Ron Mark who I had known for many years. I had sold him a business in the late

1980s when he had come out of the army. I discovered that ideologically we had a lot in common. He was keen to meet with me in his office in Parliament as he had been following my case in the media. At this stage he was part of the government and New Zealand First's whip. He assured me that he would do his best to muster some support for an inquiry including speaking to his coalition partner Bill Birch. Some weeks later he was to tell Rodney that Winston Peters wasn't willing to back my case. Ron couldn't help me.

I also spoke to John Wright, an Alliance MP from Rangiora who was on the Finance and Expenditure Select Committee responsible for the IRD. As a former tow-truck operator and small businessman, I thought that he would sympathise with my position. He expressed a willingness to do something but I have never heard back from him. Perhaps the case was just too tough for him.

Both Rodney and I wrote to Bill Birch complaining that he had misled the House. The taped conversation proved it. On 8 June the Commissioner wrote to Rodney asking him to make available the original of the tape recording. Rodney didn't have the original, while he had listened to the tape, I had only provided him with a copy of the segment of the tape covering the transcript that he had tabled. On 9 June Rodney wrote back to the Commissioner inviting him to come and listen to his copy. Two days later the Commissioner sent David Woodnorth, Corporate Legal Advisor, and his assistant solicitor to listen to the tape. They eyed the $65,000 cheque up on Rodney's wall. Rodney told them that he happened to like Max Carr. Woodnorth was surprised and claimed that Rodney was doing a good job of destroying Max's career. Rodney exploded and gave them chapter and verse about what the IRD had been doing to me and to other taxpayers for years.

On 25 June 1998 the Commissioner sent a report to Bill Birch clarifying the answer he had given to Rodney's question 4117. The four-page report fought desperately to save Max Carr's credibility. Instead of just saying someone was lying the Commissioner was blaming semantics. His conclusion was that "the answer to question 4117 was, strictly speaking, inaccurate. A more precise and therefore more accurate form should have been provided along the lines suggested at paragraph 9".

Paragraph 9 was a masterful display of bureaucratic legerdemain: "Mr Carr did not admit that the Tannadyce audit could have been completed in four weeks instead of 206 weeks and because he made no such admission,

A copy of the $65,000.12. refund cheque proudly hanging on Rodney Hide's office wall.

and nor is it his professional view that this particular audit could have been completed in that time frame, there was no failure to mention the fact in his report, as alleged by the *National Business Review*". I have read this statement many, many times. Even today as I write this I still don't have a clue what it means. It's certainly at variance with the clear and unequivocal statement Max Carr had made to me on several occasions and which I had captured on tape.

The Crown Law Office wrote to me demanding that I immediately provide the original of the tape. Here I was waiting months to receive answers to letters. I had had Official Information requests totally ignored, and suddenly I was expected to pass to the Department an original of a tape for an unclear purpose. It was clear to me that Max Carr would have known exactly what he had said in respect of how long the audit should have taken. It was a very measured observation. It was his considered conclusion. He had carefully sought my assurance that it was off-the-record before making it and he had made it to me on several occasions. What's more it was now mid-June and I had still not received a copy of the Commissioner's report to the Minister which the Minister had been sitting on now for almost three weeks.

I explained to the Crown Law Office that I would not give them the original of the tape but that I would make a copy for them. There was debate and discussion over this and an implication that I might tamper with the tape and produce an untrue copy. Rodney wrote to the Commissioner in early July and advised him that I was prepared to fly to Wellington at my own expense and play the original tape to him.

I flew to Wellington on 4 August with the original. I had agreed that I would play it to the Commissioner's legal representatives on the condition that the Commissioner would personally listen to a copy of the two-hour tape some time that week. The IRD were to make a copy as we listened to the original. I demanded this condition still believing that the Commissioner might be moved to take immediate action to clean up the mess that his department was in. Rodney was to come with me. We met at Crown Law at 4:30, with Crown Counsel Karen Clark. Also at the meeting was David Woodnorth from the IRD.

The meeting was like something out of a Marx brothers movie. Firstly, it was delayed for an hour while Crown Law staff worked feverishly and unsuccessfully to set up the recording equipment. To put them out of their misery I offered to give them a copy of the original then and there. But I wanted their assurance that there would be no nonsense about authenticity. After some debate Karen Clark finally agreed that the Department would notify me within 24 hours if there were any concerns about authenticity.

Now we could turn our attention to listening to the original. There had been so much debate and discussion about authenticity that Rodney mischievously inquired how they knew that the tape they were about to hear was in fact an authentic original. What followed caused a delay of another hour. David Woodnorth suggested that they employ the police to authenticate the tape. I saw Rodney pinching himself trying to make sure he was awake. I wouldn't let the tape out of my sight and so Rodney said they had better sort it out there and then. Karen Clark and David Woodnorth then left the room to set up arrangements with the police. Rodney and I were left in the

David Woodnorth: Works in the commissioner's office – putting out fires.

boardroom to ponder the optimal size of government.

Thirty minutes later our two legal beagles returned dejected. It seems the section of the thin blue line that exists to authenticate tapes of IRD officers had gone home for the day. After further discussion they agreed to listen to the tape and see how it sounded. Max Carr's voice filled the room with crystal clear clarity. The Crown Law's sound system was a beauty. As Max Carr repeatedly went off-record and proceeded to dig deeper and deeper holes for his Department, Karen Clark and David Woodnorth shifted ever-increasingly nervously in their seats. They didn't dare look at each other, or at us, through the whole two-hour playing.

But it was not to be the end of the matter. Up until that time the Commissioner had been suggesting that perhaps there was something in the context in which Max Carr had made his statement that might have qualified it and reduced its significance. The reverse was true.

The IRD's attempt to cover itself had gone wildly astray. Who would ever believe a bankrupt? Or a backbench MP? The IRD wouldn't even believe the tapes of their own senior staff.

The Commissioner spends $200,000 deluding his Minister

By this time I had received a copy of the Commissioner's 500-page response to my 31 March allegations. On 17 June 1998 a crown limousine pulled up my drive. This was not a usual experience. A very well-dressed driver resplendent with a chauffeur's cap delivered the report to my door. It was bigger than the Christchurch Yellow Pages. The report explained that the Department had spent over 800 hours in preparing it. Senior tax lawyer Bruce Grierson has told me that the cost of operating the Department is approximately $250 per man hour. This equates to an expense of over $200,000 for this one report alone. I had no doubt that the Department was sparing no expense to close me down and shut me up.

I had been warned by top tax professionals that the IRD would do a character assassination on me rather then deal with the issues. But I wasn't worried. I had the Minister's assurance that this would not be the case. On 16 March Bill Birch wrote to me to say: "Because the report I am seeking from the Commissioner is one which is to focus on the relevant events of the perspective of IRD having particular regard to its processes, and is not in any way an inquiry into your behaviour or affairs, it is unnecessary for me to solicit your comment on the Commissioner's report".

Of course, the Minister's assurances meant nothing. The first 13 pages of the Commissioner's report were devoted to nothing but assassinating my character. "Before answering Mr Henderson's complaints this report sets out by way of background some of the ways in which Mr Hendersons contributed to the difficulties, particularly delays, associated with the Tannadyce audit". And away the Commissioner went. Contrary to the Minister's assurances, the Commissioner opened his report on IRD's "processes" by commenting negatively and defamatorily on my behaviour and affairs. The report's headings say it all. "The Level Of Correspondence From Mr Henderson. The Barrage Of Telephone Calls From Mr Henderson. Mr Henderson's Abuse And Intimidation Of Inland Revenue Staff. Escalating Minor Mistakes Or Oversights That Had Been Resolved. Actively Engaging As Many Inland Revenue Staff On As Many Issues As Possible. Making A Large Number Of Official Information Act Requests". And so on.

That was bad enough. But the report was far worse. This massive report that the Commissioner had spent over $200,000 preparing was nothing but allegation, distortion and dissimulation.

One of the first matters I wanted to check was how the Commissioner had treated my allegation that Max Carr had told me he could have completed the audit in four weeks, yet had never recorded this in his formal reports. On 13 May – in answer to Rodney's written question – the Commissioner was stating, through the Minister, that "Mr Carr made no such comment". In his report dated 29 May the Commissioner was now saying "Mr Carr does not recall making a statement in the terms attributed by Mr Henderson". In a June report to the Minister he had a third position on it. "Mr Carr did not admit that the Tannadyce audit could have been completed in four weeks instead of 206 weeks and because he made no such admission, and nor is it his professional view that this particular audit could have been completed in that time frame, there was no failure to mention the fact in his report, as alleged by the *National Business Review*". But by the 17 August Mr Carr had achieved total recall. In yet another report from the Commissioner to the Minister the Commissioner had a fourth position on this very serious issue. He said "Mr Henderson introduced into the conversation the notion of a four week time frame for the audit. Mr Carr has described it as an overstatement, a hyperbole. A short time later Mr Carr picked up on that hyperbole, but then immediately qualified his comment with references to aspects of Mr Henderson's behaviour which had slowed the audit. By extracting a casual and off-the-record statement from the context which governs its meaning and interpretation, a significance has been attributed to Mr Carr's words which is unintended by Mr Carr. Mr Carr was, and remains, of the professional view that the Tannadyce audit could not have been completed within four weeks".

But I had the hard evidence on tape.

The Commissioner dedicated a large amount of energy and paper in trying to convince the Minster that this audit could not have been completed in four weeks. He was desperate to dismiss this observation. This is so typical of my dealings with the IRD and how they will work to try and dismiss a reality that doesn't suit them. Max Carr had investigated this audit for three months. He understood the factors involved well. He had made his observations to me freely and candidly. The Commissioner, who knew virtually nothing about it, was now taking a position contrary to Max Carr's solely to avoid an embarrassing reality.

But the problem isn't just Max Carr and the Commissioner. I have over 70 hours of tapes and twenty Eastlight files to back the allegations that I had made. The problem lies with the Commissioner right through the IRD down to Gordon Byatt. In the light of my records, the Commissioner's report to the Minister was studded with departures from the truth.

The Commissioner's report did attempt to justify why IRD had fabricated a million-dollar debt. "Where a taxpayer does not supply relevant information to justify a tax deduction or GST input credit or fails to provide evidence to dispute information held about income received or GST output liability, it may be necessary for an auditor to issue an assessment to disallow a deduction claimed or to include additional income as a means of encouraging the supply of information." The Commissioner is here admitting that it is Departmental policy to fabricate debts to intimidate taxpayers during an audit. It was entirely unnecessary in my case, even as a matter of this policy, because I had fallen over backwards to make available whatever information the Department wanted. In the end Max Carr had found that the position the Department had reached in May 1995 – long before the million-dollar debt was asserted – was the correct one.

The Department also sought to minimise the significance of their fabricating and publicising the million-dollar debt. "The only relevance of the assessments against Tannadyce in the bankruptcy proceedings against Mr Henderson was to show that no credit balance had been assessed for

Tannadyce from which funds would be available to pay Mr Henderson's personal tax debts. In the context of the bankruptcy proceedings against Mr Henderson it made no difference if Tannadyce had been assessed as owing a net of one dollar or one million dollars".

It is still going on. Even after an internal inquiry the IRD were still wasting money trying to bury me rather than confront the obvious problem and deal with it.

National Business Review outbluffs Commissioner

T hroughout this entire period the *National Business Review* continued to champion my cause. People were coming up to me in the street to give me their support and very often to tell me their own personal horrific IRD story. The Minister of Revenue himself appeared to be interested in my case only because of the publicity it was receiving. In a letter dated 25 May he said "It is my view that the Commissioner's Report should be as full and as thorough as merited by a matter which has commanded so much attention for so many weeks in *National Business Review*".

National Business Review continued to report the case and detail IRD's failings. Simon Carr wrote in his 29 May column "So, with all the natural advantage of power, prestige and resources that IRD has, it also has the capacity to lie baldly". Next week he upped the stakes further. He observed that the Commissioner "has appeared in the final stages of this drama like the Wizard of Oz, saying (off the record) the [500-page] report isn't really anything to do with him; it carries his name, as it were, in name only". The following week Simon received a letter from the Commissioner's lawyers demanding a public apology. Instead of apologising Simon, in another one thousand words restated some of my key allegations and reminded the Commissioner that "Hendo" had hard evidence. He refused to withdraw and apologise. That was the last *National Business Review* ever heard from the

February 20, 1998

INSIDE COVER

Simon Carr

THE NATIONAL BUSINESS REVIEW

Everything you were afraid to ask about Inland Revenue but never wanted to know

THE NATIONAL BUSINESS REVIEW • MARCH 13, 1998

The experience of Christchurch businessman David Henderson, who claimed a GST refund and was forced into bankruptcy by a $1 million IRD assessment, has thrown an interesting light on the inner workings and departmental processes of this great apparatus of the state.

Here is the beginnings of a glossary for taxpayers.

Promptly: According to IRD's response to an official information request, this means "as quickly as our resource situation allows us to deal with something". (That's great, can we pay our taxes "promptly"?)

$1 million: $300,000. As in, "We didn't really say you owed us a million, Dave, mate, we said it was $300,000, er plus penalties taking it up to, er a million".

Apology: The officer who agrees to apologise for breaking agreements is then told he

apologise, so he flies down to Christchurch to apologise about breaking his agreement for not now being able to apologise for breaking agreements.

No further delays: Endless delays. (Hendo was quite frequently assured resolution without further delay. The longest period between assurance and result was two years.)

Swamping the department with correspondence: Writing 39 letters in two years. The internal inquiry on Henderson, recorded in four lines the fact that no basis could be found for the $1 million assessment.

However, it gave a whopping 56 lines to the idea of swamping correspondence. The report said, "Mr Henderson h- slowed the investigation- glut of corres- during the ' year-

Only after the department's unending failure to provide an explanation for its $1 million demand did the correspondence move to another level (see the commissioner's letter page 27).

Handcuffs: It seems the commissioner himself announces his attention to audit his Christchurch taxpayers by offering to come over to their office with a pair of handcuffs.

Oh, all right, it's not Mr Holland personally – it's one of his officers who does this. But by the spooky arrangem' they have in the IP' refer to theme- mission-

has to apply his most important organ to evidence. This follows a court ruling that the commissioner can't just pluck a figure out of the air and demand it from a taxpayer – he has to "apply his mind to the evidence".

You wouldn't think, would you, that we'd need a court ruling to make a commissioner apply his mind to evide-

However, a source said, ager-

THE NATIONAL BUSINESS REVIEW

JULY 31, 1998

Why commissioner of Inland Revenue must pack his bags

Hide Sight
RODNEY HIDE

Solicitor-general John McGrath QC is cogitating on what to advise Prime Minister Jenny Shipley after my call for a judicial review of Inland Revenue's four-year campaign of harassment against Christchurch businessman Dave Henderson.

This is a case where IRD took a simple audit, blew it up into a four-year beat-up, manufactured a million dollar liability, and in the process destroyed Mr Henderson's business and personal life.

The case itself is bad enough. What's worse has been IRD's response. It has delayed, it has obstructed, it has obfuscated, it has lied.

Let me give but one example of what I mean.

Under pressure late last year the commissioner of Inland Revenue, Graham Holland, appointed his national manager (corporates), Max Carr, to prepare a report on the Henderson case. Mr Carr spent a tough three months trying to get to the bottom of what had gone on. He discovered no basis for IRD's million dollar claim.

"I think that this particular issue has caused the greatest frustration and anxiety on the part of the taxpayer and, having read practically all the correspondence on the issue, I have been at a loss to understand exactly what was the position in respect of the application of section 60 at any one point in

time."

Exactly. After much delay and hassle, the claim was quashed and Mr Henderson was presented with his $65,000 refund that had freed the original audit.

The cheque proves Mr Henderson was right all along and that IRD was wrong. I have a large copy of the cheque hanging on my wall. It serves as a trophy; a reminder of civil servants' fallibility and of their stubbornness.

Mr Carr then requested a private meeting with Mr Henderson. At this meeting he went much further than he was prepared to in his report. For example, he accepted that the biggest boo-boo the IRD made was in failing to approach the audit with an unbiased mind. That is to say, Mr Carr admitted IRD was biased against Mr Henderson: "I would have thought that if I was doing this investigation, and if we had started off in the very early days, just you and I, I think, I could have got through it in four weeks."

Once again, this is a key finding. An audit took four years when it should have been wrapped up in four weeks. Unfortunately, once again, this key fact was not in Mr Carr's report to the commissioner.

I subsequently asked Revenue Minister Bill Birch whether Mr Carr had admitted the Tannadyce (Henderson's

GRAHAM HOLLAND:
Caught out by tape's existence

company) audit could have been completed in four weeks. Following IRD's advice, Mr Birch replied: "Mr Carr made no such comment."

Unfortunately for the minister, for IRD and for Mr Carr, Mr Henderson had taken the precaution of taping his conversation with Mr Carr after his long experience of IRD officers saying one thing one day and quite a different thing the next.

It was just as well he did. I was able to help everyone involved by tabling the relevant part of the transcript that proved the minister's statement to be false.

Meanwhile, the commissioner had his staff put in 800 hours to prepare a report for the minister concerning my

limited sense", "words actually spoken" and "strictly speaking".

The commissioner goes on to say: "Mr Carr did not then and does not now recall making a statement in the terms and with the meaning attributed to him by Mr Henderson. Mr Carr was and remains of the view that the Tannadyce audit could never have been completed in four weeks."

But elsewhere on the tape Mr Henderson says, "My point is this: this audit could have been and, in fact at the end of the day, was solved and sorted out in four weeks." Mr Carr responds, "Yes."

There you have it.

The tape has been offered to the minister, to the solicitor-general, and to the commissioner. So far they have failed to take up the offer.

Commissioner Holland has been caught out by the tape's existence. He should now step aside. He has failed in his statutory duty to uphold the integrity of the tax system.

IRD desperately needs someone from the private sector who has served on the other side of the counter to sort it out and to direct what is the most powerful ship of state.

There should also be an immediate independent inquiry into IRD's mistreatment of Mr Henderson. It should now be extended to include the cover-up and lies the IRD has perpetrated in trying to prevent just such an inquiry.

call for a judicial review. The tabling of the transcript resulted in the report being changed overnight.

In his report, Mr Holland says Mr Carr now cannot recall making the statements in the terms attributed to him by Mr Henderson.

Mr Carr had gone from "making no such comment" to "I can't recall whether I did or not".

Having tabled the transcript I naturally wrote to Mr Birch asking what he was going to do to correct his answer. To date he has done nothing. But he did ask for yet another report from the commissioner, which I have now obtained under the Official Information Act.

In preparing this report the commissioner had his corporate legal adviser and his assistant solicitor come to my office and listen to the relevant part of the tape. They confirmed the transcript I had tabled in the House.

The commissioner then had no option but to use the answer which "in a limited sense the answer which was provided to question 4117 was inaccurate". And again: "Therefore, on the basis of the words actually spoken by Mr Carr, it must be acknowledged that the answer was, strictly speaking, inaccurate."

In other words, the answer by the commissioner to the minister and tabled in the House was false.

But note the weasel words: "In a

194

Commissioner or his lawyers. The Commissioner's legal representatives must have reminded him that truth is an absolute defence.

On 3 July the *National Business Review* ran a two-page article written by me titled "Five Years Fighting IRD Takes its Toll". I had tried to summarise in 4,000 words all that had happened. That was tough. But I did make some key points. In particular I was quoted as saying that "the Commissioner had misled the Minister, senior IRD staff have been shown to be telling bald-faced lies, and an inordinate amount of energy has been spent perpetuating and building the illusions". I went on to express my intentions by stating that "it is my determination that eventually the bright light of reality will shine on all this and the Commissioner and his senior staff will be shown to be the liars and cheats that they are". I concluded the article by noting that "unfortunately the whole affair highlights one very sad fact about our public service and the politicians that they are supposed to answer to: lying and dissimulation at the highest level is now acceptable practice".

I thought this was pretty hard-hitting stuff and, once again, in my naivety, I thought that it just might inspire someone in government to want to look deeper into my affair. Of course, nothing happened.

Rodney joined in with his regular weekly *National Business Review* column declaring that the Commissioner "should now step aside". According to Rodney, Graham, Holland had "failed in his statutory duty to uphold the integrity of the tax system".

In July, Rodney ripped into the IRD and the Minister in the Estimates debate. He declared the Commissioner's report "a whitewash and a tissue of lies". He wanted to know what Bill Birch's and the Department's response was to the Commissioner and the IRD having been accused of being "liars and cheats" in the National Business Review. The silence was deafening. They had no response because the allegations were true. The Government's response came from Tony Ryall. His only reply to Rodney's charges was that the Department had made great advances in the year in answering their phones.

The IRD's letter to the National Business Review showed their intimidatory tactics would extend to the media. The Government's response to Rodney was to try and ignore him.

Bill Birch not interested in the facts

Late August Rodney and I were still waiting for the Solicitor General, John McGrath, to report to the Minister and for the Minister to advise Rodney of his decision.

Given the Commissioner's dissimulation in his report to Bill Birch I didn't rate the chances of a judicial inquiry very high. I was also getting some strange and abrasive correspondence from the Minister. For example, when he wrote to me originally the Minister had called for "a checklist of your complaints". That is exactly what I provided him. I also had told him that I had all the evidence to support that checklist. He was now accusing me of having withheld my evidence. I had never been asked for my evidence. Far from withholding it I was anxious to present it. The Minister didn't look a good bet.

I decided to explore some other avenues. David Carter chaired the Finance and Expenditure Select Committee and had written to me as a consequence of the articles in the *National Business Review*. He seemed genuinely interested in the case. Over the next few weeks I met with him a number of times, but nothing ever came of it. In September, Prime Minister Jenny Shipley appointed David Carter Associate Minister of Revenue. I saw this as a very positive development as he had real power now. We were to meet again and engage in several phone conversations. He too was positive that he could move things forward. Although he wouldn't make a firm commitment he kept on assuring me that he was going to call an inquiry and get the matter cleaned up once and for all. Week after week, he kept saying to Rodney and to me, "Trust me on this". And we did.

To make matters easier for him I offered to him a proposal that I had put to Bill Birch over a year earlier. This offer was made to demonstrate my sincerity and commitment to my case. It was simple. I would present to a Queen's Counsel, nominated by the Minister, some of the evidence I had to support some of my more serious allegations. I would pay for that Q.C. to consider what I had put before him and to report directly to the Minister. If that report sustained my allegations then the Minister was to move to inquire independently into the whole affair. If the Q.C. found that my allegations did not have substance, and that I was in fact a whacko, as I suspect they believed, then I undertook that the government would never hear from me again. David Carter said my offer was unnecessary because the government would pay for the inquiry he was planning. He didn't want me to pay a further cent.

I also made it very clear to David Carter what my intentions were in seeking an inquiry. I was not looking primarily for personal financial gain or recompense but rather I wanted to help to expose what I considered to be unlawful and improper practices embedded in the Department. My offer to him was that I would accept a political outcome way ahead of a financial one.

I met with my local MP Gerry Brownlee. Gerry is a pleasant enough sort of guy but he proved of no use at all. In November alone he would cancel four meetings with me. He seemed concerned with my allegations but appeared to have no idea what to do.

Gerry kept repeating that he couldn't do anything without a copy of the Commissioner's report. I arranged to have Rodney provide him with one. I then kept a regular log on his progress in dealing with a constituent in trouble. The first hurdle he said was for him to read the Commissioner's report completely. After three months he advised Rodney that he was a quarter of the way through it. This became a standing joke with Rodney and me. A few weeks later he got forty percent of the way through it. At this rate it would take him a year just to

Bill Birch: Wasn't interested in the facts.

Gerry Brownlee: Nice guy, but proved to be useless.

get through the report. I would have thought being junior whip that Gerry would have been able to read quicker and to do something. I had hoped that as I was his constituent that he would have seen it as his responsibility to make some effort to have the matter cleaned up. I was also aware that National Party philosophy was to support small business and to stand against arbitrary and big government. David Carter had told me that complaints about the IRD dominated his constituency work. I have no doubt that it would have been the same for Gerry. I had thought too that Gerry Brownlee might have been embarrassed by Rodney Hide's efforts on behalf of one of his constituents and pitch in. He did nothing to help solve the problems.

Gerry did write to me on 28 August 1998, asking me to release publicly the very expensive report that the Commissioner had prepared and submitted to Bill Birch in May that year. He advised me that it was "causing a bit of a problem" that this report had not been made public. I found this proposition amazing.

I immediately responded by making the report available to him and confirming with him that I would immediately make the report public if he, or indeed anyone involved, could explain to me how such a release would assist in resolving the issues.

He has never responded to that letter despite repeated requests to do so. In addition I have asked the Minister and the IRD to explain how the public release of that report will assist in resolving the issues; they too have never bothered to respond.

I have been left to conclude that the National Party didn't want to support me or investigate my case further as that would only serve to validate Rodney Hide for all his efforts and commitment on my behalf.

Both the Minister's attitude and Gerry's apparent failure to pursue the matter on behalf of a constituent have been of considerable concern to Brian

Palliser. As Gerry's luck would have it, Brian is a long-standing National Party member and had been involved in Gerry's selection as the National Candidate for the Ilam electorate. I suspect Brian will be giving at least his party vote to Rodney and ACT at the next election.

Finally on 14 September 1998, seven months after Rodney wrote to the Prime Minister seeking a judicial inquiry he received his response from the Minister. The answer was no. Bill Birch provided Rodney with a copy of the advice he had received from the Solicitor General. The Solicitor General noted that he had reviewed the Commissioner's report carefully but that in advising Bill Birch he thought it "inappropriate that [he] express any view of the merits of the Commissioner's report, the Carr report, or the rights and wrongs of the various issues at dispute". The actual facts of the case were for him redundant. He gave his advice based on whether or not the Department simply *appeared* to have addressed the issues. The facts were neither here nor there. Bill Birch concluded from the Solicitor General's report that "what is involved in this case is not a matter which calls into question the integrity of the tax system".

The IRD's powers were truly amazing. The Government MPs and Ministers were quite prepared to overlook my valid complaints to protect what they saw as "their" Department.

Back to square one – "Tannadyce owes us money"

– Commissioner to Bill Birch

The Commissioner in his report had told the Minister that Tannadyce had a total of 67 outstanding tax returns. He formally advised the Minister in respect of Tannadyce that "significant tax is believed to be outstanding and Tannadyce should be granted no further extensions of time in relation to its outstanding returns".

I was now back to square one. The Commissioner was rejecting Max Carr's settlement. By my reckoning there were only five returns outstanding, all to do with income tax. The main reason Tannadyce had not completed these is that over the last four years the Department held our records relating to the periods in question. Now a significant number of those records were missing or lost. The Department itself had identified that Tannadyce had suffered considerable losses since its incorporation in 1991 and that no income tax could possibly be due. As the Commissioner well knew Tannadyce was a moribund corporation that had not traded for many years. In December the previous year we had made a settlement with Max Carr with respect to all outstanding PAYE, GST and FBT. In addition, we had reached agreement with Max Carr that until such time that Tannadyce was in a position to recommence trading there was no requirement upon us to file returns in respect of these taxes. On 9 December 1997, a year earlier, the Commissioner wrote to me and advised: "Some further work is to be considered in some areas (such as that needed in relation to the missing records) and this will be done urgently under Mr Carr's control".

What do I do? I tried to seek a way forward. I repeatedly asked the Commissioner to find a way for us to work together to solve the issue of missing records. His undertaking proved to be worthless. The lack of co-operation was such that I had to resort to making an Official Information request seeking information on his Department's procedure where the Department had lost a taxpayer's records. This request, along with a number of equally reasonable requests, was ultimately dismissed by the Department through the Crown Law Office as being frivolous and vexatious. Eventually the matter would be resolved by the Department acknowledging that Max Carr couldn't remember what he had agreed to and that it would appear that Tannadyce had not been trading.

This still did not get us over the issue of missing records and the outstanding income tax returns. I was forced to write several more letters to the Commissioner literally pleading with him to tell me how we might find a way forward. I even offered for the Department to come to my home and inspect the evidence I had that showed that the Department had received records and not returned them to us. The Commissioner firstly demanded that we reconstruct all our records and file the returns. Quotes from accountants indicated that this could cost us in excess of $30,000. After more correspondence with the Commissioner's office it was agreed that we would provide some evidence to show the level of losses that had been incurred through that period. I provided the evidence as requested. I haven't heard back. Once again I had shown that there was no tax due when the Department was claiming that it was. Once again the Commissioner and his staff broke agreements and made casual assessments of tax due.

There was one income tax audit that had been started in June 1996 that was still continuing. Anxious to bring it to a conclusion, I wrote to the Commissioner seeking details of where the audit was at. He never answered me. I made requests under the Official Information Act. He refused those. Out of desperation, I rang a customer service operator in Christchurch. She politiely asked for the company's tax number. Seconds after she had entered it into her computer she went strangely silent. She then stammered that she would need to "check something out". She came back to declare that she could have nothing to do with me and that I knew that I was only to communicate to the Department in writing. She would not answer the simplest of my questions and slammed the phone down in my ear. I then phoned a young investigator, Philip Lynn, who had worked on the audit originally. He explained that all staff were under strict instructions from the Commissioner: if Henderson rings, hang up.

It was some months later that I was to be advised that that audit was now complete with the Commissioner upholding to the cent the losses we had claimed when filing the income tax return two-and-a-half years earlier. The IRD's delays and harassment had, once more, all been for nothing.

Here was the Department's other tactic: if fear and intimidation weren't going to work, imply that the taxpayer is a tax cheat.

Henderson's files shifted north

On 11 September 1998, the Commissioner wrote to me and advised that, as a consequence of the allegations I had made against his Christchurch staff, all current and future enforcement work against myself and Tannadyce was to be conducted by a separate Service Centre. My files were shifted to Hamilton. I was advised that the person responsible for them was Neil Lewer. The Commissioner also insisted that all my communication with IRD staff be in writing. I immediately rang Neil Lewer. What transpired was astounding. I asked him for a programme to resolve the issue of the outstanding income tax returns and, in particular, resolve the matter of the missing records. He repeatedly and quite irrationally asserted that all our records had been returned. I explained they hadn't. Our conversation terminated with me inquiring whether he was suggesting I was a liar. He responded by confirming that he was. Once more I was having to deal with a biased mind.

The next day Lewer wrote, not apologising but noting that he "regretted" his comments. He demanded arguments from Tannadyce fully specifying all the propositions we were relying on together with "dates, places, parties to conversations and full details of any other occasions" to support our position on the missing records and the outstanding returns. He ignored the fact that there were letters from us that were now over two years old, setting out some of this information, that the department had never responded to.

Around the same time I received a phone call from a Hamilton businessman who had been following my case in the National Business Review. He had read how Neil Lewer was now in charge of my files. He had rung to commiserate. From all he told me it was no coincidence that the Commissioner had arranged for Neil Lewer and me to work together. This businessman told me that Mr Lewer was uncharitably known in the Hamilton business community as "Lewer the Sewer".

My relationship with Neil Lewer continued to deteriorate. I sensed the Commissioner may not have given him glowing reports about me. I also sensed that the Department was still working to wear me down.

On the morning of 8 October 1998, I returned to my flat from a meeting in town. I was poring through my files to identify some documents for another meeting when my phone rang. The caller asked for Chris Bond. I explained that he wasn't here but that I could take a message. The caller identified himself as Matt from the Telecom Malicious Calls Centre in Hamilton. He said that he was responding to Mr Bond's request of the previous day. He had some of the information that Mr Bond required but he was having difficulty in particular with identifying the bank, branch and account from which the payments had been made. He then went on to schedule for me the dates and the exact amounts that I had paid in respect of my personal Telecom accounts in recent months. He then asked me to advise Mr Bond that he would be sending all this information through that afternoon. It was clear to me that this sloppy Telecom officer had rung the number he had been asked to investigate. True to form, later that day he faxed through all the information that he had presented to me, this time to the fax number he was investigating. I was shocked at how freely Telecom was dispensing important personal information.

There was no legitimate or legal reason for the Department to seek this information. They were simply snooping, obviously desperate to find out how I was surviving and paying my bills. By now I was so numbed that I looked forward with almost excitement as to how they would explain their way out of this one.

To set the ball rolling I rang the privacy officer at Telecom. He seemed highly embarrassed at what had happened. I wanted full copies of all Telecom's correspondence with the Department and I wanted them that day. Telecom rang Chris Bond at about 3 o'clock but he had gone home for the day. I then told them that the person to contact was Neil Lewer in Hamilton as he was now in charge of all my files. The Telecom officer obliged me and phoned back a few minutes later. He had made contact with Mr Lewer. Mr Lewer could not authorise the release of all the documents as he "knew nothing about the request". Later that day, after a call to David Woodnorth, the documents were all released to me. I instructed Geoff Clews to write to the Commissioner seeking an explanation. I could hardly wait for the reply.

A week later Mr Lewer responded: "Mr Bond was making enquiries of Telecom on my behalf (the telephone numbers being Christchurch ones) as you are no doubt aware, the Hamilton Service Centre has been requested to deal with the issue of outstanding returns. The enquiry was directed at that issue". Geoff Clews wrote back. He pointed out the obvious discrepancy between Mr Lewer's advice to Telecom and now his frank admission that Mr Bond was acting on his instruction. The Commissioner had some weeks earlier assured me that Mr Bond and his Christchurch colleagues would have nothing to do with our compliance issues. It appeared that Mr Lewer was trying to justify this by claiming that they were Christchurch phone numbers. The Malicious Call Centre is just a stone's throw away from Mr Lewer's own office in Hamilton. My excitement was building. I instructed Geoff Clews to make these points and, in particular, to have Mr Lewer explain how the means by which I paid my personal telephone account in 1998 had any bearing on Tannadyce's outstanding 1997 tax return.

On 18 November, David Woodnorth, Corporate Solicitor for the IRD, phoned Telecom's Barry Cathro and questioned him at some length about his recollection of his phone call with Mr Lewer where Mr Lewer had advised that he knew nothing about the section 17 inquiry. It seemed clear to me, from what Barry Cathro has relayed to me, that Mr Woodnorth was misrepresenting the situation to try and have Cathro reconsider his recollection of events.

It took Neil Lewer a month to reply. I suspect he sensed our excitement. As the weeks went by I knew his reply was going to be a belter. He didn't disappoint. His reply lived up to his nickname. Mr Lewer explained that Tannadyce had failed to "provide evidence that there is no liability to furnish returns". As a result "enquiries are being conducted for the purpose of ascertaining whether any business and/or trading activity has been conducted during the relevant periods, in this regard evidence of such activity is being sought from third parties". He closed his letter by issuing Russell McVeagh with a section 17 demand. He wanted "details of payments made to the firm Russell McVeagh McKenzie Bartleet and Co for services rendered to Tannadyce Investments Ltd (whether such services have been rendered solely to Tannadyce, or to Tannadyce Investments Ltd and Mr Dave Henderson jointly) or Mr Dave Henderson. Details of such payments are to include the

Neil Lewer: Suggested I was a liar.

date made and amounts, method of payment, identity of the party who made the payment, if payment was by cheque, credit card, eftpost, the identity of the payer, full account details (including name of account holder, bank and branch of bank, and full account number)". Geoff Clews explained to me that none of the information sought was privileged from disclosure and that the cost of complying would be borne by Tannadyce. He advised that the request was "mischievous and improper". After consultation I instructed him to give Lewer 24 hours to withdraw his notice.

The Commissioner responded to my personal complaint about the Telecom snooping incident, written some weeks earlier, by explaining that he was "satisfied that Mr Lewer's request of a Christchurch staff member to obtain information from a third party was not an unreasonable step for Mr Lewer to take, given the performance would not involve any contact between the Christchurch staff member and Tannadyce, nor would it involve that staff member making decisions concerning Tannadyce's tax liabilities". The Commissioner was proudly approving the Hamilton office using staff in the Christchurch office to make inquiries of a third party located in Hamilton. The inanities continued.

The IRD was now using its awesome powers to pry – and to pry for reasons clearly unconnected to tax collections.

IRD make it up – again

Rodney had meanwhile complained again to new Minister Max Bradford. Max had Rodney up in his office along with his tax adviser Mike Shaw, who had previously been Bill Birch's adviser. The new Minister opened by saying that the Henderson case had come up on his "radar screen". Rodney wanted to know what his radar was telling him. Bradford said he wanted to begin with Rodney's latest letter complaining about the issuing of the section 17 notices. Bradford tried to put Rodney in his place by saying that he just had a report from the Commissioner that no section 17 notices had been issued. Rodney said that this was interesting. He asked if he could use the Minister's phone. Rodney's secretary promptly delivered copies of Chris Bond's and Neil Lewer's section 17 notices. Rodney dropped them in front of Mike Shaw and asked him what he thought they were. Mr Shaw looked them over and then looked up nervously and said that "these are section 17s Minister". Rodney reported that Max Bradford was physically shaken that the Commissioner could have so misled him. The meeting went downhill. It concluded with the new Minister saying that he would get back to Rodney about the issuing of the section 17 notices. He never has.

Mr Lewer meanwhile sought legal advice from the Crown Law Office in regard to Geoff Clew's demand that the section 17 notice to Russell McVeagh be withdrawn. He advised that the request to Russell McVeagh "although in terms of section 17 was a first and informal request". He then went on to explain that, as in essence it was an informal request, it need not be responded to. Russell McVeagh could just forget all about it. Geoff Clews had never in his career heard of the concept of a section 17 request you could ignore.

The next week at the Finance and Expenditure Select Committee Rodney grilled the Commissioner over IRD's newly advised policy of informal section 17 notices. Rodney asked the Commissioner what an informal section 17 notice was. The Commissioner replied, "It is a phrase that is used internally to … aah … identify a request for information … aah … which does not ... aah ... at the time that it is made specify that the provisions of section 17 – in terms of the sanctions – would be applied if the information is not provided". The Commissioner wasn't able to tell the committee when informal section 17s became policy. He did say taxpayers had never been informed of their existence. No tax professional had ever heard of an "informal section 17" before. Nor had any of the Commissioner's staff – as a ring around half-a-dozen IRD offices throughout the country confirmed.

One of the few things that Max Carr had criticised the Department for was Mr Bond issuing section 17 notices in September 1997. Amongst other things he said "they were technically improper in their form". The Commissioner committed to providing section 17 retraining as a matter of priority for Christchurch staff. After Chris Bond had issued yet a further improper section 17 notice in September 1998 to Telecom, Rodney Hide asked the Minister whether Chris Bond had in fact been retrained as promised. The answer came back advising that the training had gone ahead but that Mr Bond hadn't attended.

All this time the new Associate Minister David Carter had been telling me and Rodney that he was sorting it out and that we should be patient. This went on each week for months until he advised that we were not to deal with him anymore. All our enquiries on the matter were to be directed to Max Bradford. In my view, Carter was a complete failure. His "trust me" line proved completely worthless.

For his part, Max Bradford misinterpreted the Solicitor General's advice to Bill Birch. "I agree with Mr Birch and the Solicitor General that

the appropriate course is for you to follow through with the Ombudsman", he wrote. What the Solicitor General had made plain was that the decision to have a judicial inquiry was for the Minister to make. He simply suggested that, in arriving at his decision, the Minister should "take account the opportunity Mr Henderson has to make the complaint to the Ombudsman".

Max Bradford: Misinterpreted the Solicitor-General's advice.

My case was now driving national policy as the Commissioner had to explain away the improper issuing of section 17s.

Ombudsmen confirm: unable to investigate Henderson's complaints

The Ombudsmen hadn't been able to help so far. You will recall that I had approached them two years previously. Sir Brian Elwood had refused to have anything to do with me then because I was a bankrupt. I was still a bankrupt.

On 2 November 1998 I approached the Ombudsman yet again – this time with Ministerial blessing. I outlined to him in broad terms the nature of my allegations and I asked for specific detail including a timetable showing how an investigation might be progressed. Two weeks later I received a response from Ombudsman Anand Satyanand. He provided me with a timetable that showed it would take a minimum of 13 months to investigate my allegations. He concluded his letter by saying "this is maybe somewhat different from the time schedule which you may have had in mind when making your complaint. It is, however, well known that this office is presently operating in circumstances with a considerable volume of work, as well as having to accept financial cutbacks along with the entire public sector. Accordingly, I am unable to justify expenditure of any special resources for the investigation of a specific complaint when there are many pressing calls upon the service of the Ombudsman".

This seemed to identify little "opportunity" to progress my complaint through the Office of the Ombudsman. I pointed this out to Dave Carter and Max Bradford.

On Wednesday 2 December 1998, David Carter contacted me and proudly announced that the Minister of Revenue, Max Bradford, had agreed to meet with the Ombudsman and make available "all the resources necessary for him to conduct an urgent and robust enquiry" into the matters about which I had been complaining. That meeting took place the following week. The Chief Ombudsman, Sir Brian Elwood, also attended. The Minister subsequently told me that he had made the offer of resources and Sir Brian Elwood advised the Minister in turn that they did not now need any resources and that the time frames were now necessary because of the "structured process" needed for the investigation.

Furthermore, I was to be advised the following week that if an investigation was to commence then I would have to forward to the Ombudsman all the allegations that I sought to be investigated together with all the evidence I held to support each one of these allegations. Then – and only then – would the Ombudsman determine whether or not any or all of my allegations warranted investigation. The work required to comply with this request has been estimated at an excess of 800 hours – twenty-weeks' full time work. The only beneficiary of such an investigation would be the Minister who would have the opportunity to identify from an independent investigator whether or not his Commissioner and staff had acted improperly. The Ombudsman's conclusions, if he did investigate, and if he did sustain my allegations, would have no bite because any recommendations he made would not in any way be binding on the Department.

The only concession I could elicit from them was that I could provide my allegations and evidence on audio tape. This too was going to take an extraordinary amount of time. Without the absolute assurance that the Ombudsmen would investigate these complaints, I could not justify the time, cost or energy to do this.

The Prime Minister had also directed me to the Office of the Ombudsman. Under the Ombudsman Act, she has the power to direct an Ombudsman to undertake an investigation. She has never exercised this authority.

It was becoming clear to me why the Commissioner and government only wanted the Ombudsman to investigate this matter. It would be an investigation that would be a massive burden on me for many months, it would not be public and, at the end, its findings would not be binding on the Minister or the Commissioner.

I discovered in the Ombudsmens' newsletters what they were devoting their resources to. They were proudly promoting their role in recovering a small amount of petrol money that had been billed to a prisoner who had been driven, by his agents, to a funeral. That seemed to sum up the Ombudsmen.

I continued to write to the Ombudsmen. Anand Satyanand was to confirm that it was not possible to commence an investigation into the checklist of complaints I had sent to Bill Birch. As the end of 1998 approached I felt compelled to reflect on what Rodney and I had been able to achieve that year. Sadly, it was very little. We had put a massive effort in with the Minister Bill Birch but the Commissioner's seemingly endless resources and ready access to the Minister's staff confounded us.

The Commissioner, Graham Holland, has it in his power to call a properly constituted independent inquiry into this matter, at any time. He has not done so, despite repeated requests and clear policy laid down by Bill Birch, as Minister of Revenue, that requires him to do so.

David Carter and Gerry Brownlee had promised heaps and delivered nought. It was becoming more apparent that the political process had evolved to bury problems like mine and not to confront and fix them. I had sought an opinion from Geoff Clews during the year as to the costs and prospects of me bringing an action for damages against the Department and individually

David Carter: Assured me he was putting together an inquiry – nothing happened.

Anand Satyanand: Ombudsman.

against all the officers involved. He rated my chances as good but the cost of this was way outside my resources.

By the end of 1998 this process of recovering a $65,000 refund had cost me over $200,000 in out of pocket expenses, two years of my life part time, and three years full time. They had bankrupted me and had established in people's minds that I was a tax cheat. They had cost me my businesses and my health took a hammering for nearly two years.

The more fuss that I kicked up the more resources the Department poured in to discrediting me and destroying me.

I have always believed that the IRD needed to take responsibility for this cost, but that was not my prime motivation. I have told the Ministers and the Commissioner on several occasions that I would trade off any personal financial solution for a political solution whereby the Department was cleaned up and the necessary processes and policies were put in place to ensure that my experience was never repeated.

Money is the last concern of the Department. They had spent a million dollars trying to deny me my refund. They have spent at least another half million dollars in the last year trying to shut me up, misleading tax ministers and working to close down this story.

I have a passion about small business and entrepreneurship. I understand what it takes to create a business, risk your life savings, meet all the challenges and hassles that a competitive market delivers, and sometimes spending years working long hours before receiving any return.

Small businesses are the heart and soul of our economy. They employ the most people, they create the most wealth and produce virtually all the material innovations in our lives. They also pay the most tax and receive by far the most attention from the IRD's audit section.

The IRD doesn't value small business. What I discovered was an institutional attitude that is anti-enterprise. Last year the IRD initiated 46% of all company bankruptcies.

The Commissioner's awesome powers and their unchecked effect

In every IRD office in the country there proudly hangs the IRD's charter of "Your Rights and Obligations". There are seven rights trumpeted. There is one obligation that falls upon the taxpayer.

I stuck to my end of the bargain. I was honest with my dealings with the IRD. I co-operated with them in every regard. I don't like the IRD or paying tax but the consequences of not co-operating are too horrific to be worth it. Our massive tax legislation is like a gun to the head of every taxpayer. The penalties regime that supports it is now so punitive that its application can swiftly destroy a business and even lives. Small businesses and the self-employed are a soft target for IRD officers trying to look efficient and effective. The laws are so complex that even the most diligent and well meaning small business person is unwittingly breaking the law. As a rule, these small businesses and self-employed offer no resistance. They can't afford the phalanx of lawyers and accountants that are the ready response of our large corporates.

YOUR RIGHTS AND OBLIGATIONS

■ **YOUR RIGHT TO GOOD SERVICE**

You are entitled to prompt, courteous and efficient service from Inland Revenue.

■ **YOUR RIGHT TO CONFIDENTIALITY**

We will respect the information you give us, and use it for lawful purposes only.

■ **YOUR RIGHT TO BE BELIEVED**

We will presume that you are honest in your dealings with us unless we have good reason to believe otherwise. However, sometimes we are required to check information you give us.

■ **YOUR RIGHT TO INDIVIDUAL ATTENTION**

You are entitled to know the name of the staff member you are dealing with.

■ **YOUR RIGHT TO HELP**

We will give you the information you need to understand your rights, and to meet your obligations.

■ **YOUR RIGHT TO QUESTION OUR DECISIONS**

If you ask, we will explain how to object to any assessment or decision we make.

■ **YOUR RIGHTS IF YOU ARE AUDITED**

If you are selected for a tax audit, then we will explain your rights and obligations to you.

■ **YOUR OBLIGATION TO ACT HONESTLY**

You are obliged to act honestly in dealing with Inland Revenue (for example, by disclosing all your income in your tax return).

INLAND REVENUE
TE TARI TAAKE

The IRD, for its part, repeatedly trampled every right it proudly declares that I should enjoy as a taxpayer. I did not get good service. I did not get help. My affairs weren't treated confidentially. I had no right to question IRD's decisions. I wasn't believed. My rights and obligations were never explained or provided to me (despite my repeated requests). For long periods of the audit I never knew who was responsible for it.

My rights weren't trampled by just a few IRD officers, but by everyone I dealt with from Commissioner Graham Holland down. Whenever I complained about my stated rights being trampled the effect was even greater abuse.

Whenever I approached any of the several ministers I had to deal with the Department would simply mislead them. The Ministers, in turn, seemingly focused on larger issues, were always willing to take the word of the Department who buttered their bread rather than the taxpayer who produced the butter.

My case is not an isolated one, it is the tip of the iceberg. Over the last five years literally dozens of similar cases have been bought to my attention. In every instance the Department has wreaked havoc on the lives and businesses of honest toilers.

That the IRD is a law unto itself is no longer a metaphor, it is a reality. Graham Holland, as Commissioner, is literally the most powerful person in New Zealand. He holds files containing the most personal and private information on every single New Zealander. He freely delegates enormous powers that no human should ever have over another to people who lack the training or the character to use these awesome powers either wisely or well. If I had not resorted to taping phone calls and meetings I would not have been able to expose improper and unprofessional behaviour within the Department. Despite the existence of these tapes, the Department and the Commissioner have continued to mislead their Minister.

The IRD can barge into your business at will, force you to answer any questions it asks, punish you before your case is even heard, demand very personal information from you and anyone you deal with, and assert your guilt without having to prove it. These are awesome powers, far and above those of the police.

Successive governments have sanctioned a legal process that holds taxpayers guilty until proven innocent. It is this process that has allowed a culture of contempt for the very producers in our society to breed and to permeate right through every level of the Department. Totally unacceptable behaviour is now seen as routine.

With the burden of proof on the taxpayer, the sloppiest and most unprofessional investigator can easily corner taxpayers and bludgeon money out of them whether that money is legally due or not.

What saddens me most is the fear that paralyses taxpayers and further sanctions the Department's unacceptable behaviour.

That you should concede to the Department, even when you are right, has now become an unwritten tenet of business. My experience in lots of respects justifies this. But more importantly it justifies a complete overhaul of tax laws and the culture and operation of the IRD.

In January 1999 I started again going through my files to set out what had happened to me. This book is the result. As I finished this book Prime Minister Jenny Shipley announced Hon Bill English as the new Minister of Revenue. He is the sixth Revenue Minister I have had to deal with over the life of the Tannadyce audit. Ministers came and went but the improper behaviour by the IRD just went on forever. My own audit appears to be going on forever.

As I write this the Commissioner has still not resolved the issue of the missing records. Over 14 months ago he gave me his personal undertaking that this issue would be dealt with urgently. Once more he has proved his assurances and undertakings have no currency. I have no one to appeal to. If the Commissioner breaks his word or determines to treat you unfairly then there is no one you can complain to.

I have now resolved to publish the book. I hope it will inspire other tax victims to stand up and to speak out. I hope it will prove a much needed catalyst to engender the reforms our tax laws and our IRD desperately need

to ensure what happened to me doesn't happen to anyone else. That may be a long process. They will fight back, work to discredit me and this book, and do everything to avoid independent review of this case. None of that really daunts me. I feel pleased that I am now one more step further ahead to ensuring that the Commissioner of the IRD and his staff are once and for all time held to account.

Bill English: Sixth Minister of Revenue that I had to deal with.

Where Are They Today

Graham Holland: Is still the Commissisoner and Chief Executive of Inland Revenue. The most powerful public service position in the country.

Max Carr: Is still the National Manager Corporates, responsible for ensuring that all our large Corporates meet their tax obligations.

George Gray: Is still the Group Manager Customer Services, responsible for the senior staff at every service centre throughout the country.

Carson McNeill: Is still Manager South Island Service Centres. He is responsible for every IRD staff member in the South Island and for ensuring every business and individual resident in the South Island meets their tax obligations.

Peter Sivertsen: He is no longer Manager, Technical and Legal Support Group. As a result of restructuring, he is now an investigating accountant with the Corporates Unit and answers to Max Carr.

Adriaan Geerlofs: Is still Area Manager BusinessLink Investigations.

Chris Bond: Is still a Senior Investigator in Christchurch.

Gordon Byatt: Took early retirement in 1997, and no longer works for the department.

Keith Shand: Is still a Senior Audit Officer in Christchurch.

Neil Lewer: Is still Area Manager BusinessLink, Hamilton

Gib Lee: Is still a Senior Audit Officer in Christchurch.

Chris Jones: Left the Department in 1996.

Ross Gardiner: Is now a Technical Advisor in Christchurch.

Helen Sumner: Is still an IRD staff solicitor in Christchurch.

Afterword

Inland Revenue
Te Tari Taake
OFFICE OF THE COMMISSIONER

National Office
12-22 Hawkestone Street
PO Box 2198
Wellington
New Zealand
Telephone 04-472 1032
Facsimile 04-499 0806

Commissioner's Response to Mr Henderson's Book

I reject the attacks made in this book on the personal and professional reputations of a number of Inland Revenue Department staff. These attacks are unwarranted and untrue.

Mr Henderson's complaints as they stood up to April 1998, were fully responded to in a report comprising 100 pages of text and 400 pages of appendices which I provided to the then Minister of Revenue, Rt Hon Bill Birch, on 29 May 1998. Mr Henderson continues to withhold consent to the public release of that report. As long as he does so his allegations cannot be fully answered.

When my report on Mr Henderson's allegations was submitted to the Minister in May, he referred it and Mr Henderson's complaints to the Solicitor-General, Mr John McGrath QC, for advice on whether anything in Mr Henderson's complaints or the way Inland Revenue handled them gave cause to set up a public inquiry. The Solicitor-General's report includes his view that Mr Henderson's complaints would not justify the setting up a Commission of Inquiry; that on the facts as known there is no legal basis for the Government to compensate Mr Henderson; and noted the availability of the option for Mr Henderson to make a complaint to the Ombudsmen.

A request for a public inquiry was made by Mr Rodney Hide MP, finance spokesperson for the ACT political party in February 1998. On receipt of the Solicitor-General's report Mr Birch wrote to Mr Hide, a copy of Mr Birch's letter to Mr Hide is attached to this afterword. Mr Birch concluded that the criteria for a public inquiry were not satisfied and pointed to the Solicitor-General's advice as to the option available to Mr Henderson of making a complaint to the Ombudsmen.

It is my opinion too that if Mr Henderson wants to follow through with his complaints against Inland Revenue and its staff an investigation by the Ombudsmen as a totally independent and impeccably impartial organisation will provide the proper forum. Inland Revenue will cooperate fully to assist the Ombudsmen with any such investigation into Mr Henderson's complaints.

No employee of any kind of business, including the professional, competent and hardworking staff of Inland Revenue, should have to put up with the type of nasty and vicious personal attacks which have occurred in this book.

To my staff and their families for whom this kind of book can cause all sorts of stresses, I and the Department's senior management team offer our support. We continue to have confidence in the professionalism, competence and integrity of the staff of the Inland Revenue Department.

Graham Holland
Commissioner of Inland Revenue

MINISTER OF FINANCE & REVENUE

Copy for: Commissioner of Inland Revenue

14 September, 1998

Mr Rodney Hide
ACT Spokesperson for Finance
Parliament Buildings
WELLINGTON

Dear Mr Hide,

DETERMINATION OF REQUEST FOR JUDICIAL INQUIRY

You wrote to the Prime Minister on 16 February 1998 requesting a judicial inquiry into IRD's handling of the tax affairs of Mr David Henderson and Tannadyce Investments Limited. She referred your letter to me for investigation and reply. I advised you in a letter dated 9 March 1998 of the procedure to be adopted in determining your request:

(1) That the Commissioner of IRD had been instructed to report on;

- All actions taken or planned to implement findings of Mr Carr, with expected timings

- Any other areas yet to be resolved between IRD and the taxpayer, together with proposed actions and timings

- Any areas of identified concern to the taxpayer where IRD does not propose further actions; with the reasons for that position

- What kinds of factors might lead to an assessment after rising to $1 million subsequently to collapse into a refund

- Whether further steps were needed to protect taxpayers from large claims which, tested, prove unsustainable

- Why he opted for an independent internal inquiry rather than an independent external once

Parliament House. Wellington, New Zealand, Telephone (04) 471 9991, Fax (04) 473 3587

2

- And whether he had reason to believe that any conclusion in the Carr report was based on incomplete or inadequate information.

(2) That I would then refer the Commissioner's report on completion to the Solicitor-General, asking him to advise whether it revealed matter justifying judicial inquiry, and whether any other action by the Government, the Minister of Revenue or Inland Revenue was desirable in response to these issues in the interests of fairness, efficiency and good tax administration.

(3) Subsequently, Mr Henderson made further representations to me in respect of the concerns he wanted addressed, as a result of which I added something approaching 70 pages of concerns supplied by Mr Henderson to the matters I had originally asked the Commissioner to report on. As Minister, I therefore went to considerable lengths to ensure that all matters Mr Henderson regarded as significant were placed before the Commissioner for investigation and report.

The Commissioner's report became available to me on 29 May 1998. A copy was provided to Mr Henderson, and on his request, also to you. The Commissioner's report was transmitted to the Solicitor-General on 2 June 1998. Mr Henderson subsequently expressed the view that some of the Commissioner's report is inaccurate, alleging that recordings which he secretly made of his conversations with IRD staff prove this. A copy of one such recording was eventually supplied. I sent a transcript of that recording to the Solicitor General before the completion of his report to me.

The Solicitor-General's report (copy attached) is dated 24 August 1998. You will note that the Solicitor-General explicitly states that his conclusions are not dependent on the merit or otherwise of the Commissioner's report, or the Carr report, or the various issues at dispute in respect of those reports.

It may be of assistance if I quote, from the Solicitor-General's report, some of his key conclusions in respect of the other matters which I referred to him in order to place myself in an appropriate position to determine the request you made:

1. The nature of the Commissioner's report and "the rigorous nature of the process followed by the Department are such that it can be accepted as an adequate basis from which to form a view on whether the merits of the dispute have been satisfactorily addressed." Mr Henderson's complaint as referred to the Commissioner by me was "very comprehensive". The "Commissioner instructed a senior staff member to prepare the report following extensive briefings in Christchurch and National office, written responses by relevant officers to allegations made, and reference to a volume

of documentation." The Commissioner's report followed "an extensive review conducted by Mr Max Carr" of IRD. The Solicitor-General finds that there has been "acceptance and implementation by IRD of the recommendations of Mr Carr". TIL's GST liability has been "resolved by way of negotiated settlement". An apology "has been given by the Commissioner to Mr Henderson and TIL in relation to delay with the audit, and a verbal apology given by Mr Carr to Miss Cook". The dispute over official information requests with the department "has been resolved in conjunction with the Ombudsman's office, providing full access to the documents". All significant issues "from the department's point of view appear to have been addressed." he states.

2. The Solicitor General notes the jurisdiction of the Ombudsmen to investigate matters of maladministration, and his own need to avoid trespassing on the jurisdiction of the Ombudsmen to investigate such matters in this case on the complaint of Mr Henderson, TIL or Mr Hide. "It is the statutory function of the Ombudsmen to investigate 'any decision or recommendation made or any act done or omitted relating to a matter of [government] administration'." He notes that this power to investigate "covers decisions or recommendations made by departments". It is therefore "broadly within the jurisdiction of the Ombudsmen to investigate matters of government administration or maladministration such as those the subject of complaint" in this case.

3. On the question of justification for a commission of inquiry, the Solicitor General quotes in some detail the criteria normally applied to test such need—"whether there are issues of sufficient public importance or public concern at stake in the nature of corruption, illegal or grossly aberrant conduct amounting to it by officers of the Government." He also notes that "it is generally accepted that an inquiry should not be held if the matter naturally falls within the jurisdiction of the Courts", and that an inquiry "will not be appropriate if the matter is of such proportions that it can adequately be dealt with by established administrative or other means."

4. He concludes that this complaint "does not reach the tests described. The matters substantiated are simply not of that level of seriousness." Without diminishing the force of the criticism of departmental handling of the matter from Mr Hide or Mr Henderson, he says, "it seems clear to me that there were particular factors that contributed to the department's work on the matter which lead me to believe they are instances that arise from the particular circumstances, and not such that would call for the extensive special investigatory process of a commission of inquiry." In the case of allegations of maladministration, adequate remedies generally "would encompass internal administration, as has taken place, or investigation and ultimately review by

the Ombudsmen. Mr Henderson, TIL and Mr Hide can decide whether that is a procedure they wish to follow."

5. The Solicitor-General concludes that it is for the Minister to decide whether he is persuaded by the Commissioner's report that it appears satisfactorily to have addressed this matter. He advises that bearing in mind a duty to use my "best endeavours to protect the integrity of the tax system"; "consider not only what the department has put [forward] but also Mr Henderson's material"; and take into account, if the proportions of the matter are not such as to require public inquiry, that Mr Henderson "has the opportunity to make the complaint to the Ombudsmen."

6. Under a heading, "Other Action Required", the Solicitor-General addresses the question of compensation by the Government to Mr Henderson. He concludes that, on the facts known, there is no legal basis for doing so.

My office has gone to exceptional lengths to elicit Mr Henderson's concerns fully, place them before the Commissioner for investigation, and to seek the Solicitor General's advice. These processes complete, I am now in a position, therefore to determine the request you made for a judicial inquiry.

Conclusion

I am satisfied that the Commissioner's report traversed fully and fairly all of the information held by the department about the matter. Mr Henderson complains that the Commissioner did seek to review the rest of the tape recordings he secretly made of conversations with IRD officers. I appreciate that, but there was never an onus on the Commissioner to do so. It has always been open to Mr Henderson to submit the transcripts of his recordings to the Commissioner if he thought them relevant. He alone knows their content. He has always been the only person well-placed to take relevant decisions in respect of their submission.

In the event, however, the Solicitor-General's opinion makes it clear that those matters are irrelevant to the determination of your request. The Commissioner's report acknowledges administrative error, albeit, in the words of the Solicitor-General, "nowhere near the extent that Mr Henderson perceives the wrong done to him." As the Solicitor-General and the Commissioner's report both point out, a range of remedial actions have been undertaken by the department. In addition, the Solicitor-General's report is specific that what is involved in this case is not a matter which calls into question the integrity of the tax system:

"It seems clear to me," he writes, "that there were particular factors that contributed to the department's work on the matter which lead me to believe they are instances that arise from the particular circumstances, and not such that would call for the extensive special investigatory process of a commission of inquiry."

In sum, the advice to me as Minister is that this is not a matter which satisfies the criteria established as preconditions for an inquiry of the sort you requested.

I am aware, of course, that Mr Henderson, notwithstanding the settlement agreed between him and the department, continues to feel aggrieved about what he personally sees as unfair treatment. The Solicitor-General states however:

"Mere allegations of maladministration are not usually thought sufficient to found an inquiry. In the case of such allegations, adequate remedies generally would encompass internal administrative action, as has taken place, or investigation and ultimately review by the Ombudsmen. In particular, it is always open for a person in Mr Henderson's position, if dissatisfied by IRD's internal response, to make a complaint to the Ombudsmen concerning administrative decisions or practices affecting him."

I enclose for your convenience an additional copy of this   letter and the report of the Solicitor-General, if you may wish to copy them to Mr Henderson.

Yours faithfully

,sgd) R.T. HON W.F. BIRCH

Rt Hon W. F. Birch
Treasurer and Minister of Finance

This is not the end.